Palgrave Macmillan Memory Studies

Series Editors
Andrew Hoskins
University of Glasgow
Glasgow, UK

John Sutton
Department of Cognitive Science
Macquarie University
Macquarie, Australia

The nascent field of Memory Studies emerges from contemporary trends that include a shift from concern with historical knowledge of events to that of memory, from 'what we know' to 'how we remember it'; changes in generational memory; the rapid advance of technologies of memory; panics over declining powers of memory, which mirror our fascination with the possibilities of memory enhancement; and the development of trauma narratives in reshaping the past. These factors have contributed to an intensification of public discourses on our past over the last thirty years. Technological, political, interpersonal, social and cultural shifts affect what, how and why people and societies remember and forget. This groundbreaking new series tackles questions such as: What is 'memory' under these conditions? What are its prospects, and also the prospects for its interdisciplinary and systematic study? What are the conceptual, theoretical and methodological tools for its investigation and illumination?

More information about this series at
http://www.springer.com/series/14682

Jessica Gildersleeve · Richard Gehrmann
Editors

Memory and the Wars on Terror

Australian and British Perspectives

Editors
Jessica Gildersleeve
School of Arts and Communication
University of Southern Queensland
Toowoomba, QLD, Australia

Richard Gehrmann
School of Arts and Communication
University of Southern Queensland
Toowoomba, QLD, Australia

Palgrave Macmillan Memory Studies
ISBN 978-3-319-56975-8   ISBN 978-3-319-56976-5   (Ebook)
DOI 10.1007/978-3-319-56976-5

Library of Congress Control Number: 2017939103

Image credit: DOD Photo/Alamy Stock Photo

Printed on acid-free paper

This Palgrave Macmillan imprint is published by Springer Nature
The registered company is Springer International Publishing AG
The registered company address is: Gewerbestrasse 11, 6330 Cham, Switzerland

ACKNOWLEDGEMENTS

Some of the papers collected here were first given at the Australian Historical Association Biennial Conference held at The University of Queensland, Brisbane in June 2014, and we thank all those who participated as well as those who provided feedback for papers delivered at this and other venues. However, our principal debt is to all those scholars who contributed the individual chapters in this collection. The editors thank these contributors to our volume for their patience and belief in the project. Additionally, we acknowledge the assistance of Ralph Kimber for his work with the index, and wish to thank Prof. Frank Bongiorno for kindly reading this manuscript in its earlier stages. Finally, the editors thank their colleagues at the School of Arts and Communication at University of Southern Queensland for their support and encouragement in fostering a research environment in a regional University.

CONTENTS

EDITORS AND CONTRIBUTORS

About the Editors

Jessica Gildersleeve is Senior Lecturer in English Literature at the University of Southern Queensland. She is the author of *Elizabeth Bowen and the Writing of Trauma: The Ethics of Survival* (Brill/Rodopi 2014), as well as essays on other twentieth- and twenty-first-century women writers, including Rosamond Lehmann, Jean Rhys, Agatha Christie, Sarah Waters, and Pat Barker. Her monographs on Christos Tsiolkas and the film *Don't Look Now* will be published later this year.

Richard Gehrmann is a Senior Lecturer in International Studies at the University of Southern Queensland who deployed to Afghanistan and Iraq as an Australian Army reservist. A graduate of the University of Cambridge, he has published on war and society, and on representation and identity. Richard is currently researching depictions of captivity and trauma in the Age of Terror.

Contributors

Frank Bongiorno Australian National University, Canberra, Australia

Jessica Carniel University of Southern Queensland, Toowoomba, Australia

Kevin Foster Monash University, Clayton, Australia

Amanda Laugesen Australian National University, Canberra, Australia

Dashiel Lawrence University of Melbourne, Melbourne, VIC, Australia

Robert Mason Griffith University, Brisbane, Australia

Belinda McKay Griffith University, Brisbane, QLD, Australia

Christa van Raalte Bournemouth University, Poole, UK

Denise N. Rall Southern Cross University, Lismore, Australia

Rebecca Te'o University of Southern Queensland, Queensland, Australia

Kezia Whiting State University of New York at Buffalo, New York, USA

CHAPTER 1

Memory and the Wars on Terror

Jessica Gildersleeve and Richard Gehrmann

To paraphrase Virginia Woolf, on or about September 11, 2001, human character changed. The terrorist attacks in New York City on that day, and the subsequent Wars on Terror which have continued since then, have fundamentally shaped our understanding and representation of the world throughout the twenty-first century. Of course, these incidents were, and continue to be, highly significant in the United States and are deeply embedded within contemporary North American culture, so it is unsurprising that the US-centric view of these experiences, their created memory, and their aftermath have been the subject of extensive analysis. The campaigns of the militant group the Islamic State of Iraq and the Levant (ISIL, also translated as the Islamic State of Iraq and Syria/al-Sham [ISIS], and often referred to by the acronyms IS or Daesh) and Western reintervention in the region in 2014 and 2015 have reenergised these debates.

For the United States, the most significant events of the twenty-first century have been the September 11 attack, the associated wars in

J. Gildersleeve (✉) · R. Gehrmann
School of Arts and Communication, University of Southern Queensland,
Toowoomba, QLD, Australia
e-mail: Jessica.Gildersleeve@usq.edu.au

R. Gehrmann
e-mail: richard.gehrmann@usq.edu.au

© The Author(s) 2017   1
J. Gildersleeve and R. Gehrmann (eds.), *Memory and the Wars on Terror*, Palgrave Macmillan Memory Studies,
DOI 10.1007/978-3-319-56976-5_1

Iraq and Afghanistan, and the perception of an increased terrorist risk on North American soil since then—shown, for example, in President Donald Trump's attempts to block immigration into the United States from certain Muslim nations. This series of events has collectively been labelled the Wars on Terror; while it is internationally understood, the label primarily reflects American concerns and preoccupations. As David Holloway notes, the very idea of the Wars on Terror 'was in itself a representation of events, a rhetorical construction, a series of stories about 9/11 and about America's place in the world' (2008, p. 4). The September 11 attacks, the war in Afghanistan, and the war in Iraq are of course three separate events, but they are intertwined and interconnected; moreover, while they are fundamentally a part of North American cultural history, they have also shaped cultural memory outside the United States.

This collection examines the way in which Australian and British historians, journalists, writers, film-makers, and other cultural producers and cultural figures have represented and thus remembered this ongoing period of conflict, using a range of significant case studies. It proposes that this period of conflict has seen a concomitant militarisation of Western society and culture which has impacted modes of language and literary expression, press freedom, art forms, gender roles, clothing styles, a willingness by those in the West to accept potential losses of their freedom, and a hardening of attitudes towards groups that represent different cultures. Different community and ethnic groups have had particular responses to events in the Wars on Terror, responses that are based within their own cultural frameworks and remembered history. Previous cultural eras such as the Renaissance, the Age of Revolution, the First World War, or even the counterculture movement of the late 1960s all shaped different forms of cultural memory, and the conflicts of the Wars on Terror are no different. Given that, as Jane Goodall and Christopher Lee have argued, 'in the public sphere, the reverberations of trauma are bound up with live tensions over national security and cultural identity' (2015, p. 10), an understanding of the Wars on Terror within its historical context, its historical precursors, and its chronological course are crucial for interpreting the processes and impacts on its memorialisation in Britain and Australia.

GLOBAL CULTURE AND A CLASH OF CIVILISATIONS

September 11 and the associated wars in Iraq and Afghanistan have taken the form of direct military conflict involving the United States, coalition allies (including Britain and Australia), and a variety of enemies, but these conflict events have also become components of a wider global clash between disparate cultural groupings. While historians such as Peter Burke (2009) have identified the positive facets of greater levels of international cultural hybridity, the conflicts of the Wars on Terror have also come to represent a global struggle between diametrically opposed cultural opposites. American social scientist Samuel Huntington generated controversy with his publication of *The Clash of Civilizations and the Remaking of World Order* (1996), hypothesising a far more bleak future than that imagined by the observers who had celebrated the global peace dividend that came with the end of the Cold War, or even what fellow American Francis Fukuyama (1992) claimed to be the end of history and triumph of capitalist democracy. Huntington argued that whereas the basis for political and cultural conflict for much of the twentieth century had been the ideologies of communism and capitalism, conflict in this new post-Cold War era would be found in the underlying differences between human cultures. His idea of a clash of civilisations has been much debated and critiqued from a variety of perspectives (for example, Sen 1999; Said 2001; Berman 2003), but the conflict that began on September 11 appeared to many as another manifestation of this conflict, in this instance between Islamist extremism and the United States, a symbol of Western capitalism and democracy.

The idea of such a clash of cultures might have had a particular appeal for many in America, but it was not as convincing for those outside it. This volume seeks to explore such differences, emphasising that while there are many similarities between societies faced with conflict and extremism, there are also many differences. Such differences are given greater voice by societies that reject apparent American triumphalism, and by societies that seek to develop a more nuanced approach to understanding the meanings attached to the conflicts of these years of warfare. Both in the United States and throughout Western societies, such cultural divides are to varying degrees seen as having been related to American actions in the late twentieth century. Such allocation of blame to the United States does not excuse the actions of terrorist groups, but it does explain them and place them in context. From an outsider's perspective, it is easy to have a critical view of the United States' policies because the worldview and perceptions of the outsiders diverge from those of the United States. This leads to differing memories of the Wars on Terror.

Regardless of whether Huntington's explanation of a clash of civilisations is palatable, it is clear that there are vast cultural differences between the worldview of Al Qaeda militants, insurgent groups in Iraq or Afghanistan, and the governments and people of the Western world. The existence of such cultural divides shapes the representation and memory of these conflicts. Despite the apparent binary division between the Western and Islamic worlds, within the Islamic world there are millions who value aspects of Western democracy, Western-style capitalism, and a Western-style freedom of expression. Far too often observers generalise about Islam and Islamic groups in response to the actions of a small minority of Islamist militants. The actions of these militants might attract the sympathy of some within the Islamic world, but sympathy does not mean active support or even approval, and it is a mistake to assume that opposition to the United States' policy implies rejection of all Western values. Decades of interrelationships between the Islamic world of the Middle East and the United States (and its Western allies) have shaped international cross-cultural relationships, and an understanding of this historical background provides an appreciation of the way the Wars on Terror has been and continues to be remembered.

HISTORICAL FRAMEWORKS AND CONTEXTS

The Wars on Terror describe an era of challenges to Western power, shaped by key events that had impacted Islamic-Western relations in the previous three decades. The once-strong force of Arab nationalism that had fostered the Baath party governments in Syria (1963–2011) and Iraq (1963–2003), and that had validated President Nasser of Egypt's leadership in the Arab world, was challenged by a revival of Islamic beliefs. Israel's victory in the 1973 Yom Kippur War discredited Arab nationalists, and secular nationalism lost further ground after the overthrow of Iran's nationalist Shah in 1979 and his replacement by the Islamic republic of Ayatollah Khomeini. Iran's Islamic Revolution not only signalled the overthrow of a Western ally—it also legitimised the concept that Islamic values rather than nationalism could provide a valid philosophical base for governance in the contemporary Middle East.

Despite this Islamic resurgence, there remained a perception that challenges to Western primacy in the Middle East would remain at irritant level, although challenges to the West were not long in coming. Following Israel's 1982 invasion of Lebanon and defeat of the (nationalist) Palestinian Liberation Organisation, the United Nations authorised a Western-based multinational peacekeeping force. It was hoped that this deployment of first-world soldiers from Italy, France, Great Britain, and the United States would facilitate transition to peace, but a series of confrontations culminating in the October 1983 suicide bomb attacks that left 241 American and 58 French soldiers dead showed that the threat of great power intervention had little impact. France and the United States responded with ineffectual air attacks, although the ultimate representation of Western weakness masquerading as apparent strength was the United States battleship *New Jersey* shelling the Lebanon hills with outdated 16-inch gunfire. The symbolism of a World War Two battleship launching attacks on militias that did not respect great power posturing was not lost.

The fall of the Berlin Wall in 1989 and end of the Cold War led to expectations that Western liberal democratic capitalist models would have worldwide appeal, a belief reinforced by the American-led liberation of Kuwait in the 1990–1991 Gulf War. Iraq's military had been the most powerful conventional force in the Middle East, but despite their defeat by the far smaller multinational coalition, challenges to American dominance were not long in coming. Famine and the governmental collapse in Somalia led an overconfident United States to embark on a peacekeeping mission that ended abruptly after low-level militants killed 19 American soldiers in street fighting in Mogadishu in October 1993. Clearly the global superpower was vulnerable to asymmetric warfare and could quickly be forced to withdraw when attacked by poorly armed militants. Earlier that year, Islamic terrorists had tried to destroy the World Trade Center with a truck bomb, a direct attack on American soil, and throughout the decade, further attacks, such as the 1998 bombing of the United States embassies in Kenya and Tanzania (224 dead) and the bombing of the *USS Cole* in Yemen, were demonstrations of the growing capability of anti-American Islamic terrorists.

SEPTEMBER 11 AND THE WARS ON TERROR

The September 11, 2001 attacks on the World Trade Center in New York and the Pentagon in Washington shattered Western beliefs of their own immunity outside the Arab world, as did subsequent high casualty attacks in Bali (2002), Madrid (2004), London (2005), Paris (2015), Brussels (2016), Nice (2016), and Manchester (2017). Despite the previous decades of tensions, most in the West had not expected that Middle Eastern conflicts would have a global reach, despite the contemporary era of globalisation and porous borders. In the case of the September 11 attacks, the ruthless hijacking of four commercial passenger aircraft and their utilisation as flying bombs was unprecedented and shocking. The United States' response was conditioned by the magnitude and nature of the attack, the personality of newly elected Republican President George W. Bush, and also a sense that his predecessor Bill Clinton's response to the embassy bombings of 1998 with cruise missiles attacks on Al Qaeda bases had only limited impact. Bush's response to September 11 became known as the Wars on Terror and resulted in major campaigns in Afghanistan and Iraq.

The United States took the war directly to Al Qaeda by removing them from a position of influence in Taliban-ruled Afghanistan—actions which embroiled the United States and its allies in both an invasion and then a nation-building exercise. One factor behind the success of the initial 2001 American attack on both Al Qaeda and the Taliban was the existence of a long-running anti-Taliban opposition: the Northern Alliance. The combination of American air power, targeted Special Forces actions, and the tenacity of the Northern Alliance resulted in a rapid collapse of the Taliban and their Al Qaeda allies by early 2002. The Taliban regime was unpopular internationally (only three governments recognised it) and it had been long condemned for its repressive actions towards women and its callous disregard for Afghanistan's pre-Islamic heritage; a notable example was the Taliban's destruction of the fourth and fifth-century Bamiyan Buddhist statues. There was widespread international support for the new democratic Afghan government established in 2002, and when the United States turned its attention to invading Iraq in 2003 and the Taliban re-emerged, there was also international support for the NATO-led International Security Assistance Force for Afghanistan (ISAF). Although the United States and ISAF forces did not always have the same goals, the existence of clear UN mandates and the repugnant nature of the former Taliban regime allowed Afghanistan to become 'the good war' in the Wars on Terror. International support for nation building and for ISAF and United States counterinsurgency continued throughout the first decade of the twenty-first century, but Afghanistan took a subsidiary place in the Wars on Terror following the invasion of Iraq.

The apparent ease of Western intervention in Afghanistan undoubtedly encouraged the United States to invade Iraq in March 2003, and this invasion was also to result in a protracted nation-building exercise. The United States could have tried to justify their invasion on the grounds of democratic reform or responsibility to protect, but chose to use dated United Nations Security Council resolutions and a subsequently discredited claim that Iraq was redeveloping a defunct Weapon of Mass Destruction (WMD) capability. There is unequivocal evidence that Iraq had previously maintained and used such a capability prior to 1998, but as the United States' forces advanced on Baghdad, it quickly became apparent that the only sign of usable WMD capability came from inaccurate Western intelligence reports, and this failure to find anything other than residual WMD material discredited the Iraq War in its early stages. The overthrow of Saddam Hussein's authoritarian regime and its replacement by the UN-endorsed democratic regime in 2004 could have been internationally lauded, but an invasion on those grounds would have contravened international law and long-established Westphalian principles of state sovereignty unless the United States' actions were given international legitimacy (Kagan 2004). Although the subsequent occupation and reconstruction of Iraq was legalised by a series of United Nations Security Council resolutions, the United States and its allies were widely criticised and mass protests in the West condemned the war as an invasion by a self-serving United States. Despite democratic elections, the new Iraqi government lacked widespread domestic support, and a foolish American decision to disband Saddam Hussein's army in 2003, as well as a paucity of ground troops establishing law and order in the immediate aftermath of Saddam's defeat, fuelled the growing Iraqi insurgency.

The war in Iraq entered a second phase from 2004 onwards, and it appeared that the United States had become bogged down in an intractable conflict. Ethnic and religious divisions within Iraq increased, and these divisions became the basis for further anti-government and anti-American insurgency, as well as sectarian violence and mass killings. The new Iraqi government, the United States, and its allies were opposed by a wide variety of insurgent groups that included nationalists, Islamists, and Shia and Sunni sectarians who were united in their opposition to the presence of foreign troops. The Iraq War became a lodestone for anti-American Islamists worldwide and attracted foreign fighters. The War on Terror in Iraq was clearly now associated with American weakness and casualties rather than American strength and victory. Revelations of prisoner abuse at Baghdad's Abu Ghraib prison and at the US detention facility in Guantánamo Bay in Cuba further undermined the moral basis of the American-led mission. Nevertheless, the Americans and the Iraqi government did achieve success with the 2007 anti-insurgent Al Anbar Tribal Awakening and the 2007 United States troop surge, which created the conditions for the United States to establish a limited victory and set the preconditions for withdrawal in 2011. Although in the post-invasion reconstruction phase the United States was supported by more than 40 coalition allies, the war was primarily seen as being initiated and run by the United States and serving an American agenda.

The year that saw a war-weary United States officially withdraw combat troops from Iraq ironically coincided with a wave of democratic protest throughout the Middle East and the subsequent emergence of a new Islamist movement, Islamic State. The 2011 Arab Spring protests had mixed success but they did lead to the collapse of non-democratic regimes in Tunisia, Egypt, Libya, Yemen, and Syria. Syria and Libya endured civil war, and the civil war in Syria soon spread to neighbouring Iraq. The Islamic State movement seized substantial territory in eastern Syria and western Iraq in 2014 and attracted supporters with its proposal for a world-wide Islamic caliphate, while being condemned worldwide for its extremist behaviour, thus opening a new front in the Wars on Terror, an end to which seemed distant.

As the euphoria of the Arab Spring was overshadowed by the tragedy of what became known as the Arab Winter with its increasing levels of religious extremism, authoritarianism, and violence, the complexities of regional multilateral involvement also marked a clear transition from simple binaries such as Islam versus the West. The struggles in Syria, Iraq, and beyond devolved to subsume increasingly significant Middle Eastern and extra-regional actors, with the once-dominant United States and its long-term Western allies being relegated to a marginal position. The liberal presidency of Barack Obama (2009–2017) may have differed in style from his more pugnacious (and contradictory) successor Donald Trump, but regardless of leadership, the United States' public was clearly disinclined to support further expeditionary wars. A small Western-based coalition achieved some success against Islamic State by 2016 and 2017, but other actors were becoming increasingly important and diverse, ranging from the extensive Iranian and Russian support for the Syrian government, to Turkish intervention against Kurdish forces, and an emerging Saudi Arabian–Iranian proxy conflict. A danger of writing contemporary history is that we are uncomfortably close to events, yet it might be that future scholars will argue that the varied actors in this disorder mark a new era rather than a post-9/11 continuation.

This brief historical synopsis provides the necessary context for the essays in this volume. More precisely, the broader ideas of the clash of civilisations; the decades of Western attempts to comprehend, assist, or dominate the Middle East; and the September 11 attacks establish the foundation for understanding the way that the Wars on Terror became embedded in the cultural memories of communities outside the United States.

Contemporary War, Cultural Memory, and Trauma

Memory studies throughout the twentieth and twenty-first centuries—centuries marked by war and violence—have been dominated by the study of trauma. Both individual and cultural memory, following the influence of Freudian psychoanalysis, have been primarily understood through a logic of forgetting, of repression and recovery. 'Traumatic memory', as Cathy Caruth has it, 'totters between remembrance and erasure, producing a history that is, in its very events, a kind of inscription of the past; but also a history constituted by the erasure of its traces' (Caruth 2014, p. 20). Caruth's model might be seen to hold true for those directly affected by traumatic events (such as the terrorist attacks of September 11), but what of those less involved, those who bear witness to the trauma and have sympathy for those affected, but are also able to consider a more nuanced perspective, one less explicitly marked by those processes of erasure?

This collection considers the recent historical and cultural significance of terrorist attacks in New York City on September 11, 2001, and the subsequent and ongoing Wars on Terror in the Middle East with the particular aim of understanding how those events have been and continue to be perceived and remembered by those living outside the

United States—specifically Britain and Australia. As such, the essays collected here are interested in the processes of *making* memory in both individual and collective contexts, and in the ways in which our memories of the past are *changed* or altered precisely by those new memories and practices of memorialisation, and also in the ways these are affected when one is at a remove from the original trauma. These essays are thus guided by Michael Rothberg's conceptualisation of multidirectional memory, which 'draw[s] attention to the dynamic transfers that take place between diverse places and times during the act of remembrance', as part of a consideration of the ways in which 'remembrance both cuts across and bind together diverse spatial, temporal, and cultural sites' (2009, p. 11). The Wars on Terror in the twenty-first century have ignited reflections on these processes of memory-making and the ways in which they interact across space and time, as well as the ways in which those temporal and geographical contexts impact cultural and individual memories. Indeed, for Nigel C. Hunt, a study of 'the psychosocial impact of war' is simultaneously a project of 'understanding memory not just as individual memory, but also the ways in which other people, society and culture, and history, all affect how we remember' (2010, p. 2); in other words, understanding war and understanding memory are intrinsically related projects. 'History is written by the victors,' so the cliché goes, but this book is more specifically interested in the ways in which, as in Nicolas Abraham and Maria Torok's model of the transgenerational phantom, the trauma of war is experienced by others beyond the immediate witness.

Marc Redfield has made the evocative observation that the adoption of the term 'September 11' into popular discourse is a kind of 'linguistic fallout', a 'mark on ordinary language' (2007, p. 55)—it is, perhaps, a cultural wounding. But if this is true, the term's adoption into a global discourse suggests that this wound is not limited to the immediate victims or the immediate national context of the attacks. Indeed, since 'the literal damage they did to the military and commercial orders symbolised by the Pentagon and the World Trade Center was miniscule' so that 'it is of course as symbolic acts of violence that they claim culturally traumatic status' (p. 56), it follows that this 'culturally traumatic status' would extend to other nations and contexts bearing witness to the attacks and their effects. For Jacques Derrida, too, the 'mark' of the date 'September 11' suggests the

...impact of what is at least *felt*, in an apparently immediate way, to be an event that truly marks, that truly makes its mark, a singular and [...] 'unprecedented' event. I say 'apparently immediate' because this 'feeling' is actually less spontaneous than it appears: it is to a large extent conditioned, constituted, if not actually constructed, circulated at any rate through the media by means of a prodigious techno-socio-political machine. (Borradori 2003, p. 86; original emphasis)

Wounding, marking, feeling, impression—each of these terms evokes the way in which September 11 lingers in our cultural memory. Indeed, in psychoanalytic terms, memory is the result of the way in which both reality and fantasy create 'their mutual impress upon pliable screens that simultaneously conceal as well as reveal what is behind them' (Antze and Lambek 1996, p. xii).[1] Saradindu Bhattacharya, too, has shown how online environments of memorialisation have 'call[ed] upon a global audience to participate in the collective acts of recollecting, archiving and mourning the loss that occurred at the epicentre, Ground Zero', in order to create 'a deterritorialised community of witnesses who are united in their emotional response to the event' (2010, p. 64). This 'affective community' is a product of 'bring[ing] together mourners, across physical space and time' (p. 71). Yet, Bhattacharya's study depends upon a US-centric framing of the discourses discussed, and those impressions of memory, we must note, are global: 9/11 was 'an event [...] unmatched in terms of its (hyper)visibility as a "spectacle" as well as of its representational power to attract a "witnessing" audience far beyond the limits of its direct impact' (p. 64). As such, Derrida adds, the impression that the event was a crisis, a 'major event...cannot be dissociated from all the affects, interpretations, and rhetoric that have at once reflected, communicated, and "globalised" it, from everything that also and first of all formed, produced, and made it possible' (Borradori 2003, p. 88). To understand the impact of 9/11 and the Wars on Terror in this wider context, we must attend precisely to those external discourses of response. What happens when the *lieux de mémoire*, sites of memory, to borrow Pierre Nora's phrase, are relocated or dispersed? How does the space of memorialising 9/11 and the Wars on Terror work outside the US context? What happens when 'those who are outsiders to the experience deal with the challenge of its presence in their world' (Goodall and Lee 2015, p. 1)? It is to those impressions as they have been felt in Britain and Australia that this collection of essays turns.

At the same time, to attend to these instances of transnational memories is to understand the totalising, universalising, and far-reaching effects of trauma. Individual memories, to be sure, are tied to our personal circumstances and to our own identities (Goodall and Lee 2015, p. 2), and the same is true of both collective and public memories: 'memory offers a certain scope for the kind of play or freedom that enables us to creatively refashion ourselves, remembering one thing and not another, changing the stories we tell ourselves (and others) about ourselves' (Antze and Lambek 1996, p. xvi).[2] Memories are not, therefore, simply made and archived, but are subject to processes of selection and adaptation that support an individual's or a nation's or a culture's view of itself. Indeed, add Paul Antze and Michael Lambek, '[m]emories are acts of commemoration, of testimony, of confession, of accusation. Memories do not merely describe the speaker's relation to the past but place her quite specifically in reference to it' (p. xxv). Thus, this collection is concerned with ways in which memories of the Wars on Terror are both selected and altered, whether that is with an explicit intention, or as a result of the process of traumatic response. By exploring how cultural memory is both made and shaped, the essays collected here seek to understand the impact of September 11 and the Wars on Terror on national and cultural identities in Britain and Australia, and the implications of these events on the ways in which we understand our global relations in the twenty-first century.

Memory and the Wars on Terror is interdisciplinary in its scope, and addresses a range of contexts and practices in which the memory-work of September 11 and the Wars on Terror might be seen to most prominently take place. The chapters by Kevin Foster, Amanda Laugesen, Rebecca Te'o, and Jessica Carniel, for example, consider the ways in which media representations of the Wars on Terror might be seen to shape public memory. In attending to these practices, they take up Barbie Zelizer and Keren Tenenboim-Weinblatt's recent argument that although 'the very surfacing of collective memory depends often on a wide range of institutional engagements, more so today than perhaps ever before, the neglect surrounding journalism's role in the establishment and legitimation of shared memory leaves a curious hole in our understanding of memory's trappings' (2014, p. 1). Far from neglecting the influence of the media, and at odds with its stated commitment to truth and fact, Foster, Laugesen, Te'o and Carniel make clear the ways in which the media can subject its audiences to expectations of memory-making, sometimes resulting in false memories (Foster) or in traumatic experiences for journalists themselves (Te'o).

Marita Sturken makes the important point that '[c]ultural memory is a field of cultural negotiation through which different stories vie for a place in history' (1997, p. 1), or as Jay Winter and Emmanuel Sivan put it, '[c]ollective remembrance is public recollection. It is the act of gathering bits and pieces of the past, and joining them together in public. The "public" is the group that produces, expresses, and consumes it' (1999, p. 6). In Sturken's discussion of the memorialisation of several prominent events that have occurred in the United States throughout the twentieth century, she explores the political and sentimental conflicts and intersections between memory and history, and the ways in which these are represented in various cultural products, explaining that such products 'are *technologies* of memory in that they embody and generate memory and are thus implicated in the power dynamics of memory's production' (1997, p. 10; original emphasis). These 'technologies of memory', including novels, film, and visual art works, are in an ongoing dialogue, 'an ongoing process of contestation', Winter and Sivan argue—and this is 'one of the permanent features of remembrance', in itself an 'enduring social activity' (p. 39).[3] Various kinds of cultural products of the Wars on Terror are considered in detail in this collection. Belinda McKay, Richard Gehrmann, Christa van Raalte, Jessica Gildersleeve, Kezia Whiting, and Denise N. Rall all explore a range of literary, cinematic, and visual art works, suggesting the ways in which September 11 and the Wars on Terror are not only represented in those works, but the ways in which they have impacted on the medium of art itself. In particular, a number of these pieces attend to the way in which memory is made visual in cinema and art. Zelizer has argued that images can 'challenge what we think we know about the past and how we think we know it' (1998, p. 2). Gildersleeve's essay, for example, explores the way in which Pat Barker's literary representation of the artist and her art has been impacted by the Wars on Terror—violence and trauma, she suggests, might, in the popular reading, go beyond representation. Barker's novels also suggest that it is the artist's responsibility to depict and respond to that trauma as part of a process of ethical survival. Rall, too, notes the way in which images themselves can shape memory and response, while van Raalte argues for the impact of gender on such representations in film. Like Raelene Frances and Bruce Scates in their recent study of the cultural memory of the First World War as it appears in Australia, New Zealand, and Turkey (Frances and Scates 2016), this study attends to a range of cultural products that shape our memory of the war.

Finally, Robert Mason and Dashiel Lawrence turn to the ways in which particular cultural groups have been impacted by and memorialise the Wars on Terror, noting the perhaps-paradoxical formation of community and connection in addition to the transferred and reinvigorated experiences of trauma wrought by these events. Far from being a function only of the fraught relationship between the United States and the Middle East, the Wars on Terror should always be understood as conflicts with a long global history. These wars are the product of other wars, earlier conflicts, which bind the twentieth and twenty-first centuries in cycles of revenge and justice. In testament to those cycles of physical and psychological violence, the study of memory has been dominated by the discussion of the effects of trauma (Nadal and Calvo 2014, p. 1). Indeed, 'although not all memory is traumatic' (Traverso and Broderick 2010, p. 5), for Antze and Lambek, 'memory worth talking about—worth remembering—is memory of trauma' (1996, xii). This relationship is a critical one for the present study, and the essays collected here seek to interrogate the means by which the traumatic experiences of other groups or nations are incorporated into the collective psyche or cultural memory of apparent 'outsiders'.

There have been several studies of the effects of September 11 and the Wars on Terror on contemporary culture, especially to mark the ten-year anniversary in 2011.[4] However, these works either retain a focus on the significance of the Wars on Terror as they have been received and represented in the United States, or they were produced prior to the withdrawal of American and NATO troops from Afghanistan in 2014 and before the full effects of the 2011 American withdrawal from Iraq had been felt. *Memory and the Wars on Terror*, by contrast, is concerned with the international impacts of these events, and the ways they have shaped, and continue to shape, Britain and Australia's relation to the rest of the world. Most existing critical coverage therefore ignores the meaning of these events for people, nations, and cultures apparently peripheral to them, but which have, this collection shows, been extraordinarily affected by the social, political, and cultural changes these wars have wrought. *Memory and the Wars on Terror* is written at the conclusion of Bush's Wars on Terror, with a focus of legacies and perceptions outside the US. With the ending of US involvement in Iraq and the withdrawal of most foreign troops from Afghanistan, and with the challenges to state structures in Iraq and Syria, there is a fundamental shift in analysis of the Wars on Terror. These changes allow more effective reflection on what is sometimes known in the United States as 'the long war'. This book provides an up-to-date reflection on representations of 9/11 and of the Wars on Terror, but includes perspectives that incorporate analysis framed within the context of the end of the US wars in Iraq and Afghanistan.

This collection thus aims to respond to dominant perspectives on twenty-first-century war by exploring how the events of 9/11 and the subsequent Wars on Terror are represented and remembered outside the US framework. Adopting a literary and cultural history approach, it asks how these events resonate and continue to show effects in the rest of the world, with a particular focus on Australia and Britain, perhaps America's closest allies, but two nations also able to see these events within a broader (and perhaps less personally victimised) context. It argues that such reflections on the impact of the Wars on Terror help us understand what global conflict means in our modern era, as well as what its representative motifs might tell us about how nations like Australia and Britain perceive and construct their remembered identities on the world stage in the twenty-first century. The collection makes this contribution at a time of four significant historical events: shortly after the fifteenth anniversary of 9/11 in 2016, the effective end of the war in Afghanistan and of this phase of the Wars on Terror, and the Centenary of the First World War. Although the Wars on Terror cannot truly be said to be 'over', international intrusion in the Middle East has significantly changed from the large-scale US and coalition commitments of the past, meaning that the time is ripe for reflection on this historical phase. Simultaneously, the centenary of the First World War means that reflection on contemporary conflict and various strategies of memorialisation has and will be taking place between 2014 and 2018.

The essays collected here thus ask three primary questions: how have these contemporary conflict events been received and remembered by nations outside the US? How have they been represented in fictional and non-fictional works of art produced from these perspectives? How have they impacted social relations among different ethnic groups in these regions? In its close examination of films, novels, memoirs, visual artworks, media, and minority communities in the years since 2001, this collection recognises the impact of 9/11 and the Wars on Terror in these areas, and seeks to explore what that means for the cultural identity and transnational position of the old and new nations of Britain and Australia. The September 11 terrorist attacks marked a turning point in modern global history. It is those effects as they are felt outside the United States with which this book is concerned.

NOTES

1. 'The past does not correspond to the real in any direct, unmediated way since what we remember are memories—screens always already impressed by the fantasies or distortions of a series of successive rememberings. Hence memories, like dreams, are highly condensed symbols of hidden preoccupations' (Antze and Lambek 1996, p. xii).
2. Goodall and Lee point out the distinction between collective (or cultural) and public memory: 'collective memory occurs when individuals separately remember the same event; public memory forms when a people remember in and through inter-subjective relationships with other members of the public' (2015, p. 4). However, in this collection we recognise that individual memorialisation cannot occur without the influence of those 'inter-subjective relationships'; as such, we use the terms interchangeably, except where specified otherwise.
3. Winter makes the same point in his introduction to *The Legacy of the Great War: Ninety Years On*, beginning the study with the assertion that '[w]riting history is always a dialogue' (2009, p. 1).
4. See, for example, E. Ann Kaplan, *Trauma Culture: The Politics of Terror and Loss in Media and Literature* (2005), David Simpson, *9/11: The Culture of Commemoration* (2006), David Holloway, *9/11 and the War on Terror* (2008), Jeff Birkenstein, Anna Froula, and Karen Randell eds, *Reframing 9/11: Film, Popular Culture and the "War on Terror"* (2010), Véronique Bragard, Christophe Dony, and Warren Rosenberg eds, *Portraying 9/11: Essays on Representations in Comics, Literature, Film and Theatre* (2011), Phillip Hammond ed, *Screens of Terror: Representations of War and Terrorism in Film and Television since 9/11* (2011), Kate McLoughlin, *Authoring War: The Literary Representation of War from the* Iliad *to* Iraq (2011), V Seidler ed, *Remembering 9/11: Terror, Trauma and Social Theory* (2013), and Lucy Bond, *Frames of Memory after 9/11: Culture, Criticism, Politics and Law* (2015). While Cara Cilano's (ed) *From Solidarity to Schisms: 9/11 and After in Fiction and Film from Outside the US* (2009) does address the representation of 9/11 from non-US perspectives, its focus solely on narrative representations, as well as

its pre-ISIS time of publication mean that an updated study such as is presented here is necessary.

Works Cited

Antze, Paul, and Michael Lambek. 1996. Introduction: Forecasting Memory. In *Tense Past: Cultural Essays in Trauma and Memory*, eds. Paul Antze and Michael Lambek, xi–xxxviii. New York: Routledge.

Berman, Paul. 2003. *Terror and Liberalism*. New York: WW Norton.

Bhattacharya, Saradindu. 2010. Mourning Becomes Electronic(a): 9/11 Online. *Journal of Creative Communications* 5 (1): 63–74.

Birkenstein, Jeff, Anna Froula, and Karen Randell (eds.). 2010. Reframing 9/11: Film, Popular Culture and the '*Wars on Terror*'. New York: Continuum.

Bond, Lucy. 2015. *Frames of Memory after 9/11: Culture, Criticism, Politics, and Law*. Houndmills: Palgrave Macmillan.

Borradori, Giobanna. 2003. *Philosophy in a Time of Terror: Dialogues with Jürgen Habermas and Jacques Derrida*. Chicago, IL: University of Chicago Press.

Burke, Peter. 2009. *Cultural Hybridity*. Cambridge: Polity.

Bragard, Véronique, Christophe Dony, and Warren Rosenberg (eds.). 2011. *Portraying 9/11: Essays on Representations in Comics, Literature, Film and Theatre*. Jefferson, NC: McFarland.

Caruth, Cathy. 2014. After the End: Psychoanalysis in the Ashes of History, in Nadal and Calvo, *Trauma in Contemporary Literature*, 17–34.

Cilano, Cara (ed.). 2009. *From Solidarity to Schism: 9/11 and After in Fiction and Film from Outside the US*. Amsterdam: Rodopi.

Frances, Raelene, and Bruce Scates (eds.). 2016. *Beyond Gallipoli: New Perspectives on ANZAC*. Clayton: Monash University Publishing.

Fukuyama, Francis. 1992. *The End of History and the Last Man*. New York: Free Press.

Goodall, Jane and Christopher Lee. 2015. Introduction. In *Trauma and Public Memory*. ed. Jane Goodall and Christopher Lee, 1–18. Houndmills: Palgrave Macmillan.

Hammond, Phillip (ed.). 2011. *Screens of Terror: Representations of War and Terrorism in Film and Television since 9/11*. Bury St Edmunds: Anima.

Holloway, David. 2008. *9/11 and the Wars on Terror*. Edinburgh: Edinburgh University Press.

Hunt, Nigel C. 2010. *Memory, War and Trauma*. Cambridge: Cambridge University Press.

Huntington, Samuel. 1996. *The Clash of Civilisations and the Remaking of World Order*. New York: Simon & Schuster.

Kagan, Robert. 2004. America's Crisis of Legitimacy. *Foreign Affairs* 83 (2): 65–87.

Kaplan, E. Ann. 2005. *Trauma Culture: The Politics of Terror and Loss in Media and Literature*. New York: Rutgers University Press.

McLoughlin, Kate. 2011. *Authoring War: The Literary Representation of War from the Iliad to Iraq*. Cambridge: Cambridge University Press.

Nadal, Marita, and Mónica Calvo. 2014. Trauma and Literary Representation: An Introduction, In *Trauma in Contemporary Literature: Narrative and Representation*, eds. Marita Nadal and Mónica Calvo 1–15. New York: Routledge.

Redfield, Marc. 2007. Virtual Trauma: The Idiom of 9/11. *diacritics* 37 (1): 55–80.

Rothberg, Michael. 2009. *Multidirectional Memory: Remembering the Holocaust in the Age of Decolonisation*. Stanford, CA: Stanford University Press.

Said, Edward. 2001. The Clash of Ignorance. *Nation*, Oct 22. Available from: http://www.thenation.com/article/clash-ignorance.

Seidler, V. 2013. *Remembering 9/11: Terror, Trauma and Social Theory*. Houndmills: Palgrave Macmillan.

Sen, Amartya. 1999. Democracy as a Universal Value. *Journal of Democracy* 10 (3): 3–17.

Simpson, David. 2006. *9/11: The Culture of Commemoration*. Chicago, IL: University of Chicago Press.

Sturken, Marita. 1997. *Tangled Memories: The Vietnam War, the AIDS Epidemic, and the Politics of Remembering*. Berkeley, CA: University of California Press.

Traverso, Antonio, and Mick Broderick. 2010. Interrogating Trauma: Towards a Critical Trauma Studies. *Continuum* 24 (1): 3–15.

Winter, Jay. 2009. Approaching the History of the Great War: A User's Guide. In *The Legacy of the Great War: Ninety Years On*, ed. Jay Winter, 1–17. Columbia, MO: University of Missouri Press.

Winter, Jay, and Emmanuel Sivan. 1999. Setting the Framework. In *War and Remembrance in the Twentieth Century*, ed. Jay Winter and Emmanuel Sivan, 6–39. Cambridge: Cambridge University Press.

Zelizer, Barbie. 1998. *Remembering to Forget: Holocaust Memory Through the Camera's Eye*. Chicago, IL: University of Chicago Press.

Zelizer, Barbie, and Keren Tenenboim-Weinblatt. 2014. Journalism's Memory Work. In *Journalism and Memory*, ed. Barbie Zelizer and Keren Tenenboim-Weinblatt, 1–15. Houndmills: Palgrave Macmillan.

AUTHORS' BIOGRAPHY

Jessica Gildersleeve is Senior Lecturer in English Literature at the University of Southern Queensland. She is the author of *Elizabeth Bowen and the Writing of Trauma: The Ethics of Survival* (Brill/Rodopi 2014), as well as essays on other twentieth- and twenty-first-century women writers, including Rosamond

Lehmann, Jean Rhys, Agatha Christie, Sarah Waters, and Pat Barker. Her monographs on Christos Tsiolkas and the film *Don't Look Now* will be published later this year.

Richard Gehrmann is a Senior Lecturer in International Studies at the University of Southern Queensland who deployed to Afghanistan and Iraq as an Australian Army reservist. A graduate of the University of Cambridge, he has published on war and society, and on representation and identity. Richard is currently researching depictions of captivity and trauma in the Age of Terror.

CHAPTER 2

False Memories and Professional Culture: The Australian Defence Force, the Government and the Media at War in Afghanistan

Kevin Foster

One of the more remarkable effects of the September 11 attacks on the United States mainland was their apparently revolutionary impact on military-media relations in the US and how this supposedly catalysed a liberalisation of information management policies among militaries across the globe. This chapter will explain why the radical changes that eventuated in the US and far beyond were implemented much later and in a much-diluted form in Australia and how they can only be understood in the context of the history of military-media engagement through the 1980s and 1990s. It will then consider how the Australian Defence Force's continued commitment to restrictive and tightly managed relations between the military and the media rested on a stubborn fidelity to false memories of the Vietnam experience and how these shaped Australian coverage of the war in Afghanistan.

K. Foster (✉)
Monash University, Clayton, Australia
e-mail: kevin.foster@monash.edu

© The Author(s) 2017
J. Gildersleeve and R. Gehrmann (eds.), *Memory and the Wars on Terror*, Palgrave Macmillan Memory Studies,
DOI 10.1007/978-3-319-56976-5_2

In the years after its retreat from Vietnam in 1975, the US military and its supporters insisted that the media had lost a war that 'South Vietnamese and American forces actually won', that though they had 'crushed the Viet Cong in the South' and 'threw back the invasion by regular North Vietnamese divisions...the War was finally lost to the invaders *after* the US disengagement because the political pressures built up by the media had made it quite impossible for Washington to maintain even the minimal material and moral support that would have enabled the Saigon regime to continue effective resistance' (Elegant 1981, p. 73). The belief that the media was responsible for the US defeat in Vietnam shaped the military's attitudes towards and relations with the media and 'became a defining feature of the US military's public affairs policy for the next quarter century. The lesson, translated into practical advice for future operations, was that the press needed to be treated like an adversary and that media access to the battlefield should be strictly denied' (Rid 2007, pp. 62–63).

During the First Persian Gulf War in 1991, the Americans applied this lesson to the 1600 media professionals who descended on Saudi Arabia after Iraq's invasion of Kuwait on 2 August 1990. Around 200 of these reporters, formed into Media Reporting Teams (MRTs), were granted access to the troops in forward areas to provide pooled dispatches for their colleagues in the rear. Their movements closely monitored by military Public Affairs Officers (PAOs), the journalists were completely at the mercy of their uniformed minders for access to and transport within the area of operations, and for the review and transmission of their copy, which was dispatched via military communications systems. When Operation Desert Shield became Operation Desert Storm on 17 January 1991 and the bombing campaign to liberate Kuwait began, despite their greater proximity to the action, the MRT reporters were little better off than the 'hotel warriors' back in Riyadh and Dhahran, sitting through the US military's official briefings, cheering the smart-bomb footage and guffawing at General Norman Schwartzkopf's leaden jokes. The military's comprehensive control over the media seemed to provide 'a classic example of how to project a desired view of conflict in the new informational environment that had emerged during the 1980s' (Taylor 2003, p. 287). Yet this was not the media management triumph that it appeared. John J. Fialka observed that '[w]ithin hours of the launching' of the ground offensive on 24 February, '[t]he Army-designed pony express system of couriers and its teams of reporter escorts' collapsed:

'nearly 80 per cent of reports filed took more than 12 hours to get back to Dhahran. One in ten took three days or more' (1991, p. 11; Carruthers 2000, p. 141). As a consequence, despite the new 24-hour coverage of events, the reporting of the First Gulf War was notable for its significant absences, its tardiness, and its failure to provide contemporary coverage of any of the war's major battles. In the aftermath of the fighting, despite Defence Public Affairs chief Pete Williams' claim that the American people had enjoyed 'the best war coverage they ever had' (cited in Cumings 1992, p. 117). Peter Braestrup condemned the media's Gulf War experience as 'high-cost, low-benefit horde journalism' and put '[b]oth Washington policymakers and senior Army officers' on notice that they 'should not embrace the notion that handling the media Gulf War-style is the way to do things next time..."Next time" will be different' (Braestrup 2000, p. xiii).

The US experience in the Gulf demonstrated that 'the new informational environment that had emerged during the 1980s' had made the lessons of Vietnam redundant. While military commanders in the Gulf corralled the media, drip-fed them a diet of good news, and busied themselves with degrading the local infrastructure, the Iraqis seized the 'information initiative' (Rid 2007, p. 84). Minders from the Iraqi Information Ministry undercut the US effort to portray the war as a bloodless exercise in precision bombing by directing Western news crews to evidence of the human cost of the bombardment. On the night of 13 February 1991, US precision-guided bombs hit a command and control bunker in al-Amiriya that was being used as a civilian air-raid shelter, incinerating hundreds of old people, women, and children. The Iraqis bussed the international press corps to the site where they 'filmed scenes of charred human remains being removed from the ravaged building... The footage was revelatory, as grief-stricken survivors unwrapped bundles of molten human flesh' (Carruthers 2000, p. 139). Outgunned on the battlefield, the Iraqis exploited their information assets to undermine the coalition cause.

Far from demonstrating the defeat and humiliation of the media, the First Gulf War provided an object lesson in how badly the military needed them. The *Gulf War Air Power Survey* (1993) recognised that, like Saddam Hussein, future adversaries would deploy sophisticated information operations to undermine public support for a given campaign. In their efforts to achieve 'full spectrum dominance', militaries were going to need the media to tell their stories. As a result, provision for adequate press coverage had to be regarded as 'an unavoidable yet important part of military operations' (Olson 1993, p. 135). Just how important was reflected during Operation Allied Force, NATO's 1999 effort to halt the ethnic cleansing of Kosovo's Albanian population during the Yugoslav Civil War, where its greater force of arms was frustrated by Serbia's domination of the information space. Due to the exclusively airborne nature of the operation, there were no friendly ground forces with which correspondents might embed to report on events on the ground as they occurred. The Serbs adroitly exploited this gaping hole in NATO's information operations planning. On 14 April 1999, near the village of Djakovica, around 70 civilians were killed when US Air Force F-16s mistook a convoy of agricultural vehicles for a Serb armoured column and bombed it. Serb authorities transported Western journalists to the site of the bombing and expedited the transmission of their copy. The resulting images of 'mangled tractors and minibuses...burned and bloodied corpses...limbs scattered among destroyed vehicles' and their accompanying reports ran constantly on CNN over the following days and made front-page headlines in both the *New York Times* and the *Los Angeles Times* (Rid 2007, p. 98). By contrast, it took five days for NATO to concede responsibility for the mistake, by which time it had ceded the information advantage to the Serbs and paid the price in damaged legitimacy and rising public disapproval of the campaign.[1]

Three weeks later, misled by an out-dated map, NATO jets struck the wrong target again, in this case the Chinese Embassy compound in Belgrade, where three people were killed and fifteen wounded. Once again, while NATO dithered over an official response, the Serbs exploited their advantage, claiming that it was their civilian population, and not the Kosovars or the Bosnians, who were the victims of indiscriminate assault from heavily armed opponents. Information dominance brought the Serbs concrete military benefits. In the wake of the Djakovica attack, NATO cancelled daytime sorties and then abandoned the bombing of Belgrade after the Chinese Embassy incident. Its Supreme Commander, US General Wesley Clark, conceded that 'The weight of public opinion was doing to us what the Serb air defence system had failed to do: limit our strikes' (2001, p. 444). Chastened by this experience, US commanders realised that force of arms alone could not guarantee victory and that wars also had to be won in the information environment. Like their nimbler adversaries, the military had to move its approach to information management from defence to attack, to treat information as a weapon as well as a shield: 'the US military needed to engage in what doctrine would call counter propaganda activities', and to do that they had to integrate public affairs into strategic planning, to bring the media onto the battlefield with the freedom and the technical means to tell the story (Rid 2007, p. 87).

In late 2002, as the US prepared for a second invasion of Iraq in little more than a decade, the Assistant Secretary of Defense for Public Affairs, Victoria Clarke, set out to persuade her boss, the Secretary of Defense, Donald Rumsfeld, that if the military were to dominate the information sphere, they would have to take the media with them into battle. The embedding of reporters had a 'strategic function in the overall war plan and had been designed to achieve five specific objectives: to pre-empt and counter Iraqi disinformation; to encourage dissent and defection among Iraqi civilians and fighting men; to publicise the successes of the US invasion; to manage the public's expectations about what might be achieved in Iraq; and to achieve and maintain information dominance' (Rid 2007, p. 133). Having won Rumsfeld's support, Clarke's office issued the Public Affairs Guidance (PAG) document on 10 February 2003 that laid out the responsibilities and duties of the military and the media around access to the area of operations, freedom of movement within it, and the review and transmission of copy. It required the military to 'ensure that the media were provided with every opportunity to observe actual combat operations' (Office of the Assistant Secretary of Defense for Public Affairs 2003, 3G).[2] They had to furnish seats on 'priority inter-theater airlift' to make sure that reporters could get to the fighting and then assist them in the timely transmission of the copy gathered there (2.C.2). Just as 'no communications equipment for use by media in the conduct of their duties will be specifically prohibited', so there would be 'no general review process for media products' (2.C.4; 3.R). The PAG's specific provisions underwrote the broader political commitment to openness and democracy: 'Our ultimate strategic success in bringing peace and security to this region will come in our long-term commitment to supporting our democratic ideals. We need to tell the factual story—good or bad—before others seed the media with disinformation and distortions' (2.A). In light of this, the PAG explicitly forbade any attempt to 'prevent the release of derogatory, embarrassing, negative or uncomplimentary information' (4).

By contrast, the principal goals of the ADF's media management policies and practices in Afghanistan were, for almost the entire period of its deployment there, to keep the fourth estate at arm's length from the military, impede their access to the nation's forces, curtail their freedom of movement, assign escort officers to shadow the reporters, and subject their copy to review. While the US military's media relations were transformed between the First and Second Gulf Wars by bitter experience, the ADF's practices in Afghanistan and its identification of the media as the enemy were shaped by its misremembering of the 'lessons of Vietnam'. During and after the fighting in Vietnam, there was a growing conviction in Australia that if the media had not actually conspired to lose the war, it had certainly 'maligned the troops after so wholeheartedly supporting them', and so fomented public resentment against them and the war as a whole (Ham 2007, p. 415). This belief reflected a broader tendency to conflate the US and Australian experiences of the Vietnam War to the point where, Jeffrey Grey noted, 'our "memories" of the war are shaped and coloured by American responses to the American experience' (2010, p. 211). With specific regard to the media, Rodney Tiffen warned that it was 'a fundamental mistake...to think the debate about American media coverage of the [Vietnam] war can be simply translated to Australia' (2009, p. 118). The resourcing and professional practices of the Australian reporters in Vietnam and the purported effects of their coverage were far removed from those of their US counterparts: 'Just as Australia's military commitment was disproportionately smaller than America's, so was Australia's journalistic commitment...The number of Australian correspondents in Vietnam at any one time never numbered more than a handful, while during peaks of newsworthiness there were several hundred from the United States' (p. 126). During the most newsworthy peak of all, the Tet offensive of 1968, while dozens of US journalists reported from Saigon, Danang, Hue, and other key sites, Australia had only a handful of reporters in country.[3] Some Australian newspapers failed to muster a single visitor to the war: 'The *Sydney Morning Herald*, which had sent more correspondents to World War II than any other Australian newspaper, did not manage to send one to Vietnam' (Anderson and Trembath 2011, p. 231). Consequently, the principal 'source of material for Australian newspapers came from the international news agencies' (Tiffen 2009, p. 166). With the news covered, Australian media outlets were free to pursue a personal angle on the war. Pat Burgess, who covered the war for Fairfax, noted that his employers 'didn't want news, they were going to rely on the agency for news...they only wanted airmailers...a feature type story' (cited in Payne 2007, p. 17).

Despite an impasto of cooperation, the military was determined to keep the reporters at arm's length: 'A telegram from Austforce, Vietnam, to the Department of the Army in Canberra stated that their senior officers "had been advised on a confidential basis that they should as far as possible avoid contact with press representatives without making it obvious that they are doing so"' (Anderson and Trembath 2011, p. 237). But it was perfectly obvious to some. Tim Bowden recalls that 'Unlike the Americans and other allied groups fighting in South Vietnam, the Australians did not welcome foreign correspondents; they had a deep seated distrust of the press. It was known in the trade as the "feel free to fuck off" approach to public relations' (Bowden 1987, p. 141).[4] Those who chose not to fuck off were subjected to intrusive oversight. Creighton Burns of *The Age* recalled that 'you couldn't talk to an Australian soldier without the presence of an officer there' (cited in Anderson 2009, p. 127), a practice Denis Warner designated 'the most blatant attempt to impose censorship at source that I have ever encountered in any Army in any war at any time' (cited in Payne 2007, p. 5).

The military's constraints on the reporters were complemented by explicit directions from their employers. John Mancy and Alan Ramsey of AAP 'were told to stick to reporting stories and not to carry out investigative pieces or editorialise' while the ABC imposed 'strict guidelines' dictating 'what its news division staff could say and could not say' which resulted in the prohibition of 'any form of commentary' (Anderson and Trembath 2011, p. 234). As a consequence of direct government intrusion, military obstruction, and the publishers' and broadcasters' editorial policies, Rodney Tiffen argued that the Australian media's coverage of the Vietnam War 'was overwhelmingly timid,' exhibiting 'less independent probing, less willingness to devote adequate resources to reporting the war, and a far more restricted range of opinion and analysis' than their foreign counterparts, resulting in coverage somewhere between 'general support' and vociferous partisanship (2009, p. 184). In light of this damning judgment, the military concluded that its policies of limited contact with the media and strict control over their movements and copy had been vindicated. Accordingly, while the Americans learned from the First Gulf War and Kosovo that the lessons of Vietnam had failed, that the media were not the enemy but an important ally, the ADF hung onto the lessons it learned in Phuoc Tuy and carried its memories of them and the hostility they bred towards the fourth estate all the way to Uruzgan.

The nature and scope of Australian reporting from Afghanistan was also shaped by the size, purpose, and geographical location of the ADF commitment. At the highpoint of its commitment in December 2012, Australia contributed around 1550 troops to NATO's International Security Assistance Force mission, of whom a little over 1200 were deployed in Uruzgan province and the remainder in Kabul, Kandahar, and elsewhere in Afghanistan and the Gulf States.[5] This commitment was a fraction of that of the senior coalition partners, the US and Britain, making it one of the 'minor players in the Afghanistan experiment' (Cantwell 2012, p. 30).[6] Further, Uruzgan is 'one of the most remote and forgotten provinces of Afghanistan' and 'remains one of the poorest and least developed' (Yeaman 2013, p. 32). The critical front lines of the conflict were located to the east on the border with Pakistan, or deeper to the south in the Pashtu heartlands of Kandahar and Helmand. As such, whatever the ADF might have achieved in Uruzgan, it had little impact on the ultimate outcome of the struggle. Correspondingly, the fate of the Afghans and their country was of little concern to Australians for whom Afghanistan was always more a war than a country. The fighting there mattered to Australians because it revealed *who* the men and women of the armed forces were, not *what* they did. Accordingly, the ADF was highly sensitive about how it was portrayed by the fourth estate and for the greater period of its deployment it retained a tight grip over who in the media went to Afghanistan, where they could travel once there, what they saw, and who they could meet.

This determination to limit the media's access and curtail their freedom of movement put the ADF's information management practices sharply at odds with those of their coalition allies from Canada and the Netherlands. In their study of Dutch embedded journalism in Afghanistan, *Eyes Wide Shut?* (2008), Mans et al. examined seven factors that had determined Dutch media coverage of the nation's military operations—media management policy, selection of reporters, timing of their visits, facilitation of access, freedom of movement, control over content, and sanctions.[7] Given that the Australian, Dutch, and Canadian militaries performed broadly similar roles with roughly equivalent force commitments, these criteria provide a useful basis on which comparisons between their approaches to military-media relations in Afghanistan and their outcomes might be based.[8]

Dutch military-media relations were framed by an explicit communications policy document, the *Communicatieplan*, whose purpose was 'to showcase the importance and the developments of the mission and its specific assignments in a professional manner', for a variety of audiences, 'the public, visitors, politicians and others that are involved' (cited in Mans et al. 2008, p. 15). To meet these goals, Dr. Joop Veen, the Director of Communications at the *Ministerie van Defensie* (MvD) recalled, 'we decided to have embedded journalism, we decided to have combat camera teams permanently over there in the field'.[9] The MvD offered Dutch reporters free transport to Afghanistan, free accommodation and personal safety equipment, and made available three embed places of two weeks duration on a rolling basis. Robin Middel, former Spokesman for the Chief of Defence and Head of Operations in the Directorate of Information and Communications at the MvD, noted that the duration of the two-week embed was intended to ensure that the reporters retained their objectivity: 'we thought if you stay longer... you will get too much involved in what the troops are doing, you get too much...part of the family'.[10] The selection process for embed places was open and transparent. As Hans de Vreij of Radio Netherlands observed, there were 'never any problems with the defence ministry' around arranging trips to Afghanistan.[11]

The MvD did not actively select or nominate particular journalists for deployment. In theory, any journalist from any Dutch news organisation could ask to go. The MvD did seek to maintain a balance between print, television and radio reporters, defence, political and development coverage, and harder and softer news, thus ensuring breadth of coverage. Robin Middel recalled that alongside the development reporters and the defence correspondents 'we took the less serious media in, we took radio reporters in and...one of the more popular Dutch DJs, [who] made a broadcast every day for three hours from the camp. All that kind of experiments we had and we never had a problem'.[12] The timing of visits to Afghanistan was the responsibility of the MvD. Reporters submitted their requests for embeds to the MvD's Public Information Department. The department then liaised with the Public Information Officers (PIO) in Uruzgan who were responsible for the overall coordination of visits as they were affected by planned operations and developments on the ground. The commander in Uruzgan determined whether it was possible for journalists to join specific operations at particular times. The MvD and its PIOs in theatre were tasked with facilitating media access to all aspects of the Dutch mission in Afghanistan—even Special Forces. An occasional point of friction was the right of more senior officers in the field to overrule a PIO's decision about media access. When conflicts of this kind arose, Robin Middel recalled that if there was no compelling operational argument against the media's inclusion, the PIO's decision generally stood.

The Dutch reporter was free to go wherever he or she wished on base, and to visit PRT projects and accompany Dutch military patrols off it. There was, technically, a requirement that a PIO accompany the reporter at all times and that all interviews were on the record, but this regulation was rarely observed. Jaus Müller of the Dutch daily *NRC Handelsblad* noted, 'I could talk to everyone...Everything was totally open'.[13] Dutch journalists were also free to disembed from the military, to leave the base to cover accessible stories in civilian areas before re-embedding and returning to the security of the base. Peter ter Velde from the Dutch broadcaster NOS regarded the opportunity to disembed as less a choice than a responsibility to ensure that the Dutch public had access to a properly balanced account of what its troops and development partners were doing in Afghanistan and whether the goals they had set themselves were being realised: 'if you travel with the military you have a one-sided story and only if you also got unembedded then you got the other side of the story and it's the only way it works...I think in order to show what's going on here you have to do both'.[14]

The main bone of contention between Dutch reporters and the MvD was over control of copy. The MvD enforced universal copy review. All material had to be submitted to a PIO to ensure that there were no inadvertent breaches of operational security. Some journalists accepted this as a reasonable condition of access, some welcomed the clear parameters it brought, while others vigorously opposed it. Hans de Vreij 'found it quite naïve and I still find it quite naïve of journalists to think that they can go along with the military, attend meetings, hear deep background stuff and not submit their material to a censor.'[15] Jaus Müller 'wasn't happy with it...I think it's bad, I think it's, it's almost like a censor. It's a principle, it's a principle of handing over your material and get[ting] comment and then publish it, it's totally weird'.[16] However, censorship was rarely a practical issue and there were few cases that could not be resolved through discussion or appeal.[17] In the event of a reporter publishing or broadcasting forbidden or contested material, the MvD had no formal provision for sanctions against those who contravened its directives.

When the Canadian media followed their troops to Kandahar in early 2002, they did so in the context of a recent history of deeply strained relations with the armed forces. A series of military scandals through the 1990s—the torture and murder of a Somali teenager by members of the Airborne Regiment in 1993, violent hazing rituals in 1995, and in 1998, allegations that sexual assaults within the forces had been inadequately investigated—had been exposed and aggressively pursued by the media. As a result of the ensuing investigations, the military lost public respect and political support, its personnel numbers nosedived, and its budget was slashed. While the decision to commit troops to Afghanistan offered Canadian Forces (CF) and the Department of National Defence (DND) an opportunity to rebuild their relations with politicians and the Canadian public, it soon became clear that this would require a new approach to military-media relations and the development of new policy documents to articulate them. When, in late 2001, the Canadian Government agreed to commit forces to Afghanistan, 'Public Affairs doctrine had not been updated since the late 1980s, and there existed no official policy for dealing with media in-theatre' (Price 2009, p. 39). Accordingly, for eighteen months, from December 2001 to June 2003, the military worked on a detailed agreement governing its interactions with the fourth estate, the *Canadian Forces Media Embedding Program* (CFMEP).[18] From the time it came into operation in September 2003, when Canadian Forces re-deployed to Kabul, the CFMEP was regularly reviewed and revised in the light of experience and consultation.[19] Notably, from its inception the CFMEP was not only intended to address operational security requirements, media needs, and direct commanders on how to deal with information management problems as they arose, its principal goal, like the *Communicatieplan*, was to serve the public, to ensure that relevant policies were in place 'to inform Canadians about the role, mandate and activities of the Canadian Forces (CF) on deployed operation' (Canadian Expeditionary Force Command 2010, p. 1).

In its efforts to facilitate this, the agreement made provision for the embedding of 30 journalists with CF at any one time.[20] Between February and August 2002, during the first rotation of its forces in Kandahar, CF hosted 20–30 Canadian reporters. For the sixteen-month period between January 2006 and mid-April 2007, when the Canadians returned to Kandahar, 230 journalists embedded with CF, 'an average of 80–90 embeds per [six-month] rotation,' reflecting the exponential increase in public interest in the deployment (Hobson 2007, p. 12).[21] After a few teething problems, the selection process for embeds settled into a transparent and orderly routine. Reporters intending to visit Afghanistan detailed the sorts of stories they were hoping to cover (e.g., combat, political, reconstruction, women), Public Affairs personnel at the DND in Ottawa endeavoured to arrange access, and the journalists were then allocated a spot on a relevant rotation.[22] The timing of media visits to Afghanistan was dictated by the availability of places and the matching of reporters to the issues they hoped to cover. Technically, any Canadian or foreign reporter could embed with CF provided a spot was available, though the prohibitive cost of insurance largely restricted participation to the national media.[23] The Canadians required the media to make their own way to Kandahar and to furnish their own protective equipment.

While some Canadian reporters spoke approvingly of the CFs readiness to facilitate their access to operations and projects in Afghanistan— Gloria Galloway of the *Globe and Mail* thought that the PA officers she had worked with were 'terrific'—others were less complimentary.[24] Stephen Thorne of the Canadian Press (CP) described the PAOs he had dealt with in Kandahar and Kabul earlier in the campaign as 'a real pain the ass'.[25] Canadian reporters, unlike their Dutch colleagues, retained control over their copy. Briefed about forbidden topics and warned off operationally sensitive issues, they were free to write and shoot as they saw fit. The CF reserved the right to sanction reporters for breaches of the policy, rescinding their embedded status and excluding them from Kandahar Airfield when such infractions occurred. Stephen Thorne recalled 'a couple of times when [Canadian PAOs] kicked me off the base…and then once I got kicked off the base by the US commander'— for photographing the return to Kandahar Airfield of the bodies of four US Engineers killed in an explosion.[26] More often, where problems arose, as with the Dutch, the reporters and the PA personnel on the ground, or their editors and more senior PA officers in Ottawa, did their best to resolve disputes, and where appropriate amended the embedding agreement to reflect changed conditions.

In the absence of any publicly available doctrine detailing the goals shaping Australian coverage of the fighting in Afghanistan and the means by which they might be achieved, it is a moot point whether the Department of Defence and the ADF actually had a policy dictating its relations with the media in Afghanistan.[27] The former Director General of Communication Strategies for the Department of Defence, Brian Humphreys, noted that as of 2009, the ADF, like the Department of

Defence, 'has no formal strategy for media relations' (Humphreys 2009, pp. 31–32). In the absence of a developed media strategy, the ADF's dealings with the fourth estate were mostly reactive, shaped by historical antagonism, false memories of the Vietnam experience, and short-term, tactical considerations, as was reflected in its approach to embedding. By its own admission, the ADF followed the 'slow road to media embedding' and took almost a decade to implement a basic program (Logue 2013, p. 14). In late 2010, nine years after Australian forces first arrived in Afghanistan, the Department of Defence claimed that 'Following a review of embedding policy and a trial deployment in 2009,' the ADF 'now conducts an embedding program.'[28] They were a little quick off the mark. In 2010, just as there was no trace of the 'embedding policy' referred to by Defence, there was no evidence of the system, routine, or procedures that one ordinarily associates with a 'program'. There was no publicly available information about how a correspondent might apply or qualify for an embed place or about Defence and the ADF's priorities in their allocation. While Defence noted that 'The ADF embed program offers access to the MTF [Mentoring Task Force] for two representatives from a single media agency for up to 21 days,' there was no information about what might dictate the timing of embeds or how they might relate to specific operations.[29] The scarcity of Australian embed places—'Each MTF rotation will host a minimum of two embed cycles'—should be set beside the Canadian average of 80–90 embed cycles per rotation when its system was working at its height.[30] While the Canadians had almost twice as many troops as the Australians in Afghanistan, they offered their media 40 or 45 times as many embed opportunities per rotation. A difference of this magnitude suggests far more about the priority the CF and the ADF accord to public information than it does about their relative capacity to absorb and facilitate the media. It implies that the purpose of the ADF's 'program' was less to ensure that public were kept informed about what its troops were doing in Afghanistan than it was to forestall criticism that it was not informing them at all.

Reporters who embedded with the ADF in Afghanistan offered mixed reviews of its readiness to facilitate access to operations. Some praised the energy and understanding of PA officers who did everything in their power to ensure access to operations.[31] Others complained about command interference in their plans and movements and the inability of the PAO to exercise any leverage in these disputes.[32] Notably, many Australian reporters seem to have had a mixed experience. Nick Butterly of the *West Australian*, noted that on his first embed, in 2010, he was 'incredibly lucky to have been partnered with the media liaison officer I was given. He was keenly interested in newspapers and always wanting to push the bounds of the embed as far as we could.' He went on to observe that he had 'since heard some horror stories of other reporters being saddled with media liaison officers who saw their jobs purely in terms of shutting down awkward stories and pedalling positive ones' (cited in Logue 2013, p. 48). A number of mid-ranking officers showed an admirable openness to the media and did their utmost to facilitate coverage. 'Unlike some of his colleagues', the Commanding Officer of Mentoring and Reconstruction Task Force (MRTF) 1, Lieutenant Colonel Shane Gabriel, believed that it was important for the fourth estate to bear witness from the front lines: 'The media has a right to be there. We have nothing to hide' (cited in Masters 2012, p. 200). Likewise, when Chris Masters and his film crew arrived at Patrol Base Wali, the officer commanding, Major Jason Groat, emerged from his command post to inform the reporters that 'We are welcome inside at any time and have an open invitation to every daily briefing' (p. 227). But it wasn't all 'hail-fellow-well-met'. When Paul McGeough and photographer Kate Geraghty of Fairfax travelled to Tarin Kot in January 2013 to report on the current state of affairs in Uruzgan as the ADF began its withdrawal, they were 'met on the tarmac by several Australian military officers' who told them 'You have no permission to be here.' Determined to avoid the ADF's restrictions on reporters, McGeough and Geraghty sought accreditation for their assignment from an Afghan agency and travelled to Uruzgan independent of the ADF. Apprised of this strategy, McGeough alleges, the ADF set out to 'derail the Fairfax assignment', and so 'block independent reporting in the province'. They did this by holding a meeting with spokesmen 'from a raft of government agencies in southern Afghanistan' where the Afghans were pressured to withdraw any offers of assistance they may already have made to the Fairfax journalists. Farid Ayil, a spokesman for the Uruzgan Chief of Police, Matiullah Khan, corroborated McGeough's account, claiming that 'The [ADF] guy went around the table getting everyone to say they had refused.' When it became clear that the Chief of Police had not refused and had determined to host the journalists, the unnamed ADF officer 'demanded to know why we were taking you' and presented 'a litany of reasons' to back his arguments for excluding the reporters: 'the Fairfax team was in Oruzgan to "write wrong stories"; it had travelled to Tarin Kowt "without permission"; and it had entered Afghanistan "without a letter from the Australian government"' (McGeough 2013, p. 9). Though the journalists had neither written nor photographed anything at this point, in the eyes of the ADF officers on the ground, the fact that they were intending to work beyond military oversight was evidence of their hostility towards the Australian armed forces and a legitimate basis for excluding them. Thus the Australian military's corporate memory of Vietnam strikes again.

For Australian reporters who made it to Afghanistan, there was no such thing as an off-the-record interview with ADF personnel. *The Statement of Understanding for Accredited Media* notes that 'the correspondent will be escorted at all times', and must 'adhere to the direction and advice of the military escort officer at all times' or face removal from the area of operations (Department of Defence).[33] In reality, the escort system worked in a variety of ways. Some reporters relied on their PA escorts for advice and direction, others ignored them, and some dispensed with their services altogether.[34] A number of journalists have noted that it was easier to secure off-the-record comments once they were beyond the wire.[35] Others were given total freedom to talk to whomever they wanted.[36]

There was no provision for or experience of Australian reporters moving between embedded and disembedded status. Reporters were expected to remain under the direction of the responsible commander. Should the correspondent elect to forfeit the protection of the ADF, the embed would be considered at an end. The review of copy was also a grey area. Despite Defence's assertion that it 'does not exert editorial control over reporting by journalists during [their] visits other than ensuring that operational security is not breached', the process for ensuring that there were no breaches of operational security was the moot point here.[37] Writing in 2013, Jason Logue noted that the ADF exercised '100 per cent review of all media embed participant material before filing' and that 'Australia is the only nation in ISAF that still requires this level of oversight' (Logue 2013, p. 33). In practice the system worked a little less rigidly in that, while some reporters had their work routinely screened, others did not.[38]

That the ADF was offering any embeds at all was a notable advance on the earlier situation. Ian McPhedran notes that by 2009 the ADF's restrictions on media reporting had grown so obstructive that 'there is more value in Australian reporters seeking help from British or American or Dutch or Romanian forces on operations than there is from the Australians' (2009, p. 71). Prior to the introduction of a formal embedding program, the only way for Australian reporters to access their troops in Afghanistan was via the 'bus tours' that the ADF used to bring the Australian media to the joint Dutch-Australian base outside Tarin Kot (Middleton 2009, p. 148).[39] The tours ran intermittently from 2002, and then more regularly from 2008. ADF PA officers not only 'fixed' the reporters' itineraries 'well in advance' but 'chaperoned' them 'every step of the way' once they were on base (Hobbs 2009, p. 92). The standard schedule took the journalists past a selection of prestige training and reconstruction projects—most notably the trade-training school and the Tarin Kot Provincial Hospital—and exposed them to selected personnel primed to respond to the reporters' questions. Little was left to chance. SBS's Chief Political Correspondent and a regular visitor to Afghanistan, Karen Middleton, noted that the ADF's determination to minimise the scope for surprises or negative publicity ensured that, as a journalist with the ADF, 'You can't be sure what will happen during your allotted time in country or what kind of stories you will be able to do...You can be absolutely certain you will be subject to considerable restriction' (Middleton 2009, p. 152).

The ADF considered the bus trips a vital means of promoting its mission in Uruzgan, but later conceded that they had persisted with them for too long: 'The decision to operate this way made sense during the initial phases of the conflicts [in Iraq and Afghanistan] with their heavy Special Forces presence, but once large bodies of conventional troops were on the ground, Defence's ongoing justification became untenable. The negative comparison between the coalition approaches became the subject of increasing political pressure' (Logue 2013, pp. 13–14). Though the bus tours may have been 'of very limited value' to the media, they were highly revealing of the military's practices and priorities (McPhedran 2009, p. 71). The *Australian*'s Mark Dodd noted that the centrepiece of any media visit to Camp Holland was the Tarin Kot Provincial Hospital, recently refurbished by the Australians. Yet the renovation of the hospital, and the addition of a maternity wing, was not the good-news story it seemed. While the ADF was 'rightfully proud' of this achievement and visitors were 'inevitably...briefed about the showcase project', few saw it in operation, as 'no foreign aid organisation has been willing to staff the hospital or provide the sort of support envisaged' (Dodd 2008, p. 11).[40]

After repeated complaints from the media about lack of access, the ADF conducted an embedding trial in August 2009 and introduced a formal embedding program in early 2010.[41] Even then a number of Australian journalists pointed out that the ADF version of embedding was 'more constraining than it needs to be' (Middleton 2009, p. 155).[42] Jason Logue's 2013 review of the ADF embedding program reveals that its tardy introduction and unnecessarily restrictive nature ultimately did the military more harm than good. His analysis of the 2011 coverage revealed that while 'the overall trend of Australian media reporting concerning operations in Afghanistan was favourable...the coverage sourced from media embed participants, a relatively small percentage of overall coverage, was of considerably higher favourability than reporting from afar.' Better still, the embeds' reporting was not only favourable, it 'showed a strong correlation with the identified favourable messages', the preferred narrative of the war that the ADF was keen to promote, namely 'the ADF supporting its personnel, the military/personal conduct of ADF personnel as "beyond reproach" and that ADF operations were making progress towards strategic goals' (Logue 2013, pp. 26–27).[43] Logue's findings suggest that ADF commanders may look to sanction the more-timely introduction of embedding in future conflicts.

The ADF's determination to retain strict control over how it was portrayed, and the false memories of the Vietnam Experience that helped shape this policy, had far-reaching and inadvertently negative effects on the broader representation of the war, and thereby on public support for it. Excluded from the front lines, the conflict dropped off the nation's front pages and the Australian media tended to focus on the war only when members of the ADF were killed or seriously wounded. This narrowed public discussion about the war and distorted the nation's understanding of and responses to it. For example, for the greater part of a decade 'at least half of Australia's Afghanistan story...the other story, of the fight being taken to the Taliban...had gone untold' and, as a consequence, the public had little idea of just how aggressive the ADF campaign had been (Masters 2012, p. 255). Chris Masters notes that 'In 2007 alone, Australian Special Forces killed and identified more than 400 Taliban' (p. 14). Four years later, in May 2011, the *West Australian* reported that 'Australian forces have killed about 1500 insurgents in the past 12 months, during some of the most vicious fighting seen by the military since the Vietnam War' (Probyn and Butterly 2011). Perhaps surprisingly, the ADF 'drew no attention' to these numbers, while the

Special Forces personnel responsible for them were 'determinedly off limits' to the media (Masters 2012, p. 14, 255). The resulting focus on the casualties suffered by the ADF rather than those they had inflicted ensured that the only body count the Australian public became familiar with was its own.

In parliament, where there was bipartisan support for the deployment, the conflict most often attracted broader public attention when the Prime Minister rose to lead a condolence motion. Over the succeeding days, in a now familiar choreography of collective grief, the media revealed more about the age, marital status, dependents, affiliations, and personal qualities of the casualty ('the fallen'), before focusing on the formal farewelling of the body from Afghanistan ('sombre procession'), its repatriation to Australia ('solemn ramp ceremony'), and the funeral, with full military honours ('flag-draped coffin...an awaiting gun carriage'), attended by the nation's most senior political and military officials ('supreme sacrifice'). In light of this focus on the ADF's losses, and the sacramental vocabulary used to commemorate them, 'It is not hard to understand why a sense of Australians as more victim than victor had formed', and why, as a result, public disapproval of the war continued to rise (Masters 2012, p. 14).

Yet blame for the poverty of Australian coverage of the war does not rest with Defence and the ADF alone. Throughout the course of the war in Afghanistan, at the very time that reporters and editors should have been leading—or at least prompting—a national conversation about the ADF's role and purposes there, they were distracted by the greatest crisis confronting the mainstream media in its modern history: the demise of its traditional funding model. The collapse of the industry's conventional sources of funding threw it into turmoil and led to massive job losses among editorial staff.[44] Foreign bureaux were closed, specialist reporters with foreign and defence experience took redundancy packages, and their expertise was lost to the industry.[45] As a consequence, the mainstream media in Australia today employs only a handful of dedicated defence correspondents.[46] The macroeconomic circumstances meant that already 'one of the toughest assignments on the media horizon', the truth about what was happening in Afghanistan was 'harder than usual to come by' (Masters 2012, p. 207). Yet while Government and Defence routinely spun the news to 'shape and misshape the truth' for their own ends and the ADF maintained its stranglehold over access to and freedom of movement within the area of operations, it became increasingly apparent that the 'lack of evidence based coverage' of what Australian forces were doing in Afghanistan was 'not only down to the ADF being obstructive' or fourth estate's straitened resources (p. 207; also Masters 2011, p. 37). Journalists recognised that among the newspapers and broadcasters they served, 'editorial commitment' to reporting the war was 'weak' and there was 'no appetite for sustained and detailed coverage except when there was an extraordinary event' (p. 37).[47] This was evidenced in both incidental and more substantial demonstrations of the media's reluctance to vigorously pursue the story. In some cases, media organisations were disinclined to meet the full costs of transporting or insuring reporters who went to cover the war.[48] In others, they baulked at the bonuses and allowances to which their employees were entitled.[49] More damningly, over the course of the conflict the media were loath to invest in the requisite personnel or resources to ensure that the public had access to sustained and comprehensive coverage. For more than nine years no Australian media outlet stationed a permanent correspondent in Afghanistan. In January 2011, the ABC finally opened a Kabul bureau headed by Sally Sara, yet when her posting ended twelve months later, it promptly mothballed the office.[50] In the absence of a permanent cadre of well-informed specialists, coverage of the war was left to a shifting band of differently qualified reporters who dropped in on brief embeds before leaving the country, and their readers, little wiser about the conflict than they were before. As a consequence of these arrangements, the greater portion of the reporting from Afghanistan struggled to illuminate the war's complex origins, geography, and alliances, falling back on the reliable staples of death, injury, and the occasional scandal.

The distinguishing features of Dutch, Canadian, and Australian information management systems reveal the critical components enabling fruitful relations between the military and the media. The success of the Dutch system can be traced back to the highest levels of government. Driven by the political imperative to inform the people about what its forces were doing in Afghanistan, the military observed the directions of their political masters and collaborated with the media to ensure that a balanced picture of the Dutch deployment emerged. Relations with the media remained cooperative because they were founded on doctrine that both parties had had a hand in developing and fine-tuning, that clearly set out each party's rights and responsibilities and provided a baseline for dispute resolution. In Canada, the military and the media gradually worked through their mutual suspicion and with the assistance of doctrine that both parties had invested in, arrived at a working relationship that, for a couple of years, delivered the media 'excellent access' to the troops and mutual benefits for both parties. In Australia, by contrast, there was neither political leadership driving an open information policy nor the military doctrine needed to manage the operation of such a system. For the greater part of the conflict, while the government was focused on minimising bad news, the ADF held fast to the antagonism towards the fourth estate that its memories of Vietnam fed. In the absence of information management doctrine to which both parties had contributed and in which both could invest, there was little or no common ground on which fundamental issues might be raised or minor disputes resolved. The ADF's principal media operations goals focused on promoting the actions of its personnel in Afghanistan and defending its reputation from what it believed was a media cohort intent on finding fault and besmirching the military brand. While the military and the media squabbled over access, freedom of movement, and control of copy, the biggest loser was the Australian public. Denied the detailed, comprehensive, consistent coverage that a thorough understanding of the war in Afghanistan demanded, they were left to decipher the relations between an unbroken flow of upbeat press releases celebrating military and civil society gains and the steadily rising body count. The revolution in information management that had catalyzed a new age of military-media relations in the US, Canada, and the Netherlands barely registered in Australia. While there is no guarantee that more information would have improved public support for the war in Afghanistan, it would certainly have ensured that the nation's longest war was not also its worst reported and least understood.

NOTES

1. Of the 23,000 bombs dropped by NATO during Operation Allied Force, Jamie Shea claims, implausibly, that only 30 or 0.0013% failed to hit the intended target (see Shea 2002, p. 157). Whatever the accuracy of his claim, it is a mark of the deftness of the Yugoslav information campaign that it was able to make effective propaganda capital out of a small amount of misdirected ordnance.
2. For further information on how the policy was sold to politicians and the military hierarchy and then implemented (see Rid 2007, pp. 129–143).
3. Back in Adelaide, John Brittle tried without success to convince his employers at the *Adelaide Advertiser* that he should be in Vietnam. They

rebuffed his proposal because 'they did not think it was worthwhile' (Anderson and Trembath 2011, p. 231).

4. For a further explanation of the origins of this description of the Australian 'policy', see Anderson and Trembath (2011), p. 238.

5. Troop numbers fluctuated slightly as personnel rotated. The figures quoted here are sometimes specific, and sometimes reflect the average over a particular period. These numbers fell gradually through 2013 until the final withdrawal of ADF forces in December 2013. That said, a little over 400 Australian military personnel remain in Afghanistan in training and support roles.

6. At the height of its 2010 'surge', the United States had 130,000 personnel in Afghanistan, well above its long-term average of 90,000. It too has now drawn down its forces to slightly more than 10,000. From a high point of more than 9500 troops, the last British forces withdrew from Afghanistan in October 2014. Comprehensive information on troop commitments can be found at 'Troop Numbers and Contributions'.

7. For more on this, see Mans et al. (2008, pp. 7–8).

8. The ADF had a shifting force commitment that, from 2007 onwards, stabilised at around 1500 personnel. For more detail on Australia's role in Afghanistan, see Smith (2010). Until they withdrew the bulk of their personnel in August 2010 and December 2011, the Dutch and the Canadians had, respectively, around 1600 and a little under 3000 troops in Afghanistan. For exact figures, see 'Troop Numbers and Contributions' (2015). For a more independent view, see Tanter (2010). For more information on the Dutch deployment, see 'Missions Abroad'. Chris Masters notes the subtle differences of culture between the ADF and the Dutch military and their view of their roles in Afghanistan (2012, pp. 106–110). For detailed analyses of the Canadian deployment and the political manoeuvring leading up to it, see Piggott (2007) and Stein and Lang (2007).

9. Author interview with Joop Veen, 21 June 2012.

10. Author interview with Robin Middel, 23 September 2010.

11. Author interview with Hans de Vreij, 22 September 2010. To put this in context, Kim Sengupta, Defence and Diplomatic correspondent for London's *Independent* described the British process as a 'bizarre Stalinist exercise which no one could quite understand', while Thomas Harding of the *Daily Telegraph* observed that in the early days of the British commitment to Iraq and Afghanistan, 'dealing with the MoD [Ministry of Defence], getting the embed itself' was 'more stressful than dealing with the Taliban or the Iraqi militia, more stressful than dealing with the army, more stressful than dealing with your news desk' (Author interview with Kim Sengupta, 12 October 2010; Author interview with Thomas Harding, 11 October 2010).

12. Author interview with Robin Middel, 23 September 2010. The media did not recall these experiments quite so fondly. In a meeting with Middel, Peter ter Velde, defence correspondent for Dutch television broadcaster NOS, recalled that he and other journalists expressed their disapproval at the inclusion of entertainment reporters in the embedding scheme (Author interview with Peter ter Velde, 23 September 2010).
13. Author interview with Jaus Müller, 22 September 2010.
14. Author interview with ter Velde, 23 September 2010.
15. Author interview with de Vreij, 22 September 2010.
16. Author interview with Müller, 22 September 2010.
17. Some journalists noted the inconsistency of the policy in that while material produced in the field was subject to review, reports written on the aircraft on the way home, in other foreign bureaux, or back in the Netherlands, that might reveal more sensitive information, were not.
18. The final iteration of the CFMEP-JTFA dates from April 2010. It was available on the Canadian Department of National Defence website but, given the cessation of Canadian combat operations in Afghanistan, the link has since been disabled.
19. The original document was written by Don Roy, a strategic planner with military public affairs. For a history of its evolution, see Price (2009, pp. 37–43). The commitment of CF to Kabul in July 2003 put these reporting arrangements under some strain (see Price 2009, pp. 49–53).
20. This number was later reduced to 15.
21. In the first 10 weeks of 2007, the Dutch facilitated 370 external visitors to Afghanistan, a significant proportion of whom were reporters (see Mans 2008, pp. 25–26).
22. Author interview with Gloria Galloway, 18 October 2010.
23. Author interview with Galloway, 18 October 2010.
24. Author interview with Galloway, 18 October 2010.
25. Author interview with Stephen Thorne, 20 October 2010.
26. Author interview with Thorne, 20 October 2010.
27. Doctrine on *Information Activities* (ADDP 3.13) was first published in 2002, with a second edition in 2006, though neither was publicly available. The third edition of the doctrine, published in November 2013, was only made available to the public in April 2014 after a Freedom of Information request.
28. Author correspondence with Captain (now Major) Chris Linden of the Ministerial Support and Public Affairs Branch of the Department of Defence, 22 November 2010.
29. Author correspondence with Linden, 22 November 2010.
30. Author correspondence with Linden, 22 November 2010.
31. Thom Cookes of the ABC and Hugh Riminton of Network Ten spoke highly of the efforts of their PA escorts to facilitate access for them (see Logue 2013, pp. 53–55).

32. Ian McPhedran of News Limited laid out his discontents in the "'Embedding" Trial Report' he wrote to the then-Chief of the Defence Force (CDF), Air Marshal Angus Houston, after his trial embed in August 2009. For a full transcript of the report see 'Embedding in Afghanistan' (2009, ep. 35). Notably, Sally Sara of the ABC, who was also part of the trial embed, has remained silent about her experiences.

33. Chris Masters enjoyed virtually unlimited, and mostly unsupervised, access to the troops when making his documentary for the ABC, *A Careful War* (2010), although this marked the exception rather than the rule.

34. Compare the experiences of Kathy McLeish, Chris Masters, and Thom Cookes. Masters notes that the PA officer who accompanied him on his 2010 trip to Afghanistan was known by the troops as the FONC—the 'friend of no cunt' (see Masters 2012, p. 219).

35. On his 2009 'sponsored visit', Hyland noted that it was easier to talk to the troops once you had moved off base and beyond the wire. Masters noted the same phenomenon.

36. When Masters was filming his ABC documentary, *A Careful War*, he was free to talk to anybody who was prepared to be interviewed.

37. Author correspondence with Linden, 22 November 2010.

38. Tom Hyland did, Thom Cookes and Nick Butterly did not.

39. McPhedran describes them as 'bus trips' (2009, p. 71).

40. As of 1 June 2011, AusAid indicated that it had 'provided equipment for the Trade Training School in Tarin Kowt and the Tarin Kowt Hospital', yet there was still no indication that the hospital was staffed or operational (see 'Australia's Aid Program').

41. The trial was contentious and resulted in a highly critical report by one of its participants, Ian McPhedran, to the CDF (see 'Embedding in Afghanistan' 2009, ep. 35) The first reporters to embed under the new program, Nick Butterly and Lee Griffith of the *West Australian*, visited Afghanistan in February/March 2010.

42. This, she noted, was the 'sense among a number of my colleagues'.

43. For more detail on the methods and findings of Logue's study see pp. 22–29.

44. Figures from the Australian Bureau of Statistics indicate that in the five years between 2006 and 2011 the newspaper industry shed almost 13% of its workforce. In June 2012, Fairfax Media, owners of *The Sydney Morning Herald* and *The Age* announced 1900 job losses, including 380 journalists. News Limited cut 500 editorial positions in 2012 (Trute 2012). The Media Entertainment and Arts Alliance, the main trade union for media employees, estimated that over the winter of 2012, 1 in 7 journalism jobs disappeared (see 'News Limited Redundancies Should Be the Last' 2012).

45. Early in 2013, Crikey reported that *The Australian* was soon to close its London, Washington, and Tokyo bureaux, while Fairfax was also looking at closing its London bureau (it didn't), having mothballed its Kabul office (see Knott 2013).
46. They include Max Blenkin at AAP, Ian McPhedran at News Limited, David Wroe at Fairfax, Nick Butterly at *WA News*, and a few others.
47. Author telephone interview with Tom Hyland, 19 December 2012.
48. Nick Butterly notes that 'insurance is a killer for newspapers going to Afghanistan' (Logue 2013, p. 47).
49. Chris Masters recalled that while the ADF applied a maximum threat level to Afghanistan, thereby entitling its personnel to an extra $141.36 per day, tax free, when he notified his superiors that he and his film crew would be travelling to Uruzgan to make a documentary 'the ABC asked that we take a reduced travel allowance, advancing the rationale that we would have no use for it' (2012, p. 219).
50. Masters regarded this situation as 'a scandal' (2011, p. 37).

Works Cited

Anderson, Fay. 2009. The New and Altered Conventions of Reporting War: Censorship, Access and Representation in Afghanistan. In *What Are we Doing in Afghanistan?* ed. Kevin Foster, 119–141.

Anderson, Fay, and Richard Trembath. 2011. *Witnesses to War: The History of Australian Combat Reporting.* Melbourne: Melbourne University Press.

Australia's Aid Program. n.d. *Australian Government: Department of Foreign Affairs and Trade.* Available at: http://dfat.gov.au/aid/Pages/australias-aid-program.aspx.

Bowden, Tim. 1987. *One Crowded Hour: Neil Davis Combat Cameraman, 1934–1985.* Sydney: Angus and Robertson.

Braestrup, Peter. 2000. 'Foreword' in Fialka. *Hotel Warriors,* ix–xiv.

Canadian Expeditionary Force Command. 2010. *Canadian Forces Media Embedding Program: Guidelines, Ground Rules and Documentation for Joint Task Force Afghanistan.* Ottawa: Canadian Expeditionary Force Command.

Cantwell, John. 2012. They Died in Vain. *Monthly* Oct.: 30–33.

Carruthers, Susan. 2000. *The Media at War.* Houndmills: Palgrave.

Clark, Wesley K. 2001. *Waging Modern War: Bosnia, Kosovo, and the Future of Combat.* New York: Public Affairs.

Cumings, Bruce. 1992. *War and Television.* London: Verso.

Department of Defence. n.d. *Statement of Understanding for Accredited Media (Ground Rules).* Canberra: Department of Defence.

Dodd, Mark. 2008. Battle for Progress. *Australian,* Oct 9.

Elegant, Robert. 1981. How to Lose a War. *Encounter* 57 (2): 73–90.

Embedding in Afghanistan. 2009. *Media Watch*, 5 Oct., episode 35. Available at: http://www.abc.net.au/mediawatch/transcripts/s2705312.htm.

Fialka, John J. 1991. *Hotel Warriors: Covering the Gulf War.* Washington, DC: Woodrow Wilson Center Press.

Grey, Jeffrey. 2010. In Every War But One? Myth, History and Vietnam. In *Zombie Myths of Australian Military History*, ed. Craig Stockings, 190–212, Sydney: New South Press.

Ham, Paul. 2007. *Vietnam: The Australian War.* Sydney: Harper Collins.

Hobbs, Sean. 2009. How to build a pergola: with the ADF in Afghanistan. In *What Are We Doing in Afghanistan?* ed. Kevin Foster, 89–101.

Hobson, Sharon. 2007. *The Information Gap: Why the Canadian Public Doesn't Know More About Its Military.* Calgary: Canadian Defence and Foreign Affairs Institute.

Humphreys, Brian. 2009. The Australian Defence Force's Media Strategy: What It Is and Why, and Why It Needs to Change. In *What Are We Doing in Afghanistan?* ed. Kevin Foster, 31–46.

Knott, Matthew. 2013. Foreign Bureau Get the Chop as News, Fairfax Cut Costs. *Crikey*, Jan 9.

Logue, Lieutenant Colonel Jason. 2013. *Herding Cats: The Evolution of the ADF's Media Embedding Program in Operational Areas.* Canberra: Land Warfare Studies Centre (Working Paper No. 141).

Mans, Ulrich, Christa Meindersma, and Lara Burema. 2008. *Eyes Wide Shut? The Impact of Embedded Journalism on Dutch Newspaper Coverage of Afghanistan.* The Hague: The Hague Centre for Strategic Studies.

Masters, Chris. 2011. The Media's Left and Right of Arc. In *The Information Battlefield: Representing Australians at War*, ed. Kevin Foster, 33–40, North Melbourne: Australian Scholarly Publishing.

———. 2012. *Uncommon Soldier: Brave, Compassionate and Tough, the Making of Australia's Modern Diggers.* Sydney: Allen and Unwin.

McGeough, Paul. 2013. How the ADF Tried to Control the Real Story of Oruzgan. *Saturday Age*, March 16.

McPhedran, Ian. 2009. 'War! What War?' In *What Are We Doing in Afghanistan?* ed. Kevin Foster, 65–74.

Middleton, Karen. 2009. Who's Telling the Story? The Military and the Media. In *The Military, the Media and Information Warfare*, ed. Peter Dennis and Jeffrey Grey, 147–157, Canberra: Australian Military History Publications.

Missions Abroad. n.d. *Ministry of Defence.* Available at: https://www.defensie.nl/english/topics/missions-abroad/contents/current-missions.

News Limited Redundancies Should be the Last. 2012. *Media Alliance*, 4 Sept. Available at: http://www.alliance.org.au/oldsite/news-limited-redundancies-should-be-the-last.

Office of the Assistant Secretary of Defense for Public Affairs. 2003. *Public Affairs Guidance (PAG) on Embedding Media During Possible Future Operations/Deployments in the US Central Commands (CENTCOM) Area of Responsibility (AOR)*. Washington, DC: Department of Defense.

Olson, RL. 1993. *Gulf War Air Power Survey, Volume Three: Logistics, Support*. Washington, DC: Government Printing Office.

Payne, Trish. 2007. *War and Words: The Australian Press and the Vietnam War*. Melbourne: Melbourne University Press.

Piggott, Peter. 2007. *Canada in Afghanistan: The War So Far*. Toronto: Dundurn Press.

Price, Dominique L. 2009. *Inside the Wire: A Study of Canadian Embedded Journalism in Afghanistan*. Unpublished MA diss., Ottawa: Carleton University.

Probyn, Andrew, and Nick Butterly. 2011. Enemy Toll as High as 1500. *West Australian*, May 25.

Rid, Thomas. 2007. *War and Media Operations: The US Military and the Press from Vietnam to Iraq*. New York: Routledge.

Shea, Jamie P. 2002. The Kosovo Crisis and the Media: Reflections of a NATO Spokesman. In *Lessons from Kosovo: The KFOR Experience*, ed. Larry Wentz, Washington, DC: Department of Defence Command and Control Research Program.

Smith, Stephen. 2010. Fact Sheets on Afghanistan. In *Australian Government: Department of Defence*, 17 Oct. Available at: http://www.defence.gov.au/defencenews/articles/1017/1017.htm.

Stein, Janice Gross, and Eugene Lang. 2007. *The Unexpected War: Canada in Kandahar*. Toronto: Penguin.

Tanter, Richard. 2010. Australia in Afghanistan Briefing Book. In *Nautilus Institute for Security and Sustainability*, 1 Dec. Available at: http://nautilus. org/publications/books/australian-forces-abroad/afghanistan/.

Taylor, Philip. 2003. *Munitions of the Mind: A History of Propaganda from the Ancient World to the Present*. Manchester: Manchester University Press.

Tiffen, Rodney. 2009. The War the Media Lost: Australian News Coverage of Vietnam. In *Vietnam Remembered*, updated ed, ed. Gregory Pemberton, Sydney: New Holland Publishers.

Troop Numbers and Contributions. 2015. *NATO*, 1 Dec. Available at: http://www.rs.nato.int/troop-numbers-and-contributions/index.php.

Trute, Peter. 2012. News Limited Announces Redundancies. *Sydney Morning Herald*, Dec 6.

Yeaman, Stuart. 2013. *Afghan Sun: Defence, Diplomacy, Development and the Taliban*. Brisbane: Boolarong Press.

AUTHOR BIOGRAPHY

Kevin Foster is Head of the School of Languages, Literatures, Cultures and Linguistics at Monash University. He has published widely on war, cultural history, and national identity and his work has appeared in a range of national and international journals. He is the author of *Fighting Factions: War, Narrative and National Identity* (1999) and *Lost Worlds: Latin America and the Imagining of Empire* (2009). His most recent book is *Don't Mention the War: The Australian Defence Force, the Media and the Afghan Conflict* (2013).

CHAPTER 3

The Limitations of Memory and the Language of the War on Terror in Australia, 2001–2003

Amanda Laugesen

Richard Jackson, in his provocative study *Writing the War on Terrorism: Language, Politic, and Counter-Terrorism* (2005), examines the ways in which language was deployed in the aftermath of 9/11 to 'justify and normalise a global campaign of counter-terrorism'. The language of the War on Terror, he argues, is a carefully constructed public discourse, with a clear political purpose (pp. 1–2). Jackson goes on to examine the key elements of the ways language constructed public understandings of 9/11 and the subsequent military and political actions of the Bush Administration. Australia joined the War on Terror, insofar as Prime Minister John Howard pledged Australian support for the United States and for military actions in Afghanistan and Iraq. But while the Australian experience of the War on Terror shared many elements with the US, it also had its own distinctive features. The public discourse of terrorism in Australia shared features with the US discourse, but only certain aspects truly resonated in the Australian context. Howard and his government

A. Laugesen (✉)
Australian National University, Canberra, Australia
e-mail: amanda.laugesen@anu.edu.au

© The Author(s) 2017
J. Gildersleeve and R. Gehrmann (eds.), *Memory and the Wars on Terror*, Palgrave Macmillan Memory Studies,
DOI 10.1007/978-3-319-56976-5_3

49

brought distinctive ideas to their articulation of the reasons for supporting the fight against terrorism, and their attempts to engender public support.

This chapter first discusses some of the key elements of the American language of the War on Terror, as identified by Jackson and other scholars. It then examines the ways in which Australian media and politicians spoke about terrorism and its consequences in the year following the 9/11 World Trade Center attacks. The next section considers the language used to frame understandings of the Bali bombing which occurred in October 2002, and which arguably had a more immediate impact on Australian society. Finally, this chapter reflects on the lingering consequences of 9/11 in terms of public discourse. As will be seen, the ongoing asylum-seeker issue can be closely connected to Australian concerns about terrorism. Indeed, it can be argued that 'asylum-seeker issues' have generated more fear and problematic public discourse than has terrorism in Australia, in contrast to the US, where concerns about terrorism are arguably stronger. In addition, it should be noted that military intervention by Australia has been somewhat minimal by comparison to the American commitment (and even other nations who supported intervention in Iraq and Afghanistan, such as the United Kingdom), and the Bali bombing, while stoking concerns about regional security, did not lead to direct regional military intervention.

Memory has played an ambiguous role in the construction of Australian understandings of the War on Terror. John Howard evoked the memory of Australia standing side by side with the United States in World War Two when calling for Australia to join the fight against the Taliban in Afghanistan, and also connected the War on Terror to Australia's Anzac tradition. Yet in other ways, responses to 9/11 required a sense of amnesia. While Vietnam would later be the war to which America's war in Iraq would be compared, there was only limited evocation of that memory in the immediate years following 9/11 (at least in mainstream political and media discourse). Similarly, in both the US and Australia, there seemed to be little memory of a longer history of terrorist activities that had shaped the modern world. For Australia, it is also notable that a great deal of the political language relating to terrorism seemed to borrow from an American or international discourse (for example, the invocation of 'good' versus 'evil') rather than echoing a distinctive Australian political rhetoric and tradition. It is perhaps timely to reflect on the ways public understandings of 9/11, Bali, and the War on Terror have been constructed, especially as we start to make sense of Australia's military experiences in Iraq and Afghanistan, and as Australian society continues to grapple with the politics of the issue of asylum-seekers, as well as terrorism.

THE US LANGUAGE OF THE WAR ON TERROR

Richard Jackson's 2005 study remains the most comprehensive and useful overview of the construction of the dominant public discourse of the War on Terror in the US. Using a corpus of official speeches, press releases, and other outputs of leading political figures (p. 17), Jackson identifies a number of discursive elements that were used to shape public understandings of the War on Terror. Jackson operates from the premise that 'words are never neutral'; language shapes the way we see and understand the world (p. 21). Using Critical Discourse Analysis, he asks a series of questions that go to the heart of the way in which language can shape our understanding, in this case, of terrorism and the actions taken to 'wage war' on terrorism (p. 25).

Jackson's study is particularly useful in identifying some of the major elements of public (especially political) language about 9/11 and terrorism, and how these elements helped construct a public narrative that gave meaning to the tragic 9/11 attacks. He identifies several key aspects of this narrative. The first is that the United States cast itself as a victim of terrorism—Americans were victims and often presented as 'innocent victims' (p. 32). Another significant element of the narrative involved seeing 9/11 as a 'defining moment', a day 'that changed the world forever' (p. 33). Importantly, the US also cast the attack on the Twin Towers as an 'act of war' that could justify a counter-attack or pre-emptive action (p. 38). Jackson also suggests that Americans placed 9/11 in a meta-narrative that linked it to other American understandings and memories of war, especially Pearl Harbor and World War Two (a surprise attack; Hitler as 'evil'), and the Cold War (fighting global networks of 'evil') (pp. 41, 45). The construction of 9/11 and the subsequent War on Terror pivoted on notions of 'good vs evil' and 'civilisation vs barbarism', ideas well-entrenched in American culture and dating back to colonial settlement. Historian John Dower has similarly linked public understanding of 9/11 into historical meta-narratives and understandings of the past, particularly Pearl Harbor (2010). In these ways, history and memory have been used in instrumentalist ways to construct popular understandings of the War on Terror.

The US language of the War on Terror demonised the enemy and cast Americans as victims. This is not an unusual feature of any wartime propaganda, and it certainly was the case after 9/11. Terrorists (notably al-Qaeda) were typically described as 'savage', 'barbarous', and 'perverted' (Jackson 2005, pp. 62, 65). They were most commonly described as 'evil' (p. 66). Such language, Jackson argues, helped to moralise the conflict (p. 69), and thus made it easier to justify taking military action or to engage in questionable actions at home. It also served to cast Americans as the 'good guys' of the conflict, typically depicted as peaceful and freedom-loving (Jackson 2005, p. 77). Jackson further points out that the 'us' and 'them' language deployed in the wake of 9/11 helped to forge unity in the US and suppress dissent (pp. 69, 88). Terry Anderson observes that the very use of the term 'war on terror' (which makes no sense because terror is a tactic, not an enemy) served to provide an idea of an enemy that was so vague as to include anyone deemed to be a terrorist in the eyes of the public or authorities (2011, p. 72).

Jackson goes on to outline what he calls the 'discourse of danger' and threat created in the wake of the 9/11 attacks. While in fact the chances of being a target of a terrorist attack are very small (then and now), a climate of crisis existed and could enable and permit certain political and military actions in response. The terrorist enemy was often portrayed as consisting of all-pervasive, highly organised global networks (2005, p. 109); the language frequently evoked apocalypse and spoke of 'mass destruction'. A language of threat and danger can be effective in suppressing dissent and, like the victim narrative, justify subsequent actions taken. Peter Stearns argues that American responses to terrorism were neither 'natural' nor 'inevitable', and argues that emotions can be seen as culturally constructed (2006, p. 12). His analysis of 'American fear' demonstrates the ways in which American culture constructed particular understandings of terrorism based on fear, which in turn made the American public particularly vulnerable to manipulation and accepting of repression, torture, and military aggression (pp. 217, 219).

These discursive elements helped to justify military actions subsequently undertaken by the US, which included military intervention in Afghanistan and, more problematically, Iraq. It also justified questionable invasions into individual privacy in the domestic sphere (primarily through the US Patriot Act). Much of this action was seen as acceptable in order to combat the threat of terrorism. But as Jackson suggests, a discourse of threat, fear, victimhood, and the notion that America was once again fighting a 'good war' against 'evil', prevented a realistic, rational, and balanced discussion of how best to deal with terrorist acts, and led to initially broad public support for a War on Terror.

THE LANGUAGE OF 9/11 IN AUSTRALIA UP TO THE BALI BOMBING

The 9/11 attacks led to terrorism becoming much more central not only to Australian foreign and security policy (Ungerer 2008, p. 9), but more generally made terrorism a central feature of political and cultural discourse. Australian media reported extensively, of course, on the events of 9/11 and American responses, and the language of the American media and politicians found its way into Australian public discourse. A number of elements identified above can be seen as being used and picked up in the Australian media, while a number of other or additional elements found their way into Australian public understandings of the War on Terror.

One of the key features of Australian discourse was the identification of Australia with America, and a casting of the 9/11 attacks as a global attack (typically considered as an attack on 'the West', or an attack on 'all of us'). Newspapers on the conservative side of the political spectrum, such as *The Australian*, were particularly sympathetic towards the United States over the attacks and keen to identify Australia with America. For example, an article published a week after 9/11 noted that Australia 'shared the loss' and argued that the West thus had 'pledged to fight this terror' ('War on Terror Requires Time' 2001). John Howard sought to present 9/11, as the US did, as a 'defining event' that demanded a response (2001d).

The language of some Australian politicians, including the Prime Minister (who was in Washington D.C. at the time of the attacks), connected the attack on the US to an attack on Australia. Howard made much of the importance of the 'Australian spirit, as much as for the American people the American spirit, triumph over these sorts of challenges and this kind of adversity' (cited in Shanahan 2001). In his later autobiography, Howard commented that 9/11 was 'an attack on the American way of life', and as a consequence, 'on our [Australian] way of life, because so much of what we hold dear as basic freedoms are the things that Americans also hold dear as basic freedoms' (2010, p. 382). Howard also saw the attacks as generally an attack on Western democracy. In an interview with right-wing radio commentator John Laws (who called 9/11 an 'attack on the civilised world'), Howard called it 'an attack on all of us' (2001a). In another speech, he asserted that 9/11 was a 'global challenge' that called for a 'global response' (2001d). This language served to closely align Australia's interests and sense of self with the US, preparing the way for a political argument that Australia should support the US politically and militarily.

Thus a key consequence of 9/11 was the overwhelming emphasis on the importance of the Australian-US relationship. Australia and the US already had a close relationship, but John Howard firmly articulated support for the US, both in sympathy with the attacks and more concretely in offering support for military and other actions taken. It should be noted that while the Howard government committed Australia to a global War on Terror, most foreign policy and security concerns and activities continued to be more regionally focused (White 2006; Shearman 2006; McDougall 2006). But the commitment to supporting the US served to function as symbolic of the broad support of a number of nations to US action, and placed Australia at the forefront of offering support (McDougall 2006, p. 107).

Not long after 9/11 took place, military action was taken against al-Qaeda networks in Afghanistan, to which Australia made a small military contribution. Howard justified this participation by drawing on a public discourse of good and evil. In a press conference held on 8 October, John Howard stated that Coalition military action had commenced against the Taliban. He argued that 9/11 was 'an obscenity' and 'evil' and the American-led offensive in Afghanistan was 'an attack on evil'. What was at stake was 'the capacity of countries of goodwill, peace loving men and women around the world, to live their lives free of the insidious threat of terrorist attacks.' He reminded Australians of US support in World War Two, and also reiterated that this was a fight between those who believe in freedom, peace, and liberty and those 'who would seek to intimidate and cow great people and mighty nations by terror' (2001b).

Howard defended the decision to commit troops to Afghanistan primarily on the basis of ANZUS (Australia-New Zealand-United States Security Treaty, 1951), but also argued that the cause was 'just' (Wright 2001). In farewelling SAS troops in October 2001, Howard reiterated the importance of fighting terrorism, but also sought to place the operation as part of a 'very great Australian military tradition' that 'has never sought to impose [its] will on others but rather to stick up for what is right and to defend what we believe in' (2001c). Deaths in combat (of which there were very few before the end of the 2000s) were seen by Howard as sacrifices 'as part of the global effort to make the world a safer place from the threat of terrorism' ('Aussie Soldier' 2002).[1]

In both countries, the language of World War Two was important to public rhetoric. In the US, this was through the comparison to Pearl Harbor, but also through a moral language of good and evil. While that language continued into the Cold War period, it was challenged and arguably undermined through the 1960s and 1970s until revived by Ronald Reagan. For Australia, the connection to World War Two was made in order to help make sense of Australia's participation. Howard frequently called on a historical meta-narrative of Australian and American co-operation in wartime, as much as any reality of ANZUS. In an address to the joint houses of American Congress in June 2002, Howard reiterated Australia's support for the US, invoking again the historic relationship of both World War Two and Vietnam. 'As we meet', Howard said, 'Australian and American troops are fighting side by side in Afghanistan' (cited in Grubel 2002). The moral certainties of World War Two also were invoked. In another speech, he commented: 'Even a cursory reflection on history must lead you to the irrefutable conclusion that passive indifference in the face of evil achieves absolutely nothing...There is a saying that for evil to triumph, it requires only good men to do nothing' (2001d). The media also made the connection to World War Two: Adam Cobb, writing in *The Australian*, invoked Franklin Delano Roosevelt's Four Freedoms in arguing for the West to clearly articulate an ideological approach to the War on Terror (2002).

The language and memory of Anzac (Australia's military tradition stemming from the Australian-New Zealand landings at Gallipoli and subsequent development as effective fighters during World War One), by contrast to the more general invocation of a moral language of war, was (interestingly) more muted in 9/11 public discourse but did occasionally appear. One report in *The Australian* on an American memorial service for Australian and New Zealand victims of the 9/11 attacks called the victims 'Anzacs'. One speaker at the service (an Australian minister) was seen to be 'recalling the Anzac sacrifices' in arguing that the lives lost 'need not be wasted' (Romei 2001). When SAS soldier Andrew Russell was killed, his story was articulated in the media through the lens of Anzac. The Anzac Day of 2002 was noted as having received 'almost unprecedented' public interest (Dunn 2002).

Patriotic rhetoric was central to much of the American discourse of 9/11. In Australia, patriotism was more complex in its expression after 9/11, especially because of the historically fraught relationship of America and Australia. While the *Adelaide Advertiser* reported on a 'surge in demand for flags and flagpoles' in the immediate aftermath of 9/11 ('Flying the Flag' 2001), it was unclear that Australian patriotism was a central part of Australia's 9/11 language. Nevertheless, 9/11 prompted some reflection on what it meant to be Australian, especially in invoking the spectres of terrorism and asylum-seekers; both threatened the 'Australian way of life'. This language would be intensified to a much greater extent after Bali.

Another distinctive element that shaped public discourse in Australia was the issue of asylum-seekers. September 11 came right before an Australian federal election (held 10 November) in which John Howard sought re-election to a third term in office. The election would be defined not just by 9/11 and the Australian commitment to the War on Terror, but also by the issue of people arriving by boat to seek refuge in Australia. The issue of boat people arrivals was not a new one for Australia, and through the 1990s, a fear of so-called 'illegal' arrivals was apparent (Marr 2003, pp. 48, 262). But the situation escalated dramatically in 2001. In particular, the 'children overboard' affair, where asylum-seekers were accused of throwing their children off a ship into the ocean in an attempt to be allowed to reach Australia (an incident later found to be untrue but used to political ends by the Howard government), led to considerable anti-refugee sentiment being expressed in Australia. The incident, David Marr argues, had a lasting impact on the Australian public, who increasingly saw 'illegals' as people desperate enough to do anything (and not welcome in the country) (p. 277).

The Howard government's approach to refugees was to implement the 'Pacific solution' of offshore processing (by designating areas such as Christmas Island as no longer being part of Australia). Some scholars have argued that the Australian approach to asylum-seekers in this period cynically played on the notion of regional threat (Perera 2009, p. 67; Southphommasane 2012, p. 55). Marr suggests that Howard and Peter Reith deliberately linked the refugee boats to terrorism, although this was denied (2012, p. 233).[2] Whether or not the government deliberately used 9/11 to manipulate public fears of refugees, the result was that fear of terrorists and the arrival of refugees by boat were intertwined in the public mind as 'border security' issues. A language of fear prevailed and informed public debates, and ultimately policy, on both. The media, especially right-wing radio 'shock jocks' such as Alan Jones, played on 9/11 to increase public fear and dislike of so-called 'queue jumpers' (Marr 2012, p. 133).

September 11 and the fear of terrorism undoubtedly helped provide a language and context that the hard-line approach to asylum-seekers taken by government could play into. Coupled with a long history in Australia of xenophobia and fear of invasion, fears of terrorism, as well as fears of undeserving 'queue jumpers' arriving in Australia, guaranteed an election victory for John Howard and a defeat for Labor leader Kim Beazley, who had only a few months before been seen as the likely winner of the 2001 election.[3]

But the official responses to 9/11 in Australia were by no means the only responses, nor was Australia's decision to support America something unanimously agreed with. Indeed, criticism was articulated at a number of levels. For Howard, providing military support not only upheld ANZUS, but was also about asserting Australian forces as 'highly respected and highly prized comrades in arms' (2001d). For many, this support of America was highly suspect and led to criticism from many on the Left. A linked issue was that of David Hicks, an Australian detained by the US as a suspected terrorist. The decision to allow Hicks to be held at Guantanamo Bay prison led to Australia's relationship to the US being described by Mark Latham, a Labor politician, as 'arse-licking' and former Labor Prime Minister Paul Keating as 'the Age of the Americans'. Keating challenged Americans' decision to approach the War on Terror as a military (as compared to a diplomatic) challenge (cited in Coorey 2002). This language of opposition arguably drew on a long tradition and cultural memory of Australia's supposed dislike of being told what to do, and occasionally prickly attitude towards the US (especially their dislike of what was perceived as American cultural imperialism).

Criticism of Bush's 'shifting definition' of the War on Terror was increasingly articulated by the *Sydney Morning Herald*, as Bush talked of an 'axis of evil' that included Iraq, Iran, and North Korea ('The World Since September 11' 2002). As Bush began to talk of links between terrorists and states suspected of developing weapons of mass destruction, criticism in the Australian press escalated. The *Hobart Mercury* reported on growing concerns about the 'US obsession with the war in terrorism' (Woolford 2002). There were also concerns voiced during the passing of the 2002 budget about the amount spent on defence and security, and ongoing concerns about the level of surveillance and other security measures that violated privacy as 2002 wore on.

Despite growing concerns about the nature of the War on Terror and the consequences of Australian support for the Bush Administration, such support continued and was justified by the primary elements of the official discourse, which included the US-Australian relationship and the necessity of fighting the evil of terrorism. In July 2002, Alexander Downer flagged that Australia would provide military support for any attack on Iraq. Downer argued: 'A policy of appeasement is a policy that is going to allow Saddam Hussein to continue to develop weapons of mass destruction' ('Our Troops' 2002). Invoking the spectre of appeasement connected the Iraq issue to Hitler and World War Two, and, building on the official discourse of the War on Terror by now entrenched in the public mind, allowed enough public support to agree to a contribution to an attack on Iraq. This would only occur, however, after the Bali bombings, an attack that once again redefined public discourse on terrorism.

BALI AND ITS AFTERMATH

In October 2002, just over a year after the American attacks of 9/11, a bomb exploded in a Bali nightclub, killing 88 Australians, and injuring more than 200 others. The bombing was the work of an Indonesian radical Islamic extremist group called Jemaah Islamiyah.[4] If 9/11 had shocked Australians at an abstract level, Bali, a popular Australian tourist destination, was much closer to home and involved considerable numbers of Australian casualties. Perera notes that Australians generally viewed Bali as 'our territory' or 'our backyard'; Bali was often imagined as an extension of Australia (2009, p. 101). In *Lazarus Rising*, John Howard acknowledges this relationship, writing that 'because of our links with Bali it felt almost like an attack on Australian soil' (2010, p. 415).

In the immediate aftermath of Bali, the language of the War on Terror was reinvigorated: there was an invocation of both moral certainty and the language of victimhood. The language of the Bali attacks was framed in much the way Americans framed 9/11. John Howard saw the attack as terrorism 'dispensed in an indiscriminate, evil, hateful fashion' (2010, p. 411). He called the bombing 'wicked' and 'cowardly'; the attacks were 'indiscriminate, brutal and despicable', and he called for 'unrelenting vigour' and 'unconditional commitment' to continuing the War on Terror (cited in 'War on Terror Must Go On' 2002). Howard also commented that Australians needed to be less complacent: 'People should get out of their minds the idea that it can't happen here. It can and it has happened on our doorstep' (cited in Dodson 2002). Howard's speech to parliament on 15 October reiterated that the bombing was a 'foul deed' and warned that Australians shouldn't be complacent about something happening on their own soil (2002a).

The media responded with commentary that suggested, in the words of one of them, 'paradise lost' (Martin 2002). *The Sun* commented: 'The laid-back land of the surfer, the beach babe and the barbie struggled to come to terms with the loss of its innocence, the massacre of its youth' ('We Cry for the Victims' 2002). Bali was also commonly seen as an extension of Australian soil by the media and politicians: Ross Peake said that Kuta Beach was 'little Australia' and the blast 'a direct strike against this country' (cited in 'We Cry for the Victims' 2002). Alexander Downer argued that the attack was a 'de facto attack' on Australia (cited in 'Attack Brings Terror Closer' 2002). Greg Sheridan, a right-wing political commentator, argued that the terrorists hated Australia for 'our oddly persistent goodness' and said that Australians were now in a 'war of survival, survival as the nation we know and cherish'. Any argument to say that the attack was a result of Australian foreign policy was, to Sheridan, 'demeaning and almost demented' (2002). He also connected his rhetoric to an argument for going into Iraq to remove WMDs. While letters to the editor (to newspapers that supported a more leftist position, such as the *Adelaide Advertiser*, the *Melbourne Age*, and the *Sydney Morning Herald*) suggested that many members of the public in fact saw Howard's support for the US to blame, Howard rejected such a position, reiterating the bombings as being a result of 'evil' and 'moral bankruptcy' (cited in 'Howard Denies' 2002).

On Sunday 20 October, Australia held a day of mourning for the victims of the attack. The focus was the Australian victims, and the Sydney Domain ceremony was called 'Australians Together' with people wearing a sprig of wattle (Smith 2002). Shortly after, Alexander Downer commented that Bali was Australia's 9/11 and had brought the two countries closer together (cited in 'Australian to Remain in War on Terror' 2002). Little of the media coverage said much about the non-Australian victims of the attacks. The Australianising of Bali continued with Howard using the event to invoke a sense of Australian nationalism. In John Howard's speech for a memorial held at Parliament House on 24 October, he particularly invoked the spirit of Australian mateship: 'in crisis we are all mates together' (2002b). In another speech not long after, Howard further invoked the importance of Australians coming together in response to the Bali 'crisis': 'There is no nation on earth that can better respond to a national challenge or crisis than Australia because we are a classless country and that means that when a [crisis] confronts all of us, we come together' (2002c).

While Australia chose not to pursue any kind of military option at a regional level in response to 9/11, and to instead work through diplomatic channels and more closely with Indonesia to combat terrorism, the analysis in the media of Bali placed it firmly in a 9/11 framework, ignoring any role that past Australian foreign policy might have had, or the complex nature of Jemaah Islamiyah. The father of one Bali victim, Brian Deegan, openly questioned Australia's intelligence leading up to the attacks and called for Howard not to lead the country into any more wars. Howard rejected any question of an intelligence failure and argued that it was important for Australians to realise that if they lived in a time of heightened anxiety, it was only due to the 'behaviour of terrorists'. He argued that the attacks were 'not our fault. There is nothing this country has done which justifies the bilious hatred that has been directed against it by the behaviour of these terrorists' (cited in 'PM Rejects Plea' 2002). A number of domestic security campaigns were initiated in the wake of the attacks, justified by the Bali attacks and the language of crisis. One was the 'Let's Look Out for Australia' campaign, which encouraged people to report suspicious behaviour to a free-call telephone line. This was criticised as encouraging people to report against any person of Muslim background ('Keep an Eye on People' 2002). A number of raids led to arrests of suspected terrorists or members of radical Islamic groups in Australia.

One year on from the Bali bombing, media noted that Australia could never be the same again after the bombing. John Howard urged Australians to fulfil their duty to the victims of the bombing and keep fighting the war on terrorism (cited in 'Aust Parliament Remembers' 2003). Doug Conway, a journalist, commented that Australia was 'now and forever part of that painful and unpredictable world, prey to influences beyond its control that might affect its security, its economy, its politics, its way of life'. Near the end of his commentary, Conway wrote: 'They [Australians] seem uncertain whether this is America's war, or the world's, whether it is unwinnable or whether it is another Vietnam' (2003). If the public language of 9/11 and Bali had been couched in terms of the moral certainties of World War Two, after the invasion of Iraq, the language would shift ever closer to the language and memory (and moral uncertainties) of Vietnam.

CONSEQUENCES AND AFTER-EFFECTS

The most problematic consequence of the construction of the public language of 9/11 was to justify American military actions in Iraq. John Howard committed Australia to military support for the American invasion. Howard, in justifying this support, told parliament that a failure to disarm Iraq of WMD s encouraged other 'rogue states' to think the world would do nothing to stop them, and allowed the danger 'of such weapons coming into the hands of terrorist groups', which he believed to be 'the ultimate nightmare'. He also reiterated in the speech the historic alliance with the US. Howard also added, near the end of his speech, that the decision had been 'taken in a world environment changed forever by the events of 11 September 2001. The world faces new and previously unknown menaces' (2003).

As numerous scholars have subsequently shown, 9/11 was used as a justification for invading Iraq, a regime that in actuality had nothing to do with the 9/11 attacks, whatever else it might have been guilty of (see, for example, Anderson 2011). While Australian military involvement in the war in Iraq was limited, Australia (along with other nations) provided rhetorical support for the war, thus helping to legitimise it. The US justified the invasion of Iraq by claiming that Saddam Hussein possessed 'weapons of mass destruction', a term that dominated public discourse about the war and, as already seen, evoked apocalyptic visions of the end of the world. With a shift to a policy of pre-emption that was integral to the 'Bush doctrine' for dealing with terrorism, an invasion of Iraq was constructed as necessary. The attack on Iraq began in March 2003, and Saddam's regime quickly collapsed. However, military occupation in Iraq would last for years, and the country would suffer through years of tragic chaos. As Anderson has argued, American plans for invading Iraq were effective, but their plans for occupying it were largely non-existent (see Anderson 2011).

The invasion of Iraq, although having the support of international leaders such as Howard and British Prime Minister Tony Blair, did engender domestic protest in a number of countries.[5] As I have already suggested, even before the invasion occurred, there was criticism in Australia. South Australian RSL President John Bailey warned the government of a 'new Vietnam' (cited in 'Beware the New Vietnam' 2003). Those who supported a War on Terror failed to see why a war on Iraq would benefit the world, and some even argued that it was counter-productive for regional security or regional interests (Mackie 2003). Political debate over the war was widely reported in the media (for example, 'War on Iraq, the Debate' 2003).

Unlike Afghanistan, there was considerable criticism at the global level of the decision to invade Iraq, borne out by the problems of occupation and reconstruction. The Bush, Howard, and Blair regimes all came under fire when, by 2005, it was conclusively proven that the regime of Saddam Hussein had no weapons of mass destruction. The moral certainties of the War on Terror would be further undermined from late 2003 onwards as scandals such as the torture of prisoners in Abu Ghraib prison by American soldiers was revealed. Other controversies included the ongoing detention without trial of prisoners in Guantanamo prison (including Australian David Hicks), and the obvious problems of America's occupation of Iraq with high numbers of civilian and military casualties.

A number of consequences of 9/11 continue to shape contemporary Australia. For example, the extension of ASIO and the Australian Federal Police's domestic security powers after 9/11, although subject to criticism, remain in place. Lawyer and legal scholar George Williams has criticised the fact that anti-terror laws remain on the statute books (they have been repealed or scaled back in a number of other countries); he argues that this 'poses a long-term challenge for the Australian legal system and Australian democracy' (2013, p. 15). A 2012 public opinion survey found that while Australians' concern about terrorism is not that highly ranked in a list of concerns, there is nevertheless a sense, according to Juliet Pietsch and Ian McAllister, that anxieties about terrorism have become the 'new normal' (2012, p. 83). They note that the public generally do not feel concerned about anti-terrorist legislation, and indeed are less concerned than the American public, who have a stronger sense of their legal and civil rights (pp. 86, 91). The continuing general state of anxiety over terrorism could be seen in the framing of the 2014 incident, known as the 'Sydney siege', where a lone gunman, Man Haron Monis, took a number of hostages in a café in Martin Place in Sydney's CBD. The government and media immediately called it terrorism, but Monis, while invoking the Islamic State, had limited links to political extremist groups, had been previously charged with being an accessory to the murder of his ex-wife, and was suffering mental health issues.

Australia only withdrew the last of its combat troops from Afghanistan in 2013. On the whole, the purpose and nature of Australian military involvement in Iraq and Afghanistan has had limited public understanding or debate.[6] Media coverage has been seen as limited, to some extent deliberately so, by a military and government reluctant to have the armed services' activities scrutinised by journalists. James Brown has suggested that veterans are poorly recognised and supported (2014). Australian participation in twenty-first-century wars remains poorly understood, perhaps obscured by a language that initially served to justify the actions but which has done little to make clear exactly what these wars are about, why they continue, or how they are conducted. Indeed, the situation may be such that while terrorism and its discursive features remain central in public debates and understandings about world affairs, Australian participation in and experiences of recent military encounters may impact the construction of public memory in only marginal ways.

The cultural and political discourse of Australia continues to be shaped by 9/11 and the War on Terror, especially if considered alongside the asylum-seeker issue. Perera suggests that the global war on terror provided a context for the 'staging and reaffirmation of Australia as a white nation' (2009, p. 119). Perera sees the period following 9/11 as one where Australia sought to re-assert its white colonial identity against external threats by various non-white 'others' (e.g., asylum-seeker, terrorist, recent non-Anglo migrant). Perera's ideas are necessarily provocative, but they have some explanatory power. The election of 2001 effectively played on the average Australian's fears of terrorists and boat people; the 2013 election played on the average Australians' fears of boat people (terrorism being the new normal) to an alarming degree. In a 2011 Lowy Poll, it was revealed that 61% of people believe that boat people pose a threat to the security of Australia (cited in Marr 2012, p. 248).

What is also clear is that much of the handling of the boat people issue (and militarised 'solutions' to the problem) is, like Australia's overseas military operations, not open to media and public scrutiny. We rarely question why it is that twenty-first-century Australia operates on the principles of fear, or try to understand the cultural construction of that fear. Yet a language of fear that plays on abstract and ahistorical (or 'selective memory') ideas and emotions obscures rational discussion. The world has indeed 'never been the same' since 9/11. But this says much more about the way responses to highly destructive and tragic events were framed and understood. Australia stood in support of the US in the wake of 9/11 but justification of that support had its own particular features in Australian public discourse. Bali had some claim to be Australia's 9/11, but largely served to prompt greater politicisation of the asylum-seeker issue, an issue that continues to be of concern to Australia.

NOTES

1. Howard made this comment in relation to the death of SAS soldier Andrew Russell, killed in Afghanistan.
2. John Howard denies this in *Lazarus Rising* (2010, p. 389). Peter Slipper (then a Liberal MP) did however make the link.
3. Media commentary at the time noted the domination of security issues (to which both 9/11 and boat people were tied) in the election. For example, see Parkinson (2001).
4. For a discussion of Jemaah Islamiyah (JI), see Sally Neighbour, *In the Shadow of Swords: On the Trail of Terrorism from Afghanistan to Australia* (2005). This book, which won a NSW History prize, has its own issues in how it constructs the narrative, but does provide an accessible overview of the story of JI and its Australian links.
5. John Howard continues to argue that the decision to go into Iraq was correct as a 'legitimate act of anticipatory self-defence' (2010, p. 425).
6. Soldiers' attitudes to this are discussed in Masters 2012. Kevin Foster has discussed the media coverage of the war at length in several works, including *Don't Mention the War: The Australian Defence Force, the Media and the Afghan Conflict* (2013), and *What Are We Doing in Afghanistan? The Military and the Media at War* (2009).

WORKS CITED

Anderson, Terry. 2011. *Bush's Wars*. New York: Oxford University Press.

Attack Brings Terror Closer. 2002. *Townsville Bulletin*, 14 Oct.

Aussie Soldier Killed in Afghanistan Identified. 2002. *AAP*, 18 Feb.

Aust Parliament Remembers Bali Bombings. 2003. *AAP*, 9 Oct.

Australia to Remain in War on Terror Even if it Takes Years. 2002. *AAP*, 21 Oct.

Beware the New Vietnam, Warns RSL. 2003. *Advertiser*, 17 Jan.

Brown, James. 2014. *Anzac's Long Shadow: The Cost of Our National Obsession*. Collingwood: Redback.

Cobb, Adam. 2002. As an Antidote to Terror, Try Well-Targeted Aid. *Australian*, 14 Jan.

Conway, Doug. 2003. Bali Events Change Psyche of Australia. *AAP*, 2 Oct.

Coorey, Phillip. 2002. Dubbya Calls the Shots. *Advertiser*, 15 July.

Dodson, Louise. 2002. We're All at Risk. *Age*, 14 Oct.

Dower, John W. 2010. *Cultures of War: Pearl Harbor/Hiroshima/9-11/Iraq*. New York: W.W. Norton.

Dunn, James. 2002. Talk of War in the Air on Anzac Day. *Illawarra Mercury*, 27 Apr.

Flying the Flag in Show of Patriotism. 2001. *Adelaide Advertiser*, 25 Oct.

Foster, Kevin. 2013. *Don't Mention the War: The Australian Defence Force, the Media, and the Afghan Conflict*. Clayton: Monash University Publishing.

———. 2009. *What Are We Doing in Afghanistan? The Military and the Media at War*, Melbourne: Australian Scholarly Publishing.

Grubel, James. 2002. September 11 Continues to Impact on Australia. *AAP*, 27 Aug.

Howard Denies he has "Blood on his Hand". 2002. *Age*, 16 Oct.

Howard, John. 2001a. Interview with John Laws. Radio 2UE, 12 Sept.

———. 2001b. Press Conference, Melbourne, 8 Oct.

———. 2001c. Farewell to SAS Troops, Campbell Barracks, Perth, 22 Oct.

———. 2001d. Address to the Australian Defence Association, Melbourne, 25 Oct.

———. 2002a. Bombing of Bali. A Day that Evil Struck. *Advertiser*, 15 Oct.

———. 2002b. National Memorial Service Reflection, 24 Oct.

———. 2002c. Address at the NSW Liberal Party State Council, 23 Nov.

———. 2003. Speech to Parliament, 18 Mar.

———. 2010. *Lazarus Rising*. Sydney: HarperCollins.

Jackson, Richard. 2005. *Writing the War on Terrorism: Language, Politics and Counter-Terrorism*. Manchester: Manchester University Press.

Keep an Eye on People Living Next Door. 2002. *Advertiser*, 28 Dec.

Mackie, Jamie. 2003. Wake Up Australia War on Iraq Is Dangerous. *Age*, 23 Jan.

Marr, David. 2003. *Dark Victory*. Crows Nest: Allen and Unwin.

———. 2012. *Panic*. Collingwood: Black Inc.

Martin, Lorna. 2002. Paradise Lost for Australian Visitors as Death Toll Mounts. *Herald*, 14 Oct.

Masters, Chris 2012, *Uncommon Soldiers*, Allen and Unwin: Crows Nest.

McDougall, Derek. 2006. Australia and the "War on Terrorism": A Preliminary Assessment. In *Australian Security After 9/11: New and Old Agendas*, ed. D. McDougall and P. Shearman, 105–120. Aldershot: Ashgate.

Neighbour, Sally. 2005. *In the Shadow of Swords: On the Trail of Terrorism from Afghanistan to Australia*. Sydney: Harper Perennial.

Our Troops Set to Join Attack. 2002. *Daily Telegraph*, 13 July.

Parkinson, Tony. 2001. Will History Make Howard? *Age*, 6 Oct.

Perera, Suvendrini. 2009. *Australia and the Insular Imagination: Beaches, Borders, Boats and Bodies*. New York: Palgrave Macmillan.

Pietsch, Juliet, and Ian McAllister. 2012. Terrorism and Public Opinion in Australia. In *Australia: Identity, Fear and Governance in the 21st Century*, ed. Juliet Pietsch and Ian McAllister, 79–94. Canberra: ANU EPress.

PM Rejects Plea from Sari Victim's Father. 2002. *Australian*, 23 Nov.

Romei, Stephen. 2001. Attacks Unite Anzac Spirit in Shared Grief. *Australian*, 1 Oct.

Shanahan, Dennis. 2001. Helping US is Risky, but we must. *Australian*, 22 Sept.

Shearman, P. 2006. Identity Politics, New Security Agendas and the Anglosphere. In *Australian Security after 9/11: New and Old Agendas*, ed. D. McDougall and P. Shearman, 47–68. Ashgate: Aldershot.

Sheridan, Greg. 2002. This Nation We Love Must Face the Threat, and Fight *Australian*, 17 Oct.

Smith, Michael. 2002. Australia Stops to Mourn Bali Bombing Victims. *Reuters*, 20 Oct.

Soutphommasane, Tim. 2012. *Don't Go Back to Where You Came From: Why Multiculturalism Works*. Sydney: New South.

Stearns, Peter N. 2006. *American Fear: The Causes and Consequences of High Anxiety*. New York: Routledge.

The World Since September 11. 2002. *Sydney Morning Herald*, 11 Mar.

Ungerer, C. 2008. Introduction: Australian Foreign Policy after 9/11. In *Australian Foreign Policy in the Age of Terror*, ed. C. Ungerer, 1–22. Sydney: UNSW Press.

War on Iraq, the Debate—What Our MPs Say. 2003. *Advertiser*, 15 Feb.

War on Terror Must Go On After Bali Bombs. 2002. *Reuters*, 13 Oct.

War on Terror Requires Time, Resolve, and Sacrifice. 2001. *Australian*, 18 Sept.

We Cry for the Victims and Our Lost Innocence. 2002. *Sun*, 15 Oct.

White, H. 2006. Old, New, or Both? Australia's Security Agendas at the Start of the New Century. In *Australian Security After 9/11: New and Old Agendas*, ed. D. McDougall and P. Shearman, 13–28. Ashgate: Aldershot.

Williams, George. 2013. The Legal Legacy of the "War on Terror". *Macquarie Law Journal* 12: 3–16.

Woolford, Don. 2002. Seeking a Smart War on Terrorism. *Mercury*, 11 May.

Wright, Lincoln. 2001. Australia "Justified" in Sending Troops. *Canberra Times*, 26 Oct.

AUTHOR BIOGRAPHY

Amanda Laugesen is a Senior Fellow in the School of Literature, Languages and Linguistics at The Australian National University and is currently Director of the Australian National Dictionary Centre. She has many publications in Australian and United States history, as well as language and lexicography. Her most recent book, *Taking Books to the World: American Publishers and the Cultural Cold War*, will be published by University of Massachusetts Press in 2017.

CHAPTER 4

Enemies of the State(S): Cultural Memory, Cinema, and the Iraq War

Richard Gehrmann

Nearly 17,000 Australian Defence Force (ADF) members ('Award Statistics' 2010) were awarded the Iraq Campaign Medal for service in the Iraq War,[1] yet for the vast majority, their experience of war had nothing in common with what was depicted in films such as *The Hurt Locker* (2008), *Generation Kill* (2008), and *American Sniper* (2014). Despite government rhetoric suggesting Australia stood by the United States as a key ally, Australia made only a limited commitment (see Doig et al 2007; Blaxland 2014). Some Australians had a combat role in the 2003 invasion, but few experienced combat in the subsequent and very different insurgency phase of the war, and while some Australians were wounded, none were killed in battle. For most, the war experience was one of tasks such as land, naval, or air patrols, occasional dangerous routine transport flights, or training the new Iraqi army, and many Australian soldiers who had anticipated direct combat action felt alienated by their marginal role.

For Australians at home, there were few realistic frames of reference regarding the war. Consistent with the significant American presence in Iraq, numerous American war films were produced and many

R. Gehrmann (✉)
University of Southern Queensland, Toowoomba, Australia
e-mail: richard.gehrmann@usq.edu.au

© The Author(s) 2017
J. Gildersleeve and R. Gehrmann (eds.), *Memory and the Wars on Terror*, Palgrave Macmillan Memory Studies,
DOI 10.1007/978-3-319-56976-5_4

were distributed in Australia. Yet these cinematic images watched by Australians spoke to an American cultural memory: US-made, about Americans, and exploring an American understanding of the war. The messages in them might have resonated for a US society intimately connected with this conflict, but such messages were not necessarily relevant or appropriate for an Australia whose military role in Iraq was peripheral. Australian soldiers' experiences generated memories that were far removed from the action and conflict of these American films, and the distorted cinematic images of the American films contributed to an ongoing dissonance and the perpetuation of an unrealistic representation of the Australian war in Iraq.

WAR, FILM, AND MEMORY

People who haven't experienced war inevitably base their understanding of [it] on the mediated versions of news or Hollywood. These representations are often limited and can't quite reveal the humour, boredom, and confusion inherent in combat. It's something we felt was important to represent. (Hetherington cited in Hetherington and Junger 2010)

In the twenty-first century, the experience of war can be told and remembered through forms that include memoir, fiction, news reports, and film. Despite persistent debate regarding the authenticity of such narratives in both fictional and non-fictional accounts, war stories nevertheless appear to achieve totemic status, becoming defining texts shaping cultural memory. The *Iliad* might have primacy for the Trojan War because of a lack of alternative cultural memories, but in more recent conflicts represented by multiple accounts, the most dynamic narratives can assume positions of hegemonic dominance. Most of us in the Western world have not personally experienced war and as Hetherington observes, it is easy to turn to popular narrative forms, such as film. Film's crafted memories can have resonant effects, especially as cinematic representation becomes ever more realistic and authentic (Gates 2005, pp. 277–278). Although David LaRocca points out that restaged fictional war films still face a challenge from documentaries with the capacity to reprise the tangible action of authentic bomb explosions and real casualties (2014, p. 13), the technically 'perfect' war film still surpasses its documentary rivals; indeed, it now mimics the documentary handheld camera, adding apparent realism (Bjerre 2011, pp. 224–225).

Despite the veracity of documentary reconstructed from spliced footage of the journalist's camera and the soldier's battlefield headcam, the re-enacted drama of the war film captures the imagination and feeds into collective memory.

These repeated and realistic (if not 'real') images can shape the soldier's own self-perception. For example, Australian Lieutenant-Colonel Chris Smith reported that some of his young soldiers in Afghanistan lacked discipline and took risks because of their 'distorted and fanciful perception of wartime soldiering derived from movie stereotypes' (Wroe 2013). Moreover, it might be seen that these stereotypes become even more persistent as techniques of realism in cinema improve: the sophistication of current film-making technology means the D-Day beach landing scene from *Saving Private Ryan* (1998) has greater impact than the once well-regarded *The Longest Day* (1962). Likewise, *The Green Berets* (1968) pales in comparison to more complex Vietnam films such as *Apocalypse Now* (1979) and *Born on the Fourth of July* (1989). Films about the war in Iraq have also shaped expectations and understanding of the contemporary war experience; *Generation Kill, The Hurt Locker*, and *American Sniper* have enjoyed particular critical and box office appeal.

THE 2003 AMERICAN INVASION: GENERATION KILL

Generation Kill was a seven-part HBO television series. Released in America, it was subsequently shown in Australia on both cable and free-to-air television channels. Although *Generation Kill* was made during the post-2004 insurgency phase of the war, it did not focus on its contemporary events—bomb and rocket attacks, guerrilla warfare, and the ever-growing list of dead and maimed in an apparently intractable conflict—which were becoming a staple of nightly television news in the United States. Rather, it looked back to a comparatively happier time for Americans: the emphatic victory against Saddam Hussein's army in March–May 2003 (see Keegan 2004). The *Generation Kill* miniseries was based on *Rolling Stone* journalist Evan Wright's successful book on the invasion experience, which chronicles the travails of a Marine company as they fight their way towards Baghdad, accompanied by their own embedded amanuensis.[2]

The series explores a trope common in war memoirs: the disconnection between soldiers and civilians. Marines are socialised into a culture detached from the middle-class reporter's world. Wright's arrival reveals deep divisions of class, culture, and experience. In his book's prologue, Wright also demarcates the division between this new generation and the young Americans of John F. Kennedy's more ordered and idealistic era:

> These young men represent what is more less America's first genera-tion of disposable children. More than half the guys in the platoon come from broken homes and were raised by absentee, single, working parents. Many are on more intimate terms with video games, reality TV shows and Internet porn than they are with their own parents. (Wright 2005, p. 19)

Such cultural divisions are amplified through the series, and Wright only gradually becomes accepted into the world of the combatants. They have an ability to sift through the ephemeral and focus on what unites them with their fellow soldiers, a profane hard-working warrior tribe owing a primordial loyalty to its members and disdaining the low-effort, superficial slacktivism of twenty-first-century American life. As Sergeant Antonio Espera puts it,

> Back home in the civilian world, a fool slaps a 'protect the planet' sticker on his car, suddenly he's all about the environment and shit. Don't matter that he still drives that fucking car, fires up his computer and video games and cell phone every night with electricity made from nuclear power, coal, and fucking melted baby seal oil. Nuh-uh-uh, I got a dolphin sticker on my shit, so I'm all about saving the fucking planet. In our fucking Marine Corps civilisation, it don't matter what a motherfucker says. Only thing that matters is, dawg, would you charge that motherfucking machine gun when the motherfucker tells you to charge the motherfucking machine gun. (White and Jones 2008)

Generation Kill portrays the invasion of Iraq, cultural misunderstandings, both planned and unanticipated fighting, military confusion, and disa-greements with commander's decisions. The war is conducted at a fast pace, accompanied by heavy metal soundtracks, and as the Marines head towards their inevitable victory in Baghdad, the series conveys a road-movie feeling of action that sometimes quite literally becomes a series of seemingly random drive-by shootings. This metaphor is apt—historian John Keegan has noted that the great mystery of the war was the lack of an organised conventional Iraqi opposition to the United States advance (2004, p. 4). The Marines are detached from their surroundings, and appear to lack an understanding of Iraqi civilians who disregard the war in order to carry out their daily business, and of Iraqi soldiers who seem desperate to avoid the war entirely. After the successful invasion and overthrow of Saddam (and his monumental Stalinist statues), the cheering of the grateful liberated Iraqis peters out, only to be replaced by a montage of angry mobs, rampant looting, and the first sign of an anti-American Iraqi insurgency and social dystopia.

This is a series that records constant fighting in the successful United States mechanised *blitzkrieg* with Americans wounded and killed in battle with their enemies. As a collective group, the warriors of Second Platoon Bravo Company have no doubts about victory, and there is an ever-present confidence that their military juggernaut will defeat all in its path. This invasion has no option but to succeed where its 1991 predecessor failed, and will result in not only the destruction of Saddam's armies but also in the liberation of Baghdad. This is a film chronicling the subculture of the combat forces of a highly confident superpower at war with a hubristic reality check in the final episode.

INSURGENCY AND BOMB DISPOSAL/DISARMING IEDS: THE HURT LOCKER

A winner of six Academy Awards, *The Hurt Locker* was, like *Generation Kill* first shown in 2008, but it reflects a later phase in the Iraq War and a different sentiment about war itself. Kathryn Bigelow's film focuses on the interactions of a much more intimate group, the team members of a small bomb disposal squad, professionals who rely on each other to save human lives rather than kill their enemies. *The Hurt Locker* screenwriter was Mark Boal, who, as an embedded war journalist, spent two weeks with an explosive ordnance disposal team, an involvement that informed his script (Johnston 2009). While he lacked Wright's extended experience with his subjects, Boal's understanding provided insights into the bomb disposal specialists' world.

In *The Hurt Locker,* the complexities of the post 2004 Iraq occupation and insurgency are revealed. This is a time far different from the earlier 2003 defeat of Saddam's army. Following elections in 2005, Iraq had its own democratically elected government but they and the American-led coalition were challenged by diverse militant groups in an increasingly violent and effective insurgency. Unable to present a conventional

challenge to United States power, insurgents utilised bombs or impro-
vised explosive devices (IEDs) to attack government and coalition forces
as well as their own ethnic rivals. In this phase of conflict, Iraq was to
become ever more ungovernable and civilians would increasingly become
victims. *The Hurt Locker* shows the unpalatable intricacies of a conflict
where shades of grey dominate. The scenes of Americans and Iraqis
working together to secure the site of unexploded IEDs were a daily
reality. Confronting insurgent tactics are revealed, such as the use of a
disembowelled Iraqi corpse to conceal an IED, and an innocent Iraqi
civilian forced to wear a suicide bomb vest. Despite an American soldier's
desperate attempts, it cannot be defused in time and detonates with
fatal consequences. Such events were not emphasised in contemporane-
ous analysis that was still viewing Iraq through a simple binary equation
(Americans versus Iraqis) and pursuing legal issues of the 2003 invasion,
rather than addressing the insurgency's multidimensional complexities.

   The Hurt Locker follows some well-established genres of the war
film. The hero, bomb disposal expert Sergeant William James (Jeremy
Renner), is a maverick rebel who ignores then breaks the rules, even if
this disconcerts fellow team members and risks their lives. TJ Sanborn
(Anthony Mackie) performs the role of conformist, level-headed soldier
who challenges James's idiosyncratic behaviour, while their subordinate
Owen Etheridge (Brian Geraghty) is an archetypal subordinate soldier admiring both his seniors before being accidentally shot by James,
reminding us that in war all protagonists are vulnerable. Physically
huge in his protective bomb disposal suit, James is primarily a saviour
rather than a killer, and throughout *The Hurt Locker* there is a constant
expectation of possible danger, rather than sustained combat. While not
necessarily an anti-war film, it explores the horrors of war and is not tri-
umphalist. As reviewer and Iraq veteran Kate Hoit (2010) points out,
there are some dramatic scenes and inaccuracies that test credibility, but
overall the film gained praise for its realistic depictions of the American
counterinsurgency experience in Iraq. Richard Adams (2010) might
have deplored an absence of developed Iraqi characters, with most Iraqis
being portrayed as 'mute, anonymous and threatening figures, seen
away in the distance', but this representation accurately replicates the
American soldiers' experience.

   A significant post-combat phenomena was post-traumatic stress disorder (PTSD), which can relate to individual events of trauma, but is
exacerbated by trauma's repetition.[3] *The Hurt Locker* ends with James

returning from Iraq to relax with his partner and child, undertaking mundane shopping tasks yet clearly dissatisfied with what should be idyllic home life. He longs to return to the euphoric and adrenaline-filled world he has left behind, and the final scene shows him in action once again, suited up and ready to undertake another bomb disposal task, this time in Afghanistan—his war is unending. The idea of endless war resonated with an American understanding of their nation's Iraq experience as the repeated cycles of deployments saw many undertaking a second, third, or fourth tour of duty in quick succession. In most cases, these deployments were 12 months long and in some instances whole units endured three-month short-notice extensions. Discharged individuals could also have their service unilaterally extended through the Stop Loss program. Such deeply resented features of the American military experience were significantly different from the shorter six-month deployments of their Australian allies, and for many in the United States military, repeat tours were a reality that could push them to the limits of endurance.

INSURGENCY AND WARFIGHTING: AMERICAN SNIPER

In contrast to *The Hurt Locker*, *American Sniper* focusses on an uncomfortably dark side of war. This film not only portrays the act of deliberate killing, but the act of killing by a sniper, a dispassionate and calculating individual sitting high on a building, watching over the urban battlefield, preparing to shoot an unsuspecting victim perhaps 1000 metres or more away. Snipers often evoke moral repugnance, yet here the sniper is a protector whose post-deployment psychological interviews do not reveal the trauma of having killed so many people (at least 160), but rather his distress at not having protected as many of his fellow American soldiers as he might have by killing even more enemies.

Based on the autobiography of a decorated Special Forces Navy sniper, Chris Kyle (played by Bradley Cooper), filmmaker Clint Eastwood turns an ultra-patriotic and narrow book into a film that, while still very loyal to the United States, manages to be less jingoistic and far more appealing to a broader audience. The focus in *American Sniper* is on Kyle, the individual soldier hero either working alone or with a spotter-assistant, in contrast to the platoon-sized teams of *Generation Kill* or the bomb disposal squad of *The Hurt Locker*. Kyle is overtly macho, Texan and American in a manner unsettling to many in a non-American audience, but this had great domestic appeal, resulting in the highest earnings of any war film ever (Shapiro 2015). Like James in *The Hurt Locker*, Kyle serves on multiple deployments (four tours of Iraq) and he also breaks the rules (risking lives) by abandoning his sniper position to lead soldiers clearing an insurgent stronghold room-by-room. However, on the whole we see Kyle lying prone on the rooftop of a war-battered building, watching over his fellow Americans as they advance through the battle-scarred urban landscapes of Iraq.

Fighting in the urban battlespaces was alien to most Australians, but was an integral part of the American Iraq War experience. Troops who patrolled insurgent-dominated towns were under constant threat from IEDs and snipers. The iconic Second Battle of Fallujah (late 2004) resulted in over 700 American, Iraqi, and British military casualties, with more than 600 of these being Americans killed and wounded in the first major combat operation against the insurgency. Casualties in individual units were heavy—one Marine company reported 17 wounded out of the 39 who occupied just one location over a six-day period (Bolger 2014, p. 172). Up to 1500 insurgents were killed in attacks on their strongholds in a virtually abandoned city. When Eastwood's film shows Kyle in position on the rooftops overlooking the tentative advance of American combat teams, memories like Fallujah resonate with a American audience. However, this was not a memory shared by Australian soldiers.

American Sniper was favourably reviewed in *The New York Times* in a piece that emphasised how the film showed an understanding of Kyle but did not sanctify him (Scott 2014). Extensive criticism followed this, and the film's subsequent Oscar nominations only fuelled debate. Yet, its box office success revealed that despite such criticism, the film's themes resonated with United States viewers. Indeed, it was praised by First Lady Michelle Obama, who felt the film reflected 'the complex journeys that our men and women in uniform endure' (cited in Thompson 2015), while others saw the military as a subculture that the film had tried to restore 'to an approved place in the American narrative' (Beck 2015, p. 218).

American Sniper concludes by exploring PTSD and the American community's support for war veterans. Following his retirement from the military, Kyle was shot dead while helping a schizophrenic fellow veteran rehabilitate—ironically the rehabilitation consisted of a trip to a shooting range. The final scenes show the real-life footage of Kyle's coffin following a 200-mile-long funeral procession route, a route lined by thousands of flag-waving Americans. This depiction of United States patriotism and mass community support for the troops was far removed from the Australian experience.

The Military in Australian Public Memory

These films and others like them provided a reference point for explaining the Iraq War experience to Australians, but using them to shape an Australian cultural memory of the war could be problematic both for veterans and members of the wider community. During the war, the ADF exercised tight control over the news media and restricted information regarding Australian actions, providing little footage and few stories of the Australian deployment—a deployment that involved only limited fighting and thus few opportunities for action images of warfare. Even in Afghanistan, where Australians would engage in far greater combat action, the restriction on media reporting (see Foster 2013, as well as Foster's chapter in this volume) meant the shrouding of a decade's worth of Australian military history 'with many battles simply not featuring in public consciousness due to tight government management of media access to Australia's forces' (Blaxland 2014, p. 279). Television news of Americans at war and American films about the Iraq War were the dominant visual products available in Australia. Australian veterans would find their actions and experiences did not match those of their fictional United States avatars, and they returned home to an Australian public whose expectation and assumptions of war were conditioned by Hollywood film industry products. These dissonances between the fiction film and lived experience emphasise the stark reality that the Australian military role in Iraq was quite different to the American role in Iraq, and was further complicated by the way Australian cultural memory enshrines the ideal of the soldier, something deeply embedded in Australian national culture.

The image of the Australian digger is part of the broader national culture linking the Army with national identity (Blaxland 2014, pp. 13–14), with the most significant Australian military tradition developing after the landing of the Australian and New Zealand Army Corps (Anzac) at Gallipoli in Turkey on 25 April 1915. In an era when concepts of nationhood suggested a heroic sacrifice could shape national character, reports of the exploits of Australians shaped national unity in a newly federated country. Critiques of Anzac's place in national identity have noted its associations with warfare and masculine achievements, but Anzac remains a highly recognised symbol in Australian national life (see Brown 2014; Damousi 2010; Dixon 2014; McKenna 2010; Ross 1985; Stockings 2012). The primacy of Anzac Day in Australian cultural memory is enhanced through its position as a national holiday and strong community support across the political spectrum. For soldiers, being the legatee of a century-old military ideal can have deleterious effects—some returning from combat in Afghanistan have reportedly felt ashamed that their service did not meet community expectations of an idealised Anzac role (Brown 2014, pp. 111–112).

The construction of Anzac in Australian national memory shaped a narrative later applied to the Second World War, Vietnam, and other conflicts. Memorialisation of the achievements and sacrifices of Australians in war was linked to an ideal of egalitarian democratic Australians who were natural combat soldiers, far better than their enemies or allies. Vietnam memories contributed to a widespread belief that unlike Australians, many Americans were second-rate fighters (McKay 1996, pp. 214–220): when, as a young officer, future Major General Jim Molan eventually trained with American soldiers, he was surprised at their unexpectedly high degree of competence (Molan 2008, pp. 23–24). As a private soldier, the author and his fellow recruits were told during basic training that Australian soldiers were the best in the world, and that the British did well with limited resources, but that the over-resourced Americans were poorly trained and unable to fight well, so achieved victory with destructive firepower.

In the early stages of the Wars on Terror, Australians also expressed ambivalence about those undertaking non-fighting support roles and peacekeeping. Both soldiers and the wider community assume that soldiers who go to war will fight. The stated role of the Australian infantry clearly articulates this concept of soldiering: 'to seek out and close with the enemy, to kill or capture him, to seize and hold ground and to repel attack by day or night, regardless of season, weather or terrain' (Royal Australian Infantry Corps 2015). However, the vast majority of ADF members are not in infantry or related combat arms, but perform combat support or combat service support roles. Since the end of the Cold War, thousands of Australians had deployed on United Nations peacekeeping operations (including Somalia, Cambodia, and Rwanda) and on regional peacekeeping missions in Bougainville (Papua New Guinea),

East Timor and the Solomon Islands, but the ADF had not engaged in offensive operations since Vietnam. Since the Iraq War was clearly not a low-level peace operation, there were expectations that Australian troops would once again perform a warfighting role.

The experience of those who were embedded with mostly American coalition colleagues in Task Force Troy's Combined Explosive Exploitation Cell (CEXC) was not warfighting but did entail a high degree of risk, and has been described as Australia's 'hurt locker' (McKenzie 2010). CEXC was the Multi National Force, the Iraq Counter-IED Taskforce, and an international team of explosives experts and analysts. For instance, Australians such as Drew Martin attended more than 15 IED incidents, while Andrew Street was shot at, and during his 70 missions faced the risk of secondary IEDs planted to target bomb disposal experts and other response crewmembers. Tony Gilchrist undertook 102 missions with roles that included defusing a live suicide vest by hand and detecting an IED in an area where two IEDs had exploded that day, killing four Americans and wounding one of his colleagues (McKenzie 2009, 2010). *The Hurt Locker* may have contained dramatic exaggerations, and did reflect a memory of Iraq to which a few Australians could relate, but their experience was not shared by most other Australians serving in Iraq.

ON THE SIDELINES: THE AUSTRALIAN WAR IN IRAQ

There was a contradiction at the centre of our Iraq policy that should be addressed because it impacted on our soldiers. We went to Iraq to impress our allies. We took a good force in 2005 to Muthanna at a time when the US desperately needed assistance. We put that force into the quietest province in Iraq where nothing was happening, then restricted the force in what it could do to the extent that we impressed no one. (unnamed Australian senior officer cited in Blaxland 2014, pp. 251–252)

At a lower level the diggers, NCOs and junior officers are starting to question the infantry's role and their part in it, which is having a tangible effect on morale. (Colton 2008, pp. 52–53)

Australians served in two distinctly different Iraq conflicts. The first was the invasion in 2003, and this was followed in 2004 by a counterinsurgency war. In the invasion, about 500 Australian Special Forces soldiers had a successful patrolling and fighting role in the deserts of western

Iraq, a role completely eclipsed by the nearly 200,000-strong United States and British invasion from the southeast. Australian naval and air force units also participated in the invasion but again performed a negligible role compared to their coalition allies. Almost all Australians were withdrawn from Iraq following Saddam's defeat, apart from a small number of security and liaison staff. In the post-invasion reconstruction stage, an army training team was sent to Iraq and by 2005, as the Iraqi insurgency grew in strength, Australia also deployed logistics units and a 500-strong battle group to protect Japanese reconstruction engineers in the southern province of Al Muthana (Noble 2006). The following year the Australian force was reassigned to the neighbouring Dhi Qar province with responsibility to provide backup to the Iraqi police and army if requested by the Iraqi government (Blaxland 2014, p. 238). These two provinces were among the most secure provinces in Iraq. Troop numbers were reduced in 2008 and a year later almost all Australian troops had left Iraq (Blaxland 2014). Australians performed well in a wide variety of roles that included embassy security, training teams, supporting coalition and Iraqi headquarters, air transport, and naval patrols.[4]

Significantly, even at the height of the United States surge in 2007 and 2008, Australia did not have a warfighting role in Iraq, and the casualty statistics reflect this. Throughout the entire war, only one of the nearly 17,000 Australians who served died—not in combat, but when he accidentally shot himself. In contrast there were 4486 Americans fatalities, 218 deaths among nearly 40 coalition partners, and more than 103,775 Iraqi soldiers, civilians, and insurgents killed (Bolger 2014, p. 276). Many coalition countries (including Italy, Romania, Thailand, Spain, Georgia, Denmark, Latvia, and El Salvador) suffered more war deaths than Australia. These statistics place the Australian mission in context and illustrate the point that the vast majority of Australian troops were undertaking defensive or protective roles (Colton 2008, p. 52) that related to peacekeeping and reconstruction rather than warfighting. This contrasts to the stated role of Australian combat corps, such as the infantry, and to the combat role undertaken by the Americans. Australia and the United States had a shared experience of war in Vietnam, the Second World War, and the First World War, but in Iraq most Australians did not share the American experience of fighting in a war. Australians served with dignity and courage, whether in the embassy security detachment convoying diplomats through the Baghdad streets, or manning a base perimeter logistics store while under sporadic fire. Some were critically wounded in attacks, and insurgent rockets and IEDs were an ever-present risk, but Australians were not tasked to attack enemies, only to respond when directly attacked. Journalist Chris Masters might have found it 'a remarkable fact' that in six years of war in Iraq no Australians were killed in action (2012, p. 93), but the actual tasking of the Australian military significantly reduced the risk of casualties.

A survey of major operational incidents involving the Australian Overwatch Battle Group in southern Iraq (2006–2008) provides contrast with the American war experience, as does the attitude of coalition allies towards Australia's cautious role. John Blaxland details an exchange of fire with insurgents at Al Rumaythah on 26 September 2006 lasting less than one hour, an IED attack damaging a vehicle in 2007, and a further machine-gun and rocket-propelled grenade attack in 2007 (2014, pp. 240–243), all incidents occurring when the United States was engaged in major offensive operations against insurgents and experiencing hundreds of casualties. Obviously Australians on patrol anticipated possible attack every time they left a base,[5] and undoubtedly their preparedness and professional skills mitigated risks (Reynolds 2006), but apart from numerous rocket attacks on their bases, the Australian taskforce experienced a relatively safe war for two years. This was not lost on allied soldiers, despite official allied praise for Australia's role. The British were incredulous that the Australians with their armoured vehicles often remained safely on base while British forces patrolled in open Land Rovers (Hammett 2008, pp. 45, 49). On several occasions, the constraints imposed by the risk-averse Australian government meant Australian troops in Iraq were not permitted to fight to assist their British and Iraqi allies, resulting in British accusations of cowardice on more than one occasion (Blaxland 2014, pp. 241–242, 246–247). The lack of combat tasking for the well-fed, body-armoured Overwatch Battle Group with pennants fluttering from their heavy vehicles led to some American comments that the initials of the force meant Overweight Banner Group.[6] Such criticisms frustrated and humiliated many Australian soldiers who were prepared for war in Iraq but were not permitted to perform an offensive role.

Not only did most Australians not fight, but the small size of the Australian deployment further confirmed Australia's marginal role. The raw statistics of contributions to George Bush's 'coalition of the willing' shows that the major troop contributions were from the United States and Great Britain, but until the detailed figures are examined it is not so obvious how minimal Australia's role was in comparison to that of its major ally, or even to other American allies. In the Multi National Force-Iraq statistics listing the troop contributions of coalition members, Australia's 'combat' numbers in-country appeared lower than America's new allies such as Georgia, Ukraine, and Poland (Blanchard and Dale 2007, pp. 10–18). The limited Australian role is also apparent when military contributions are assessed in proportion to the size of the Australian military overall and to the Australian population. Most Australians familiar with the government's rhetoric of the importance of Australian support for the United States would have been astounded to realise Australia's assistance to the United States' war in Iraq was (proportionally) overshadowed by that of one of its small Pacific island neighbours. A significant percentage of the Tongan military (and of the Tongan population as a whole) served in the Iraq War, with one in nine Tongan soldiers deployed in Iraq at any one time (Susman 2008). In political terms, the Australian government's decision to contribute a very small number of troops for maximum diplomatic gain was an excellent example of carefully calibrated decision-making, but this did not match the government's rhetorical flourishes or the self-perceptions implicit in Australian military ideology, and led to further distance between the real experience and film image of American soldiers in Iraq, and the experiences of Australians.

In contrast, for Americans, Iraq was a national conflict in terms of government commitment, size of deployed forces, popular support, and community engagement. Their deployment was based on the existing Navy and Air Force, a small increase in the size of the Army and the Marine Corps, and on the mobilisation of part-time volunteer National Guards and Reserves. Bolger argues this final decision meant that while public support for the war declined, the public continued to support those who served, as through the part-timers the military had community links to 'every county in America' (2014, p. 425). Although a small number of Australian reservists deployed to Iraq,[7] most of the Australian contingent were full-time military and in units that mostly lacked the local community affiliations of the American Reserves and National Guard. Thus Americans were more likely to know and understand fellow citizens with Iraq experience due to the sizeable United States deployments, and also because many veterans were neighbours, friends, and workmates encountered on a daily basis.

Many Australian soldiers were uncomfortable with the restricted Australian role and small contingents, and there was widespread interest when one infantry officer published an emphatic critique of this in the *Australian Army Journal*.[8] This article emphasised that Australia's allies were sending conventional arms-corps troops (such as infantry) to undertake war-fighting, whereas Australia reserved such tasks for Special Forces,[9] leading to a loss of morale among Australian infantry (Hammett 2008). His sentiments were echoed by a fellow junior infantry officer who pointed out that for a decade the operations faced by conventional troops had 'been defensive, or at the most protective, in nature' (Colton 2008, p. 52). Few serving soldiers put such criticisms in print, but this sentiment was widely held throughout the Army, and this policy of using Special Forces for high risk combat operations was also followed in Afghanistan, causing more frustration for conventional troops (Blaxland 2014, p. 278). At a time when Great Britain was sending reserve soldiers to Iraq and Afghanistan (some with only two days more training than the six weeks pre-deployment training of their regular counterparts) and when Canada and the United States also deployed significant numbers of part-time infantry, Australia was reluctant to even deploy regular Army infantry for warfighting in Iraq (Stewart and Fisher 2007).

Conclusion

The messages of *Generation Kill*, *The Hurt Locker*, and *American Sniper* resonated for American society and had meaning because they conveyed American experiences of the war. This was a significant event for them, with many killed and wounded, massive commitment by National Guard and Reserves, extending of 12-month tours by three extra months, and Stop Loss, all of which influenced the wider American community. The images of recently killed Americans were shown nightly on PBS News and yellow ribbons became a widespread symbol on trees, car stickers, outside homes, and at workplaces (Lilley et al. 2010). During the war, many Americans genuinely believed this was a just cause to which they must commit. While there was opposition to the war, overall there was support from an American public who distinguished between support for the troops and support for the government, a legacy of the Vietnam-era discrimination.[10] Australia's was a minor commitment, involving a very small number of Australians and did not touch the lives of most people. That moving yet unpretentious Iraq War film of the repatriation of a soldiers' body, *Taking Chance* (2009), could never have the impact on Australians that it would have for Americans.[11]

The films discussed here did attract Australian audiences but *American Sniper*'s overt American patriotism jarred some viewers. *American Sniper* was a film that came at the end of an inglorious war, and its box office success arrived only because '[i]t just seems to have hit a nerve in the US' (Weaving 2015). In 2012, *The Hurt Locker* was included in the Australian Chief of Army's recommended reading list for officers and senior warrant officers, as was Pat Barker's *Regeneration* trilogy (Grey 2012; see Gildersleeve's chapter in this volume for a discussion of Barker's work). Then Chief of Army David Morrison pointed out that in a digital age, film had many benefits, as it could help tell the story of soldiers, and had the advantage of being 'both instructional and entertaining, and also resonates an immediacy and heightened sensitivity that can be difficult to bring to life through the printed word' (Morrison 2012). Nevertheless, there is a lack of representation of war in Australian contemporary popular culture. An exhaustive search through 13,000 episodes of Australian popular television soap operas, *Neighbours* and *Home and Away*, found only one military veteran character in each; both were dysfunctional former army officers, and neither had served in Iraq (Brown 2014, pp. 107–109). For many Australians, the lack of an Australian cinematic representation of the Iraq War meant that they used American war films to fill the gap of understanding and experience in order to understand the greatest contemporary conflict of the decade and Australia's small part in this.

Fundamentally, it remains a reality that for most Australians who served, the Iraq War was more about alliance politics, and that this differed from the American experience and the American cinematic memory of the war. Just as the films of the Second World War and Vietnam created memories of these events, films of the Iraq War shaped the remembered understanding of the war for viewers in countries that participated. Intended primarily for an American audience, their representation of the Iraq War mediated an image of war to an audience in the similar yet different environment of a minor United States ally, Australia. There remains a stark inconsistency in the way such films are consumed and understood by viewers in different social contexts, and the way meaning and understanding of the Iraq War is derived from viewing experiences. While interesting in themselves, these films did little to explain Australia's defensive-protective war to the public, and their reiteration of United-States-related warfighting experience did little to help Australian service personnel accommodate themselves to the warfighting legends of Anzac.

NOTES

1. This medal covers service in Iraq between March 2003 and November 2013.
2. The authenticity of *Generation Kill* is supported in unit member Lieutenant Nathaniel Fick's memoir *One Bullet Away* (2005).
3. For a social constructivist account of this, see Jerry Lembcke's *PTSD: Diagnosis and Identity in Post-Empire America* (2013).
4. For a more detailed summary of the Australian commitment at its height in 2007, see Blaxland (2014, pp. 250–251).
5. The embassy security detachment in the high risk conflict zone of Baghdad would face more significant dangers (see Robinson 2006).
6. Author's experience, Iraq 2006–2007.
7. Larger reserve forces undertook peacekeeping in East Timor and the Solomon Islands (Smith and Jans 2011, p. 309).
8. This criticism was subsequently taken up by the media (Hyland 2008).
9. Major General Hindmarsh subsequently admitted the original task of Special Forces in the invasion phase of the war could have been achieved by conventional armoured cavalry units (Blaxland 2014, pp. 119, 222).
10. This continues today: I have repeatedly had Americans say to me 'thank you for your service', and while this sentiment can be appreciated for its sincerity, it is culturally awkward for an Australian to experience on several levels.
11. While Blackmore sees this as a film with 'little emotional impact on the viewer' (2012, p. 302), in the Middle East, the author observed the total absorption of American soldiers watching *Taking Chance* (Gehrmann 2015, p. 635).

WORKS CITED

Adams, Richard. 2010. *The Hurt Locker* is Empty, *Guardian*, 9 Mar. Available from: http://www.theguardian.com/commentisfree/cifamerica/2010/mar/09/oscars-kathryn-bigelow-hurt-locker-iraq.

Award Statistics. 2010. *It's an Honour*, 30 June. Available from: https://www.itsanhonour.gov.au/honours/awards/statistics.cfm.

Beck, Bernard. 2015. If I Forget Thee: History Lessons in Selma, American Sniper and A Most Violent Year. *Multicultural Perspectives* 17 (4): 215–219.

Bigelow, Kathryn dir. 2008. *The Hurt Locker*, Summit Entertainment.

Bjerre, Thomas. 2011. Authenticity and War Junkies: Making the Iraq War Real in Films and TV Series. *Journal of War and Culture Studies* 4 (2): 223–234.

Blackmore, Tim. 2012. Eyeless in America: Hollywood and Indiewood's Iraq War on Film. *Bulletin of Science, Technology and Society* 34 (4): 294–316.

Blanchard, Christopher M., and Catherine Marie Dale. 2007. *Iraq: Foreign Contributions to Stabilisation and Reconstruction*. Washington, DC: Congressional Research Service.

Blaxland, John. 2014. *The Australian Army from Whitlam to Howard*. Melbourne: Cambridge University Press.

Bolger, Daniel. 2014. *Why We Lost: A General's Inside Account of the Iraq and Afghanistan Wars*. New York: Houghton Mifflin.

Brown, James. 2014. *Anzac's Long Shadow: The Cost of Our National Obsession*. Melbourne: Redback.

Colton, Greg. 2008. Enhancing Operational Capability: Making Infantry More Deployable. *Australian Army Journal* 5 (1): 51–64.

Damousi, Joy. 2010. Why Do We Get So Emotional About Anzac? In *What's Wrong with Anzac? The Militarisation of Australian History*, ed. Marilyn Lake and Henry Reynolds, 94–109. Sydney: New South Publishing.

Dixon, Chris. 2014. Redeeming the Warrior: Myth-making and Australia's Vietnam Veterans. *Australian Journal of Politics & History* 60 (2): 214–228.

Doig, Alan, James P. Pfiffner, Mark Phythian, and Rodney Tiffen. 2007. Marching in Time: Alliance Politics, Synchrony and the Case for War in Iraq, 2002–2003. *Australian Journal of International Affairs* 61 (1): 23–40.

Eastwood, Clint dir. 2014. *American Sniper*, Warner Bros. Pictures.

Fick, Nathaniel. 2005. *One Bullet Away: The Making of a Marine Officer*. Boston: Houghton Mifflin.

Foster, Kevin. 2013. *Don't Mention the War: The Australian Defence Force, the Media and the Afghan Conflict*. Melbourne: Monash University Publishing.

Gates, Philippa. 2005. 'Fighting the Good Fight': The Real and the Moral in the Contemporary Hollywood Combat Film. *Quarterly Review of Film and Video* 22 (4): 297–310.

Gehrmann, Richard. 2015. The Hidden Reality of War in Afghanistan and Iraq: Challenges for the Fiction Film. In *The London Film and Media Reader 3*, ed. Phillip Drummond, 630–641. London: The London Symposium.

Grey, Jeffrey (ed.). 2012. *Chief of Army's Reading List*. Canberra: Land Warfare Study Centre.

Hammett, Jim. 2008. We Were Soldiers Once…The Decline of the Royal Australian Infantry Corps? *Australian Army Journal* 5 (1): 39–50.

Hetherington, Tim and Sebastian Junger. 2010. The Making of *Restrepo*: Behind the Scenes: An Interview with the Filmmakers, *National Geographic: Nat Geo Movies*. Available from: http://movies.nationalgeographic.com.au/movies/restrepo/junger-hetherington/.

Hoit, Kate. 2010. *The Hurt Locker* Doesn't Get This Vet's Vote, *Huffington Post*, Apr 6. Available from: http://www.huffingtonpost.com/kate-hoit/the-hurt-locker-doesnt-ge_b_449043.html.

Hyland, Tom. 2008. Our War Rhetoric Is Deflated by an Unlikely Source, *Age*, 1 June. Available from: http://www.theage.com.au/world/our-war-rhetoric-is-deflated-by-an-unlikely-source-20080531-2k7g.html.

Johnston, Sheila. 2009. *The Hurt Locker*: Interview with Mark Boal, *Telegraph*, 25 Aug. Available from: http://www.telegraph.co.uk/culture/film/starsand-stories/6055329/The-Hurt-Locker-interview-with-Mark-Boal.html.

Keegan, John. 2004. *The Iraq War*. New York: Knopf.

LaRocca, David. 2014. War Films and the Ineffability of War. In *The Philosophy of War Films*, ed. David LaRocca, 1–80. Lexington: University of Kentucky Press.

Lembcke, Jerry. 2013. *PTSD: Diagnosis and Identity in Post-Empire America*. Lanham, MD: Lexington Books.

Lilley, Terry G., Joel Best, Benigno E. Aguirre, and Kathleen S. Lowney. 2010. Magnetic Imagery: War-Related Ribbons as Collective Display. *Sociological Inquiry* 80 (2): 313–321.

McKay, Gary. 1996. *Delta Four: Australian Riflemen in Vietnam*. Sydney: Allen and Unwin.

Masters, Chris. 2012. *Uncommon Soldiers*. Sydney: Allen and Unwin.

McKenna, Mark. 2010. Anzac Day: How Did It Become Australia's National Day?. In *What's Wrong with Anzac? The Militarisation of Australian History*, ed. Marilyn Lake, and Henry Reynolds, 110–134. Sydney: New South Publishing.

McKenzie Nick. 2009. The Endless Battle, *Sydney Morning Herald*, 28 Mar. Available from: http://www.smh.com.au/national/the-endless-battle-20090327–9eao.html.

———. 2010. *Hurt Locker* Team Forgotten, *Brisbane Times*, 10 Mar. Available from: http://www.brisbanetimes.com.au/national/hurt-locker-team-forgotten-20100310-pz3a.html.

Molan, Jim. 2008. *Running the War in Iraq: An Australian General, 300,000 Troops, the Bloodiest Conflict of Our Time*. Sydney: Harper Collins.

Morris, Linda. 2012. Army Chief Endorses War Movies, *Age*, 28 Jul. Available from: http://www.theage.com.au/national/army-chief-endorses-war-movies-20120727-23011.html.

Noble, Roger. 2006. The Essential Thing: Mission Command and Its Practical Application. *Australia Army Journal* 3 (3): 109–127.

Reynolds, Gav. 2006. Embracing Complexity: An Adaptive Affects Approach to the Conflict in Iraq. *Australian Army Journal* 3 (3): 129–140.

Robinson, Tim. 2006. Contemporary Employment of Infantry in a Combined Arms Stability and Support Operation: SECDET VIII in Baghdad. *Australian Army Journal* 3 (3): 141–152.

Ross, Jane. 1985. *The Myth of the Digger*. Sydney: Hale and Iremonger.

Royal Australian Infantry Corps. 2015. 25 May. Available from: http://www. army.gov.au/Our-people/Corps/Infantry.

Scott, Anthony. 2014. Review: *American Sniper*, a Clint Eastwood film with Bradley Cooper, *New York Times*, 24 Dec. Available from: http://www. nytimes.com/2014/12/25/movies/american-sniper-a-clint-eastwood-film-starring-bradley-cooper.html?_r=0.

Shapiro, Emily. 2015. American Sniper Tops Box Office Record for Super Bowl Weekend, *ABC News*, 1 Feb. Available from: http://abcnews.go.com/ Entertainment/american-sniper-tops-box-office-record-super-bowl/ story?id=28645673.

Smith, Hugh, and Nick Jans. 2011. Use Them or Lose Them? Australia's Defence Force Reserves. *Armed Forces & Society* 37 (2): 301–320.

Stewart, Murray, and Dave Fisher. 2007. Send the Reserve to War with Six Weeks Training: The British Experience. *Australian Army Journal* 4 (1): 107–127.

Stockings, Craig (ed.). 2012. *Anzac's Dirty Dozen: 12 Myths of Australian Military History*. Sydney: University of New South Wales Press.

Susman, Tina. 2008. Goodbye, Iraq; Hello, South Pacific, *Los Angeles Times*, Dec 5. Available from: http://articles.latimes.com/2008/dec/05/world/ fg-tonga5.

The War in Iraq: ADF Operations in the Middle East in 2003 2003, Australian Government Department of Defence, Defence Publications Service.

Thompson, Krissah. 2015. Michelle Obama Joins Bradley Cooper to Praise *American Sniper*, *Washington Post*, Jan 30. Available from: https://www. washingtonpost.com/lifestyle/style/michelle-obama-joins-bradley-cooper-to-praise-american-sniper/2015/01/30/1d957f42-a8a2-11e4-a2b2-776095f393b2_story.html.

Weaving, Simon. 2015. American Sniper Review: Clint Eastwood a Bit off Target, *Sydney Morning Herald*, 23 Jan. Available from: http://www.smh. com.au/entertainment/american-sniper-review-clint-eastwood-a-bit-off-tar-get-20150120-12u038.html.

White, Susanna and Simon Cellan Jones dir. 2008. *Generation Kill*, HBO.

Wright, Evan. 2005. *Generation Kill*. London: Corgi.

Wroe, David. 2013. 'Blast for 'Gladiator' Diggers', *Sydney Morning Herald*, 14 Mar. Available from: http://www.smh.com.au/federal-politics/political-news/blast-for-gladiator-diggers-20130313-2g0xm.html.

AUTHOR BIOGRAPHY

Richard Gehrmann is a Senior Lecturer in International Studies at the University of Southern Queensland who deployed to Afghanistan and Iraq as an Australian Army reservist. A graduate of the University of Cambridge, he has published on war and society, and on representation and identity. Richard is currently researching depictions of captivity and trauma in the Age of Terror.

CHAPTER 5

Remembering the Warriors: Cultural Memory, the Female Hero, and the 'Logistics of Perception' in *Zero Dark Thirty*

Christa van Raalte

Zero Dark Thirty (Kathryn Bigelow 2012) is a film that has a complex relationship with cultural memory. On the one hand, it plays a role in making memories of the (real) events on which it is based; on the other, it articulates (in fictional form) existing memories and interpretations of those events. The filmmakers' research included interviews with some of the 'ordinary Americans' (Barnes 2012) on whom key characters were based, and the film begins by evoking shared memories of the 9/11 attack. However, the journalistic aesthetic and the use of degraded and apparently mediated footage familiar in style from televisual war reporting may serve to reinforce, inflect, or replace the viewer's memories of actual events—not least given the film's release only eighteen months after those events took place. Steve Coll finds there to be something fundamentally problematic in the way the film 'appropriates as drama what remains the most undigested trauma in American national life during the last several decades' (2013, p. 4). Richard Powers, in his more favourable

C. van Raalte (✉)
Bournemouth University, Poole, UK
e-mail: cvanraalte@bournemouth.ac.uk

© The Author(s) 2017   91
J. Gildersleeve and R. Gehrmann (eds.), *Memory and the Wars on Terror*, Palgrave Macmillan Memory Studies,
DOI 10.1007/978-3-319-56976-5_5

review, has nevertheless characterised the film as 'an exercise in instant history and hot-after-the-fact myth-making' (2013), an epithet which suggests both the potential impact of the film on cultural memory, and the dangers inherent in that impact.

The film has given rise to much critical debate, focused primarily on its questionable historical accuracy, apparent political perspective, and the extent to which its narrative condones torture as an instrument of intelligence gathering.[1] These are indisputably important issues, however they have tended to crowd out of the critical agenda alternative approaches to the film. In this chapter, I will address two such approaches which I believe are interconnected: the way in which the narrative and visual idiom of the film is inflected by the presence of a female protagonist, and the way in which the film articulates the highly mediated, hyper-real vision of modern warfare discussed by commentators such as Jean Baudrillard and, in particular, Paul Virilio.

The film follows the fortunes of Maya (Jessica Chastain), a CIA agent who devotes ten years of her life to the hunt for Osama bin Laden. Set largely on 'black sites', the narrative hinges on the painfully slow process of intelligence gathering, together with the investigative blind alleys and bureaucratic road blocks that beset the team tasked with bin Laden's capture. Over the course of the film, Maya survives a terrorist attack and a targeted assassination attempt; several of her friends are less fortunate and are killed in an attack on a CIA compound. Undeterred, Maya pieces together evidence from existing files, recorded interviews, prisoner interrogations, and surveillance until she has determined the location of bin Laden's Pakistan compound. The final act of the film depicts the midnight raid in which bin Laden is killed.

From a feminist perspective, one of the most striking features of *Zero Dark Thirty* is the use of a female lead in such a consistently 'masculine' genre as the war film. Susan Carruthers dismisses the casting of a female lead as a 'feminist gesture' (2013, p. 52); however the gender of the protagonist is much more than an incidental detail within the film, having profound implications for the structure and dynamics of the narrative. Without a female protagonist, the central dramatic device of surveillance-as-action and the effective exclusion of the hero from direct engagement in the climatic 'battle' (the moment for which the film is named) would be problematic, if not impossible. In effect, the re-conceptualisation of the hero as female coincides with a re-conceptualisation of what constitutes 'action' for the purposes of the film. Another striking feature of this film is the extent to which it articulates the relationship between cinema and war, as proposed by Paul Virilio. The intradiegetic use of surveillance technology exemplifies the 'logistics of perception' discussed in *The Vision Machine* (1994), while the appropriation of the 'reality effect' of mediated images for the purposes of a Hollywood film speaks to Virilio's 'aesthetics of disappearance' (p. 49). I suggest that there is a relationship between these two perspectives, which intersect in the complex dynamics of the image and the gaze within the film.

In her role as professional watcher, Maya is the bearer of a paradoxical gaze. Her gaze is constructed primarily as controlling, authoritative, and the source of knowledge—bearing more than a passing resemblance to the role of the film director. However, it is also the source of misinformation, frustration, and the feelings of impotence associated with witnessing. This paradox points on the one hand to the problematic relationship between the woman and the gaze articulated throughout feminist film criticism, and on the other towards the 'paradoxical logic' (Virilio 1994, p. 63) whereby the image comes to dominate reality—a concept Virilio associates with the moral relativism which, for many, constitutes an ideological and aesthetic problem at the heart of *Zero Dark Thirty*.

LOGISTICS OF PERCEPTION AND AESTHETICS OF DISAPPEARANCE

There is no solution to this extreme situation, especially not war that offers only an experience of deja-vu, with the same flooding of military forces, fantastic news, useless propaganda, deceitful and pathetic discourses and technological deployment. In other words, as in the Gulf War, a non-event, an event that did not happen. (Baudrillard 2001)

[O]nce you can see the target, you can expect to destroy it. (W.J Perry, former US Under-Secretary of State, cited in Virilio 1989, p. 4)

Zero Dark Thirty (*ZDT*) is a generic oxymoron: a war film about a non-war, with a non-combatant protagonist and an invisible enemy. If, as Baudrillard has argued, the first 'Gulf War' was a misnomer, how much more so the endless, borderless series of military actions that followed the events of 9/11? The hunt for bin Laden (unlike that, for example, for Spielberg's 'Private Ryan') doesn't involve much by way of battlefield action—nor even of the macho 'base camp' scenarios associated with those films set in less 'heroic' wars.[2] What it does involve is a great deal of emphasis on the technologies of surveillance and the imagery of mediated reality. Such imagery has become a generic convention of the contemporary war film, as exemplified by *The Hurt Locker* (2008), Bigelow's previous engagement with the genre. For *ZDT*, however, military surveillance is not just an aesthetic or narrative feature but the dramatic and thematic centre of the film. Action has been reconceptualised as watching, and the military protagonist has been reassigned accordingly to the role of observing and controlling the theatre of war at one remove.

Virilio has demonstrated a close historical relationship between the development of cinema and that of modern warfare. This has operated on a number of levels, from the involvement of film directors in early surveillance photography and cinema's appropriation of technologies originally developed for military purposes, to the use of film as propaganda, and the evolution of the war film genre. The connection is seen as fundamental to the natures of both war and cinema. In *War and Cinema*, he argues that intelligence and vision are key technological and strategic military resources, coining the phrase 'logistics of perception' to encompass not only military surveillance and the crucial ability to get the enemy 'in one's sights', but also the use of simulation in training, the use of the media propaganda, and the way in which war is experienced by modern media audiences. For Virilio, the 'means of destruction and means of communicating destruction' (1989, p. 32) are interwoven and interdependent. Military conquest is meaningful only in as much as it is effectively communicated to the conquered; 'There is no war, then, without representation' (p. 8).

The primacy of the image and 'the instrumental splitting of modes of perception and representation' (1994, p. 49) that the technologies of vision bring give rise to an 'aesthetic of disappearance' (p. 49) which is conceptualized along similar lines to Baudrillard's 'hyper-reality'. In *The Vision Machine*, Virilio expands on the idea of technically-mediated, even automated, vision-producing images that function as a 'substitution' for reality, rather than the 'simulation' that is the province of traditional art. He argues that the development of 'visual prostheses' (p. 4) has profoundly altered the mechanics of human memory, and that their proliferation is associated with 'a steady decline in retention rates and recall' (p. 7). For Virilio, concepts of perception, interpretation, memory, and 'reality' are inextricably entwined, and key to human understanding.[3] The eponymous 'vision machine' is part philosophical conceit, allowing him to explore the processes and psychology of perception, and part prophecy, depicting a dystopian trajectory in which not only the gathering of visual information but its interpretation is automated. Both lines of reasoning raise the problem of the 'reality effect' and its ascendancy over the reality principle as the virtual and the factual become irretrievably confused (p. 60).

Virilio draws a direct connection between the development of the photographic arts and post-modern sensibilities, as 'in multiplying "proofs" of reality, photography exhausted it' (p. 22). Ironically what was originally understood as a reliably indexical sign ultimately drew attention to the functioning of point-of-view (echoing the theory of relativity, which called into question the nature of 'reality' in the physical world). Although this is not Virilio's explicit argument, it is certainly the case that cinema itself, with its realist aesthetic, its phatic, 'real-time' images, and its powerful exploitation of 'point-of-view' as it is understood in the contexts of both cinematography and narrative, meets his description of the 'vision machine'.

Patricia Pisters has argued that Virilio's 'vision of a waning reality... needs to be revised in light of the latest developments in perceptual technology and urban warfare during the Second Gulf War' (2010, p. 233). She proposes a 'logistics of perception 2.0', reflecting what she sees to be a more 'dynamic' relationship between war and the media. She argues for, on the one hand, a democratisation of media production as exemplified by the video diaries of serving personnel and the multiplicity of viewpoints represented in what she calls a 'battle of the screens', and on the other, a return of the real through the 'subjective and affective intensity of many of the images' (p. 233).

Although Pisters identifies several significant shifts in the media landscape, there are some contradictions inherent in her arguments. When, as she notes, '[v]ideo games look like war and war looks like a video game' (p. 243) the affective power of the image can serve to undermine the recognition of reality just as easily as it can reawaken the conscious, ethical response for which she looks. Virilio attributes the power of the electronic media to a 'false equation of sign-reading with knowledge' (1989, p. 47), fearing that the emphasis for modern audiences, regaled with high-definition, phatic imagery, is on seeing rather than understanding.[4]

Meanwhile the access to, and proliferation of, both the production and the distribution of media texts, made possible by modern technologies, does not always result in the democratic ideal envisioned by Pisters.

While she celebrates the way in which serving personnel 'have appropriated Hollywood and MTV aesthetics' (2010, p. 242), it could equally be argued that this is a form of conformity, as the soldiers' own perception of their situation is channelled through cultural constructions. While soldiers are, as she demonstrates, 'no longer dependent on hierarchical structures for the distribution of their images' (p. 242), that does not prevent their work becoming assimilated into Virilio's global 'reality effect' as audiences are bombarded with images, the sources and status of which are not always easy to differentiate.

The war film, as a genre, could be said to specialise in blurring the boundaries between the factual and the virtual and exploiting what might be termed a 'reality *affect*'. The 'spectacle of authenticity' which Geoff King has identified as a key feature of the serious war film (2000, p. 118), sets out to reproduce precisely the 'subjective and affective intensity' described by Pisters, often by exploiting the conventions—if not the raw materials—of recorded 'actuality' to elicit a powerful, even visceral response. Thus, *ZDT* uses sound recorded by emergency services on 9/11 to set the narrative—and affective—scene in the opening frames.[5] Similarly, Maya's investigation involves viewing CCTV footage, recorded interviews, broadcast TV, and satellite image, while her experience of the raid on bin Laden's stronghold relies on the Seals' helmet cams. The paradoxical logic whereby these explicitly mediated images produce a powerful 'reality effect' is of a piece with Virilio's vision. By emphasising the point-of-view in an intra-textual, purely visual sense, they serve to conceal the operation of point-of-view as a narrative function, suggesting both immediacy and objectivity and disavowing the role of the filmmaker even as the cinematic construct is at its most elaborate. The driving investigative narrative of the film produces a realignment of diverse points of view into one. Pisters argues that 'in the face of the multiplication of ever increasing screens, reality does not disappear but returns with an affective vengeance' (2010, p. 250). *ZDT*, however, exemplifies the power of the mainstream media text to re-assimilate differentiated perspectives and to harness the affective power of the image to manufacture its own version of cultural memory.

The tension between Virilio's 'reality effect' and the return of the real is articulated at a number of levels in relation to *ZDT*: at the level of plot, at the level of structure and aesthetics, and at the level of the secondary texts that abound around the film. Within the diegesis of the film, the CIA investigation depends almost entirely on media images that ought to provide indexical 'proof' of reality but in practice often amount to inconclusive, or even misleading, evidence. Thus, Maya's search is thrown off track for years by a wrongly identified photograph, while Jessica is deceived by what purports to be secretly filmed footage from her supposed informer—with fatal consequences. The satellite imagery of bin Laden's stronghold, meanwhile, proves so inconclusive that the raid is almost indefinitely postponed. Moreover, diegetically 'authentic' material distorts affect. Thus, the repetitive imagery of interrogation becomes numbing, rather than shocking, for the protagonist (and, potentially, for the audience), while her moment of victory elicits a response all but drained of emotion.

In terms of structural and aesthetic considerations, the style and pace of the film, along with the appropriation of factual codes and actuality, creates an impression of documentary realism. The narrative, in common with most 'detective' narratives, is explicitly structured around the protagonist's point of view, aligning the audience with her as they share in her journey of discovery; this alignment is lent particular emphasis in *ZDT*, however, by Maya's role as the viewer of media imagery. Her intense, subjective engagement with the materials she scrutinises is contrasted with a radically limited personal life. It is in the context of her dogged, repetitive viewing that we are offered a degree of access to her emotional life, through a pattern of intense close-up reverse shots. In contrast, the only scene of any length that features Maya alone and 'off duty' shows her all but hidden among the folds of a burka. The alignment of protagonist and audience is at its most explicit during the raid on bin Laden's compound which is experienced by both as mediated reality, rendered in terms of the 'synthetic perception' (Virilio 1994, p. 60) provided by helmet cameras and night-vision goggles. The audience, then, is sutured into a position where the tension between authenticity and the 'hyper-real' is palpable.

The contested nature of 'reality' has also become a critical factor in the extra-textual narratives around, and critical responses to, *ZDT*. The film's on-screen claims to being based on real events and people were underpinned by the claims to quasi-journalistic methods made by the filmmakers pre-release.[6] This stance exacerbated the subsequent outcry around the representation of 'enhanced interrogation' in the film, and the causal link it implied between torture and the success of the CIA mission. The distinguishing, and the most disturbing, feature of Virilio's 'vision machine' is the ability not only to observe but to *interpret* reality.

It is significant, therefore, that by far the greatest opprobrium heaped upon the makers of *ZDT* was not for the depiction of torture per se, but for the film's percieved *interpretation* of torture as a valid and effective military strategy.

Cinema, by virtue of its very existence, poses 'the problem of the paradoxically real nature of "virtual" imagery' (Virilio 1994, p. 61). The 'problem' is only exacerbated by those genres, such as the war film, that draw on the codes of the 'real' to enhance fictional narratives. As representations of representations, moreover, footage that purports to come from helmet cameras, CCTV, and so on raises the spectre of the infinitely deferred referent and the collapse of meaning into a pure representation which Virilio equates with moral relativism (p. 66). The 'serious' war film may set out to speak the 'truth' through the presentation of fictional (or re-presentation of 'factual') events, but is itself part of the vision machine: thus the more sincerely it engages with 'reality', more complicit it may become in the 'reality effect'.

GENDER MATTERS: AUTHORSHIP, NARRATIVE, AND THE GAZE

[N]ever before has a stone-cold-serious American war drama featured a woman both behind the camera and at its center. (Zeitchik 2012)

[I]t matters whose desire is being figured in [the] text. (Thornham 2012, p. 28)

Reviewing the film in the *Los Angeles Times*, Steven Zeitchik suggests that *ZDT* has redefined its genre, introducing 'the viscerally human but post-feminist (and post-political) war film' (2012). Gender, it is clear, plays an essential part in this generic shift: both the gender of the filmmaker and that of the protagonist. Kathryn Bigelow, the woman 'behind the camera', has forged a career from reworking Hollywood genres, repeatedly disrupting gender-based assumptions and expectations in the process despite her refusal to identify as a 'female', let alone a 'feminist', filmmaker. Maya, the woman 'at its centre', is a dominating and disturbing presence in the film; her gender, youth, and beauty are, as Robert Burgoyne has argued, 'not easily accommodated by genre codes' (2014, p. 151).

Zeitchick is just one among a small army of journalists and cultural critics who have discussed *ZDT* in terms of its status as feminist, post-feminist, or anti-feminist text—a debate that has been effectively encapsulated by Marouf Hasian, who acknowledges that 'Maya's presence is a refreshing jolt, a transgressive move that reminds us of the ambivalences of the contemporary post-feminist conditions' (2013, p. 331), but ultimately concludes that the film is misogynist because the protagonist's gender is used as a form of ideological camouflage for US militarism, ultimately reinforcing a patriarchal status quo.

What this ill-fated debate fails to recognise is that feminist perspectives cut across other political paradigms, rather than being neatly aligned with them. It also presupposes that a text, as opposed to a reading, can be intrinsically 'feminist'. I suggest that to ask whether *ZDT* is a 'feminist' text, a post-feminist text, or indeed a misogynist text may not be a particularly productive line of inquiry. Rather, I would like to consider the extent to which it is a gendered text—to ask how both the particular sensibilities of the female director and the presence of the female hero impact the dynamic of the narrative and in particular upon the way the film articulates the themes and imagery of watching.

THE SIGNATURE OF A WOMAN: THE FEMALE FILMMAKER AND ZERO DARK THIRTY

[W]e're a watched society and a society of watchers. (Bigelow cited in Smith 2003, p. 30)

Kathryn Bigelow is a director who not only utilises spectacle as an aesthetic strategy but also explicitly addresses it as a theme in her work. For her, the act of looking is more than a simple function of film-making and film viewing: it is the subject matter and narrative driver of many of her films. Indeed, Laura Rascaroli has described Bigelow's cinema as 'essentially a discourse on vision' (1997, p. 232). Bigelow's fascination with the technologies of looking is evidenced in her film-making practice: she has frequently designed and developed new pieces of camera kit in order to achieve specific effects, such as the rig famously created for the extended chase sequence in *Point Break* (1991). More critically for this discussion, it is evidenced in the work itself, which returns over and over to themes of voyeurism, surveillance, and the mediated image. Critical comparisons have inevitably been made between *ZDT* and *The Hurt Locker*, Bigelow's first take on the war film. Here 'logistics of perception' furnish a visual *leitmotif*. The main activity of the soldiers is to watch—their paranoid gaze is repeatedly mediated through helmet cameras, the viewfinders of their rifles, and 'botcams'—while they themselves are constantly under hostile surveillance. Striking comparisons can also be made, however, with other films in Bigelow's *oeuvre*, particularly those films that present an explicitly gendered dimension to the cinematic gaze: *Blue Steel* (1989), *Strange Days* (1995), and *The Weight of Water* (2000). It is in these films that Bigelow's 'discourse on vision' is at its most sophisticated, presaging the themes and tropes explored in *Zero Dark Thirty*.

The neo-noir police thriller *Blue Steel* stars Jamie Lee Curtis as Megan, a young female cop who attracts the unwelcome attentions of a voyeuristic killer. The film sets up an uncomfortable paradox, as it simultaneously exploits and deconstructs the image of woman as object of the cinematic gaze. The narrative positions Megan by turns as investigator and *femme fatale*, hunter and prey. Meanwhile the gun, (the eponymous 'blue steel') is aligned both with Megan/Curtis as fetishised object of desire and with the gaze itself, as the act of looking is explicitly associated with that of lining up a (gun)shot. Despite their very different aesthetics, there are a number of parallels between *Blue Steel* and *Zero Dark Thirty*. Both films are about, and structured by, the mechanics and meanings of the gaze. Both films feature scrappy heroines who deal quite aggressively with the low-level, casual sexism they encounter: Megan, expected to justify her career choices to every man she meets, likes to tell her inquisitors that she became a cop because she likes to shoot people; Maya bluntly tells the CIA chief who questions her right to join an otherwise all-male planning group, 'I'm the motherfucker who found him... sir'. Most worthy of note, because it so unusual in Hollywood properties, each film ends with an anticlimactic, downbeat final scene, whereby the heroine's success in her mission brings about no sense of triumph or fulfillment, but an empty, disconsolate, almost fugue state.

Strange Days, Bigelow's idiosyncratic science fiction film, further develops ideas of voyeurism, surveillance, and the relationship between the two. The plot is centred on the SQUID—a piece of technology developed as an instrument of police surveillance, but sold on the black market as a form of entertainment, offering the user the opportunity to indulge in vicarious, voyeuristic experiences. In an interview with Gavin Smith, the director describes *Strange Days* as a film about power structures, which she explicitly conceptualizes in terms of the dynamics of the gaze (2003, p. 30). Both sets of intertwined structures have a distinctly gendered dimension. The main 'genres' of content consumed on the SQUID appear to be violent action, pornography, or a combination of the two, and the consumers appear to be almost exclusively male. The material we see through the eyes of the self-pitying anti-hero, Lenny (Ralph Fiennes), consists largely of self-conscious displays by his ex-girlfriend (Juliette Lewis), which he compulsively replays. The scenes in which he finds himself watching a woman raped, tortured, and murdered, unable to look away, raises the same uncomfortable questions about the pleasures of the sadistic gaze that are explored in the seminal writing of Laura Mulvey (1975) and Teresa de Lauretis (1984). Lenny's gaze, however, is associated primarily with passivity and impotence rather than power or control; indeed, he is addicted to the SQUID and in thrall to the horrifying images which he feels compelled to watch. Meanwhile, his female bodyguard, Mace, who recognizes the destructive nature of the technology, reacts to the 'snuff' content with unadulterated unpleasure. This complex relationship between control/impotence and the gaze, together with the explicitly mediated gaze, epistemological unreliability of images, and the blurring of the boundaries between surveillance and voyeurism, are all revisited and developed in *Zero Dark Thirty*.

The Weight of Water is Bigelow's only foray into a traditional 'woman's' genre. Moving between a contemporary and a historical timeframe, the visual focus is on the (potentially destructive) desiring gaze of the woman. Of particular interest to this discussion, moreover, is the construction of Jean (Catherine McCormack), the modern-day protagonist, as a professional photographer whose desire is expressed through the lens of a still camera, and the deliberate disjunction of reverse shots that initially mislead the viewer with regard to the object of her gaze. Sue Thornham has explored the way in which writer/narrator protagonists often operate 'as textual doubles for the female maker', foregrounding notions of authorship and narrative construction (2012, p. 5). Thus, the photographer heroine who sets out to uncover a past crime and re-tell the story of the women involved can be said to function as a 'textual double' of the film-maker. Maya, in *ZDT*, arguably fulfils a similar function. She is a professional watcher whose task is to build a narrative from images, effectively editing together material selected from the endless 'rushes' represented by the interrogation videos, and directing the acquisition of additional material through the activities of interrogators and field agents. The parallels with the role of the film director are striking. So, too, are those with Bigelow personally, who has expressed a feeling of being 'without purpose all of a sudden' (cited in Brockes 2013) after completing the film. It is a feeling mirrored in Maya's final scene, when she cannot tell the pilot of the troop carrier where she wants to go.

Thornham has observed that 'a melancholic subject and an unavowable loss which figure both in the narrative itself and in the desire which it traces' (2012, p. 18) haunt the work of many female film-makers. Despite her atypical choice of genres, this is certainly true of Bigelow's work, evidenced in the all-pervasive melancholy atmosphere of *Near Dark* (1987) and *The Weight of Water*, in the oddly wistful, lyrical treatment of action sequences in *Point Break* and *The Hurt Locker*, and—perhaps most strikingly because so unusual in Hollywood movies—in the sense of emptiness that characterizes the anticlimactic final scenes of both *Blue Steel* and *Zero Dark Thirty*. Bigelow herself is resistant to the notion that she looks at the world through a gendered lens; I suggest that, on the contrary, *ZDT* is clearly marked with what Nancy Miller has termed 'the signature of a woman' (1988, p. 68).

Gender and the Gaze: The Impact of the Female Protagonist

'I'm not that girl that fucks.' (Bigelow 2012)

Asked in interviews about the significance of the female lead in *ZDT*, Bigelow is typically dismissive: 'It's extraordinary that women were pivotal, but it's also that those were the facts. That's the hand we were dealt. And that's how we chose to deal with the story' (Digiacomo 2012). However, the gender of its protagonist is crucial to the structure and tone of *ZDT*, and to the ways in which ideas of the gaze, spectacle, and the logistics of perception are articulated in the text.

Zero Dark Thirty is a war film structured as a quest narrative—a genre and a format traditionally dominated by male protagonists, often to the exclusion of any significant female characters at all. The gender reversal represented by the tough and embattled female agent single-mindedly pursuing the hero's quest is not straightforward or without textual and ideological repercussions. Thornham argues that narrative structures marked by ideologically loaded oppositions such as 'hero/heroine, activity/passivity, subject/object' are 'fundamental to our sense of identity' and that they cannot be transformed without 'cultural, narrational, linguistic, subjective' implications (2012, p. 4). Maya's blunt response to her friend's attempt to broach the subject of her personal life (given as the epigraph to this section) perfectly illustrates Thornham's point: it is quite simply impossible to imagine an equivalent response from a male protagonist.

Hasian opines that Maya is used to propagate a myth 'of gendered equality within the CIA, while erasing or obfuscating the structural barriers that are still in play' (2013, p. 323). However the film clearly marks incidents of casual and institutionalized sexism, albeit with some subtlety, and indeed uses Maya's 'outsider' status to help propel the narrative. From the start of the film, when Maya is offered—and refuses—the opportunity to avoid the interrogation, she has to work harder, and assert herself more directly, than her male colleagues. Out of her hearing, they question whether she is up to the job on more than one occasion, and repeatedly refer to her as a 'girl'. Maya's 'motherfucker' outburst at Langley (discussed previously) can be read as a response to anyone who questions her right to a 'seat at the table'—not only the CIA chief who poses the question at that particular moment. Meanwhile, her physical presence in this scene—small, youthful, and possessed of a fragile, porcelain beauty—makes an unavoidable visual impact. Burgoyne's comment about Maya's disturbing impact on the genre could equally be applied to the institutional context: her physical encroachment in itself poses a subtle challenge to the male bastion of power that is the CIA. In many ways, gender, here, is utilized much as class and occasionally race have been elsewhere in Hollywood texts: to reinforce the 'heroic' status of a protagonist by increasing the 'odds' against them. Thus one male colleague remarks to another, 'it's her against the world' (Bigelow 2012).

The 'cultural, narrational, linguistic, subjective' implications of gender in the film, however, go far beyond explicit diegetic references to workplace gender politics. That Maya is 'not that girl that fucks' is not just a statement about the character's intradiegetic sense of and/or presentation of herself. It also serves an extradiegetic function, reinforcing the film's studied avoidance of any suggestion of objectification or sexualisation of the female protagonist. This approach, which informs both the structures and aesthetics of the film, is highlighted to the point of parody by the scene in which Maya watches the 'Canaries' (Navy Seals) await their cue to raid bin Laden's stronghold, their gleaming muscles on display as they relax in the sun. Maya, by way of contrast, is clothed from head to foot in black. In fact, Maya is a woman defined almost entirely in terms of the gaze—but as its subject, not its object. The redefinition of watching as action, which is key to the narrative construction of the film, is, I suggest, contingent on a female protagonist, and the nuanced relationship between woman, narrative, and the gaze.

Burgoyne describes Maya's experience of violence, in the film, as 'a direct, intimate witnessing' (2014, p. 247) and indeed Maya's role as 'witness' frames the core narrative of the film, beginning with the torture scene she forces herself to sit though on her first day in the job and ending with her identification of bin Laden's body, marking the completion of her ten-year assignment. The position of the witness, in Hollywood genres, is often constructed as a passive and inherently feminine position. The woman who dares to look, moreover, is often punished (notably, but not exclusively, in the horror genre) by being forced to witness horror without recourse to action. Bigelow's film is informed by these tropes, yet constructs Maya's gaze with a very different inflection. Hers is never a passive gaze. Burgoyne traces her trajectory, in relation to the 'embodied violence' (2014, p. 248) of torture, from reluctant witness at the start of the film, to one who is increasingly complicit as she utilizes recorded interrogations in her investigation, to something more akin to causal agency as she orders and oversees further interrogations. Even at the start of the film, however, when she is clearly represented as uncomfortable with the brutal scene before her, repeatedly averting her eyes and turning her head away, the film explicitly implicates her as an active participant. Given the choice to abstain, she refuses; her (specifically female) gaze, moreover, is used as ammunition by her co-agent to humiliate the half-naked prisoner.

Maya's gaze in subsequent scenes is coded as primarily active—investigative, monitoring, controlling—although never sadistic (in this respect, her discomfort in the early torture scene sets the tone) and never scopophilic. On the contrary, in the successive scenes in which Maya ploughs through video footage in search of the information she needs, looking is clearly represented as labour: an exhausting and frustrating grind to be endured, and one which takes its emotional and physical toll on Maya, as successive close-ups show. Maya's agency, moreover, is 'riven by paradox' (Butler 2004, p. 3), in common with that of many female protagonists whose agency and subjectivity retain a precarious foothold in the narrative, and whose gaze is haunted by the ghosts of victim heroines. The distinctions between the active and the passive gaze, between witnessing and controlling, power and powerlessness, are frequently blurred. Her investigative gaze is misled by unreliable evidence (notably concerning the supposed death of her chief subject), her monitoring gaze is frustrated (by indistinct satellite images), and she is rendered an impotent bystander at the assassination of her friends and colleagues. It is significant, in this respect, that Maya's gaze throughout her quest is almost exclusively mediated. Hers is a war fought through the logistics of perception, and the paradoxes that mark her agency mirror those that characterize the 'reality effect'. I suggest that it is the focus on mediated engagement that makes it possible for a female protagonist to take the central role in *ZDT*—and conversely, that it is the gender of the protagonist that makes it possible to limit her involvement in the climactic scene of the film.

Maya's paradoxical agency—explicitly mediated and implicitly gendered—is most clearly articulated in the 30-minute scene that gives the film its title: the raid on bin Laden's residence. This scene is the nearest the film comes to the traditional action sequences of the war film, and represents the climax of Maya's quest—yet Maya herself, an intelligence officer and not a soldier, cannot take an active part in the raid. The film utilises a number of strategies, however, to maintain her central position within the narrative, and her function as the focus of audience identification. The critical nature of her role is emphasised by the 'canary' who makes it clear before the raid that he believes in the mission because of the power of Maya's conviction, and by the closing scene in which the commanding officer calls upon Maya to identify bin Laden's body—as she is clearly the only person qualified to do so. During the raid itself, however, the film employs a degree of cinematic sleight of hand in the use of cutaways to suggest that Maya—in reality, a passive witness— is actively involved in, even directing, events. Visually, moreover, there is no distinction between the action itself and mediated images of the action, since the entire scene is bathed in the artificial greenish light of the night-vision technology which, for Virilio, constitutes a significant step in the evolution of the nightmarish 'vision machine' (1989, p. 4). In effect, Maya is reduced to much the same position as the audience during this sequence, having the illusion of omniscience and control but no real agency.

Burgoyne remarks that Maya's act of witnessing 'sutures her to the larger social and historical world the film portrays' (2014, p. 247). Her gaze, central as it is to the narrative, also sutures the audience to the text and thus to its world—a world of ubiquitous threat, articulating Virilio's vision of 'total war' (1989, p. 83). Maya's gender serves to underline both this vision and the 'reality effect' produced when the monitoring of military action is retransmitted as public presentation (ibid., pp. 65–66). Her particular relationship to the mediated gaze articulates the idea that war is not confined to warriors; the rest of us participate (and are implicated) by watching the warriors.

EPILOGUE: MAYA'S 'VICTORY'

Maya cries because bin Laden's death is not an uncomplicated victory, since it leaves us with the national and global question of 'Now what?' (Bigelow cited in Rothman 2013)

The final scene of *ZDT* stands apart from the rest of the film as a kind of epilogue—distinguished in terms of tone, style, and its representation of the protagonist. The melancholy lyricism that characterized *The Hurt Locker* is rediscovered in the prolonged close-up of a weeping Maya, evocatively described by Guy Westwell as 'a pieta for the war on terror' (2013, p. 87). She sits in an empty troop carrier, framed by blood red webbing that produces a stark visual impact in contrast with the shades of sepia and night-vision green that dominate the rest of the film. Presented throughout as the subject of the gaze, suddenly Maya is unequivocally its object. There is no reverse shot, no suggestion of her point of view. It is as though there is simply nothing to see any more—only the ongoing non-event that is modern warfare.

ZDT is undoubtedly a politically problematic film, however, it is difficult to justify a reading of triumphant US militarism in relation to the mournful ending. Indeed, Bigelow's original film project was a meditation on failure, telling the tale of the (at that time ongoing) unsuccessful search for bin Laden, and there are moments when *ZDT* seems to be haunted by the spirit of its origins. The paradox of the victorious hero, devoid of triumph and drained of agency, offers an appropriate finale to a film beset by paradox. *ZDT* is a war film without a war, featuring a non-combatant hero and an invisible villain whose conquest brings no satisfaction. Its female protagonist at once disrupts and furnishes an alibi for a paternalist militarised hegemony, while her presence in the text makes it possible to recast watching as action. The film appropriates documentary codes to tell a fictional tale—amid extra-textual claims to truthfulness on the one hand and artistic license on the other—and articulates

Virilio's inherently paradoxical 'reality effect' through its treatment and utilisation of the 'logistics of perception'. It is almost inevitable that the moral centre of the film slips from the critical grasp.

The morality of *ZDT*, however, continues to exercise critics, for at stake is cultural memory and what Burgoyne calls 'the dominant fiction under the pressure of 9/11' (2014, p. 249). Agnieszka Piotrowska (2014) has argued for Maya as latter-day Antigone, justified by a Lacanian ethics of pursuing personal conviction. This perspective goes some way to explain the simultaneously seductive and monstrous power of a single-minded heroine in a fictional text, but overlooks the way in which our reading of such a text may be inflected by the 'invocation of authenticity and verisimilitude' (Stewart 2014, p. 37). For Evans, Maya's 'conviction' is precisely the problem: '[i]t supports a privileged point of view [which] extinguishes the imaginative viewpoint from which this film's subject matter can be fairly seen' (2014, pp. 365, 367). Bigelow, in the face of her critics, has denied any political agenda, insisting that her interest is merely 'to explore and push the medium' (cited in Anthony 2012). As Virilio's construct makes clear, however, technology is not without moral implications, any more than aesthetics are separable from meaning. Ironically, the proliferation of mediated imagery does not create, but erases, any sense of epistemological or emotional distance, such that human understanding and human memories are in danger of being swallowed up by the 'vision machine'.

NOTES

1. K.L. Evans (2014) has provided a particularly comprehensive analysis of this issue, and of the problematic relationship between 'fact' and 'fiction' in the making of film.
2. Notably Vietnam War films such as *Platoon* (1986).
3. The epigraph with which he prefaces *The Vision Machine* is taken from the work of psychologist Norman E. Spear: 'Memory content is a function of the rate of forgetting' (cited in Virilio 1978, p. 89).
4. In this he echoes Neil Postman's concerns regarding the privileging of an emotive over a more thoughtful response to political coverage on broadcast television (1985).
5. The sound is played over a black screen without recourse to any of the now familiar imagery of the Twin Towers attack as though to underline the inadequacy of the image (particularly the over-familiar image) to the task of representation at such a moment.

6. Bigelow, in early interviews, described her work as 'reported film' while
writer Mark Boal, a former journalist, went with 'docu-drama' (cited in
Hornaday 2013), claiming, 'I don't want to play fast and loose with history' (Cieply and Barnes 2012).

WORKS CITED

Anthony, Andrew. 2012. Kathryn Bigelow: Drama Queen Who Captured
Osama. *Observer*, Dec 29.
Barnes, Brooks. 2012. "As Enigmatic as Her Picture": An Interview with
Kathryn Bigelow. *New York Times*, Dec 27.
Baudrillard, Jean. 2001. The Spirit of Terrorism, trans. Rachel Bloudl, *Le Monde*,
Nov 2.
Bigelow, Kathryn, dir. 1987. *Near Dark*, DeLaurentiis.
———, dir. 1989. *Blue Steel*, Metro-Goldwyn-Mayer.
———, dir. 1991. *Point Break*, 20th Century Fox.
———, dir. 1995. *Strange Days*, 20th Century Fox.
———, dir. 2000. *The Weight of Water*, Lions Gate.
———, dir. 2008. *The Hurt Locker*, Summit.
———, dir. 2012. *Zero Dark Thirty*, Columbia/Universal.
Brockes, Emily. 2013. Kathryn Bigelow: Under Fire. *Guardian*, Jan 12.
Burgoyne, Robert. 2014. The Violated Body: Affective Experience and Somatic
Intensity in *Zero Dark Thirty*. In *The Philosophy of War Films*, ed. LaRocca,
247–260.
Butler, Judith. 2004. *Undoing Gender*. New York: Routledge.
Carruthers, Susan. 2013. *Zero Dark Thirty*. *Cineaste* 38 (2): 50–52.
Cieply, Michael, and Brooks Barnes. 2012. Bin Laden's Film's Focus Is Facts,
Not Flash. *The New York Times*, Nov 23.
Coll, Steve. 2013. "'Disturbing" and "Misleading"'. *New York Review of Books*
Feb 7, 4–6.
de Lauretis, Teresa. 1984. *Alice Doesn't: Feminism, Semiotics, Cinema*, London:
Macmillan.
Digiacomo, Frank. 2012. The Mystery of Maya: Jessica Chastain Never Met the
Agent She Plays *in Zero Dark Thirty*. *Movieline*, Dec 5.
Evans, K.L. 2014. The Work of Art in the Age of Embedded Journalism: Fiction
versus Depiction in *Zero Dark Thirty*. In *The Philosophy of War Films*, ed.
LaRocca, 355–381.
Hasian, Jr, Marouf. 2013. *Zero Dark Thirty* and the Critical Challenges Posed
by Populist Postfeminism during the Global War on Terrorism. *Journal of
Communication Inquiry* 37 (4): 322–343.
Hornaday, Ann. 2013. *Zero Dark Thirty* and the New Reality of Reported
Filmmaking. *Washington Post*, Dec 13.

King, Geoff. 2000. *Spectacular Narratives: Hollywood in the Age of the Blockbuster.* London: IB Tauris.

Miller, Nancy. 1988. *Subject to Change: Reading Feminist Writing.* Columbia, NY: Columbia University Press.

Mulvey, Laura. 1975. Visual Pleasure and Narrative Cinema. *Screen* 16 (3): 6–18.

Piotrowska, Agnieszka. 2014. *Zero Dark Thirty*—"War Autism" or a Lacanian Ethical Act? *New Review of Film and Television Studies* 12 (2): 143–155.

Pisters, Patricia. 2010. Logistics of Perception 2.0: Multiple Screen Aesthetics in Iraq War Films. *Film-Philosophy* 14 (1): 232–251.

Postman, Neil. 1985. *Amusing Ourselves to Death: Public Discourse in the Age of Show Business.* New York: Penguin.

Powers, Richard. 2013. *Zero Dark Thirty. Journal of American History* 100 (1): 303–305.

Rascaroli, Laura. 1997. Steel in the Gaze. *Screen* 38 (3): 232–246.

Rothman, Lily. 2013. *Zero Dark Thirty,* Declassified: Bigelow dishes on Deeper Meaning of Closing Scene. *Time Entertainment,* Jan 21.

Stewart, Garrett. 2014. War Pictures: Digital Surveillance from Foreign Theatre to Homeland Security Front In *The Philosophy of War Films,* ed. LaRocca, 107–132.

Smith, Gavin. 2003. Momentum and Design: Interview with Kathryn Bigelow. In *The Cinema of Kathryn Bigelow, Hollywood Transgressor,* eds. Deborah Jermyn and Sean Redmond, 20–31. London: Wallflower.

Spear, Norman E. 1978. *The Processing of Memories: Forgetting and Retention.* New York: Halstead-Wiley.

Spielberg, Steven, dir. 1998. *Saving Private Ryan.* DreamWorks/Paramount.

Stone, Oliver, dir. 1986. *Platoon.* Orion Pictures.

Thornham, Sue. 2012. *What If I Had Been the Hero?* London: Palgrave Macmillan.

Virilio, Paul. 1989. *War and Cinema: The Logistics of Perception (1984)*, trans. Patrick Camiller, New York: Verso.

———.1994. *The Vision Machine,* trans. Julie Rose, London: BFI.

Westwell, Guy. 2013. Zero Dark Thirty. *Sight and Sound* 23 (2): 86–87.

Zeitchik, Steven. 2012. *Zero Dark Thirty* Hunts for Bin Laden—and More. *Los Angeles Times,* Dec 6.

AUTHOR BIOGRAPHY

Christa Van Raalte is Associate Dean for Media Production, Bournemouth University and has published on female roles in the post-war Western, the Hollywood action film and the war film.

CHAPTER 6

Remembering the First World War After 9/11: Pat Barker's *Life Class* and *Toby's Room*

Jessica Gildersleeve

Pat Barker's most famous novels are those which form her *Regeneration* trilogy (1991–1995), culminating in the Booker-Prize-winning novel, *The Ghost Road*. Her most recent novels, *Life Class* (2007) and *Toby's Room* (2012), return to the subject of the First World War with a different focus: non-combative personnel in the war. What has changed in a global sense between the publication of the trilogy and the more recent novels is, of course, the occurrence of the terrorist attacks on September 11, 2001, and the subsequent wars in Afghanistan and Iraq. While there has been a great deal of critical focus on the significance of 9/11 for our understanding of another of Barker's late novels, *Double Vision* (2003), its influence on representations of war, trauma, and violence, and in particular, the ways we memorialise and historicise the First World War as it appears in *Life Class* and *Toby's Room* have not been discussed. Extending Fiona Tolan's recognition that 'the role and responsibilities of the artist as chronicler and interpreter of war is central to *Regeneration* and also,

J. Gildersleeve (✉)
University of Southern Queensland, Toowoomba, QLD, Australia
e-mail: Jessica.Gildersleeve@usq.edu.au

© The Author(s) 2017
J. Gildersleeve and R. Gehrmann (eds.), *Memory and the Wars on Terror*, Palgrave Macmillan Memory Studies,
DOI 10.1007/978-3-319-56976-5_6

111

clearly, to Barker's own experience as writer of historical fiction' (2010, p. 378), this chapter explores how the events of 9/11 may have altered memories and representations of earlier conflict. The First World War has constituted a primary touchstone for Barker throughout her career because, Peter Childs argues, it 'remains in the collective memory as a persistent traumatic experience that has been insufficiently addressed or acknowledged' (2005, p. 62). The *Regeneration* trilogy, in particular, draws on what Catriona Pennell calls the most ready 'shorthand' of 'modern Britons for stupidity, blind obedience, failures of leadership, appalling physical conditions, and deadlock': the trenches (2012, p. 12). And yet, while Barker's earlier novels about World War One perceive the war as it was experienced by British soldiers through a philosophy of shell-shocked victimhood, vulnerability, passivity, and 'social cannibalism' (Monbiot cited in Pennell 2012, p. 12), her post-9/11 narratives dealing with the war are less clear in their moral dichotomy. While the primary interest of these novels lies in the way the work of the war artist emphasises the need for ethical witnessing and remembering in response to trauma and conflict, the refusal of a particular character, Elinor Brooke, to acknowledge the war in either life or art, and the alignment of this belief system with her response to the personal trauma of incest, provokes an investigation of how the motif of guilt and responsibility in contemporary narratives about World War One has changed since, and may be seen as a response to, 9/11 and twenty-first-century war. 'The truth is', Elinor claims, the war's 'been imposed on us from the outside. You would never have chosen it and probably the men in the hospital wouldn't either. It's unchosen, it's passive, and I don't think that's a proper subject for art' (Barker 2007a, p. 176). This chapter will explore the ways in which Barker's representations of World War One in *Life Class* and *Toby's Room* not only trace early twenty-first-century attitudes towards 9/11 in Britain, and what Georgiana Banita calls 'an increasingly globalised theatre of war and sympathy' (2012, p. 207), but more particularly figure these attitudes through a logic of complicity that transforms individual and cultural memories of the earlier war. In this way, narrative depictions of personal and collective trauma constitute an indictment of the hero-enemy dichotomy in war ideology, and complicate a perception of guilt and responsibility from those outside the 'war zone'.

As what is arguably the most defining cultural event of the twenty-first century, what Ulrika Tancke calls 'the collective trauma of post-millennial humanity' (2009, p. 77), the terrorist acts that occurred in the United States on September 11, 2001 have dominated literary texts and literary criticism over the past thirteen years. According to Michael Rothberg, this is because 'literature and other forms of art are important sites of response to terrorism because...they illustrate the interconnectedness of the public and the private and allow us to reconnect our faculties of seeing and feeling, two forms of connection that both terrorism and mass society threaten' (2008, pp. 123–124), and because 'they allow us to imagine alternative responses to the violence of terrorism and the spectacles of mass-mediated culture' (p. 131). And in John Brannigan's terms, 'the images of 9/11...denote not just the events in New York, Washington and Pennsylvania on that day, but an apparently new state of mourning, vulnerability and terror which they ushered in' (2005, p. 153). However, this chapter is not interested in exploring direct representations of 9/11 in literary fiction, or in American reflections on the terrorist attacks, but is concerned instead with how the events of 9/11 have shaped 'outsider' literary responses to previous occurrences of war and trauma. How do we remember or read differently now? This kind of question draws precisely on the logic of the trauma narrative. Trauma, as it is viewed in psychoanalysis and literary criticism, is characterised by our failure to conceive, know, or understand the trauma, to take it in, at the time the traumatic event actually occurs. Instead, we know it only through its compulsive and unbidden return, as the traumatic past insistently and persistently haunts the present. In the terms of Cathy Caruth, perhaps the most prominent philosopher of trauma theory, the traumatic event 'is experienced too soon, too unexpectedly, to be fully known and is therefore not available to consciousness until it imposes itself again, repeatedly, in the nightmares and repetitive actions of the survivor' (1996, p. 4). The only way to rid oneself of this haunting, Sigmund Freud would argue, is to narrativise the trauma. Rothberg's position on the use and popularity of 9/11 art and literature draws on this belief, as do Ann Keniston and Jennifer Follansbee Quinn, who argue that 'the history of literary representations of 9/11 can be characterised by the *transition* from narratives of rupture to narratives of continuity' (2008, p. 3; original emphasis). By positioning the event within a linear narrative, such logic indicates, we are able to remember and mourn the trauma, rather than melancholically encrypt it in a process of refusing to know.

As is typical of the trauma narrative, such an explanation does not, however, tell us the whole story. Indeed, this kind of framework, Roger Luckhurst argues, is influenced primarily by Holocaust studies, and 'isn't necessarily helpful when transposed to contemporary events, where the urge to convey the hidden or suppressed consequences of violence in the most literal ways possible can have significant political impetus' (2012, p. 714). What happens when one feels themselves to be complicit in the trauma, and holds themselves responsible for their own traumatisation, or the traumatisation of others? 'One effect of 9/11', Siân Adiseshiah and Rupert Hildyard claim, 'was to shatter the "end of history" thesis. The moral high ground claimed by the West since the fall of Soviet Communism has unquestionably been undermined...turn[ing] toxic the ethical pretensions of neo-liberalism' (2013, pp. 2–3). Indeed, it is frequently the case that discussions about the causes of 9/11 result in, Werner Bohleber explains, 'a kind of western-national self-critique or self-inculpation that is accompanied by a corresponding sense of guilt' (2010, p. 180). The 9/11 memorial in New York City attests to this: the memorial comprises a series of concentrically arranged pools of water which cascade endlessly into a dark chasm at the centre in a relentless rendering of the perpetual cultural wound wrought on the cultural memory by this event. Such responses are not limited to the United States of America or to 9/11 itself. Indeed, the affective shift in Barker's representation of World War One following the Wars on Terror can be seen to testify to changing global attitudes to war and responsibility and to the ways we write history.

Barker's *Regeneration* trilogy has been extraordinarily influential, not only in terms of literary representations of the First World War, but even more generally for our thinking about war and its traumatic impacts on the psyche (see, for example, Barrett 2012, p. 238). In tracing the experiences of both fictional and non-fictional characters embroiled in the war, Barker emphasises the resentment felt by soldiers towards the non-combatants who ignore their sacrifice. As Rivers observes to Sassoon, then, 'The point is you hate civilians, don't you? The "callous", the "complacent", the "unimaginative"' (Barker 1996, p. 14). By focusing the trilogy almost entirely from the perspective of soldiers, rather than civilians, Barker sets up the opposition between the two groups as firmly a question of loyalty and responsibility. Although the soldier may be the one who gets his hands dirty, as it were, it is the wilfully blind civilian who 'cackl[es] on about "attrition" and "wastage of manpower"' and..."*Lost heavily in that last scrap*"' who is suggested to be guilty of the murder of those serving on both sides (p. 14; original emphasis). Under these conditions, art is firmly rejected as a site outside of war, and instead is commandeered as a means of giving voice to the sacrificed soldier masses. Thus, when, early in *Regeneration*, a nervous Wilfred Owen says, 'I s-suppose I've always thought of p-poetry as the opposite of all that. The ugliness...Something to t-take refuge in', his opinion is squarely countered by the more experienced Siegfried Sassoon: 'Fair enough...Though it does seem a bit like having a faith that daren't face the facts' (p. 78). Post-9/11, however, the debate about the ethical memorialisation and representation of war and violence in Barker's fiction becomes far more nuanced.

Barker has published four novels since 2001 (*Double Vision, Life Class, Toby's Room*, and *Noonday* [2015]),[1] and they are not unlike her earlier work in their concern with trauma and violence. The two most recent novels deal with a group of art students, Elinor Brooke, Kit Neville, and Paul Tarrant, whose education at the Slade School of Art in London, under the tutelage of the real historical figure, Henry Tonks, an artist and surgeon, is cut short by World War One. Kit and Paul initially enlist with the Red Cross, seizing the opportunity to work as war artists, but both are eventually conscripted into the army. Paul suffers an injury to his leg, but Kit's physical trauma takes the form of serious injury to his face, and he continues to suffer enormous pain and humiliation once he has returned to England. Elinor's brother, Toby, also enlists in the army, and is killed in suspicious circumstances. Elinor, however, refuses to acknowledge the war, or to play any part in supporting it, through charity work or even through conversation. Instead, she prioritises her art over what she calls the 'bully' of war (Barker 2007a, p. 245), something that does not, she thinks, '[matter] very much', something which is not 'important' (p. 244). Whereas the primary focus of the *Regeneration* trilogy, which also dealt with some real historical figures (the psychologist WHR Rivers, and the poets Siegfried Sassoon and Wilfred Owen), was on the psychological effects of the enforced passivity of soldiers engaged in trench warfare and subject to the orders and management of more senior officers, *Life Class* and *Toby's Room* are focused on the experiences of war artists, medical staff, and civilians—in other words, the two most recent novels are concerned with those primarily operating on the fringes of battle, rather than directly participating in it. In this interest in outsiders, or those at the margins of violence, *Life Class* and *Toby's Room* are quite different from Barker's earlier narratives of war, and indeed, from most other narratives about World War One which, as I have just explained, typically focus on the experience of shell shock, trench warfare, and the exploitation of soldiers (we might list, for example, *The Wars* [1977], *Fly Away, Peter* [1982], and *Birdsong* [1993]). *Life Class* and *Toby's Room* also differ from their immediate precursor, *Double Vision*, which more explicitly deals with the events of 9/11. The protagonist of that novel is Stephen Sharkey, a war correspondent whose photographer partner has been killed on an assignment in the Middle East. The novel analyses the ethics of watching, and of representing violent acts, particularly when such observations are met without response, what Sophie Smith calls the 'immunity' (2013, p. 191) or the 'anaesthetised response to the brutality of war by the newspaper-reading and news channel-watching public who appear to be suffering from a serious bout of "compassion fatigue"' (p. 192). The argument echoes Kate Finzi's expostulation in her First World War memoir:

> Have *you* seen faces blown beyond recognition—faces eyeless, noseless, jawless, and heads that were only half heads?...When *you* have seen this... and not before, will you know what modern warfare means. (Finzi cited in Acton and Potter 2012, pp. 79–80; original emphasis)

Life Class and *Toby's Room* do extend that discussion, but they are more interested in the ethics of refusing to acknowledge trauma because of a belief that such acknowledgement also constitutes an acceptance of responsibility.

Elinor is perhaps the most interesting character in this respect. Before the war, Elinor is already a militant figure, and she struggles to make those around her understand her ambitions as an artist. Once war has broken out, her professional goals are perceived as selfishness to an even greater extent. Indeed, when she compares her own ambitions to the excitement of some young nurses she meets, she decides 'that these girls needed the war and she didn't. The freedom they were experiencing on this trip to Belgium she experienced every morning as she walked into the Slade' (Barker 2007a, p. 166). Refusing to accede to the national discourse concerned with contribution and social duty, Elinor explicitly repeats the famous points made by Virginia Woolf in her long essay on the relationship between women and war, *Three Guineas* (1938), arguing that

...it didn't concern me. As a woman, it didn't concern me. To be honest, I was copying something I'd heard Mrs. Woolf say last night after dinner, about how women are outside the political process and therefore the war's got nothing to do with them. (Barker 2012, p. 71; original emphasis)

Elinor's attitude to war art takes on a similar cast. In a repetition of the disagreement between Owen and Sassoon in *Regeneration*, Elinor asserts that art should address what is chosen, rather than what is imposed (p. 176). Arguing with her, Paul says that he paints scenes of war:

'Because it's there. *They're* there, the people, the men. And it's not right their suffering should just be swept out of sight.'

'I'd have thought it was even less right to put it on the wall of a public gallery. Can't you imagine it? People peering at other people's suffering and saying, "Oh my *dear*, how perfectly *dreadful*"—and then moving on to the next picture. It would just be a freak show. An arty freak show.' (pp. 175–176; original emphasis)

Elinor's resistance to the war has less to do with a political or artistic standpoint, as is the case for Owen—she differentiates herself from the Bloomsbury 'conchies', for example—and is instead more clearly a traumatic response: a repression of memory, as opposed to Owen's 'refuge'. In both cases above, moreover, Elinor adopts a position which advocates separation and a refusal to take responsibility, but in no other respects does she engage with the ethics of the war, or of seeing or representing violence.

Compare, moreover, Elinor's response to a group of disabled veterans she encounters at a military hospital with an almost identical event experienced by Sarah Lumb in *The Eye in the Door* (one of the only times, indeed, where the narration of the *Regeneration* trilogy is from a woman's perspective).

[Sarah] backed out, walking away in the sunlight, feeling their eyes on her, thinking that perhaps if she'd been prepared, if she'd managed to smile, to look normal, it might have been better. But no, she thought, there was nothing she could have done that would have made it better. Simply by being there, by being that inconsequential, infinitely powerful creature: *a pretty girl*, she had made everything worse. Her sense of her own helplessness, her being forced to play the role of Medusa when she meant no harm, merged with the anger she was beginning to feel at their being hidden away like that. If the country demanded that price, then it should bloody well be prepared to look at the result. She strode on through the heat, not caring where she was going, furious with herself, the war... Everything. (Barker 1996, p. 143; original emphasis)

... either I [Elinor] walk quickly with my head down or extra slowly and give them a big cheery smile and say hello. I watch them watching me noticing the missing bits, looking at the empty trouser legs or, equally awful, not looking at them. And I feel ashamed. Just being what I am, a girl they might once have asked to dance, is dreadful. I feel I'm an instrument of mental torture through no fault of my own. And then I'm ashamed of feeling that because after all what do my feelings matter? I think the world's gone completely mad. (Barker 2007a, p. 151)

In the case of the earlier novel, Sarah's affective response is helplessness and anger: her emotions are the same as those felt by the soldiers throughout the trilogy, suggesting that she understands their position, the 'price' they have paid. Similarly, when she first meets Billy Prior, she tells him that her fiancé has been killed in battle, but she does so in language which expresses the terms of value shared by the soldiers: 'Loos, she said. I remember standing by the bar and thinking that words didn't mean anything any more. Patriotism honour courage vomit vomit vomit. Only the names meant anything. Mons, Loos, the Somme, Arras, Verdun, Ypres' (Barker 1996, p. 579). The first-person narration of the passage from *Life Class*, however, emphasises Elinor's focus upon herself and her own emotion (shame), rather than on the experiences of the victims themselves. Moreover, since the logic of shame suggests that one only feels this emotion under the judging gaze of another (see Gilbert 1998, p. 21), Elinor's response indicates an opposition to those who watch her (the soldiers), rather than the affinity with their suffering, as is expressed by Sarah. Thus, whereas Sarah's reactions indicate an ethical understanding of the soldier Other, Elinor's responses figure a self-centred and oppositional approach to the trauma of war. Importantly, Elinor's attitude to the collective trauma figures a repetition of her response to an event of individual trauma, her incestuous relationship with her brother, and in this way provokes an interpretation of her affective response from the perspective of complicity and responsibility.

The affair which occurs between Elinor and Toby is brief, but traumatic. One hot summer's day, trekking away from their home, the two share an unexpected kiss, which is quickly dismissed. That night, however, Elinor returns to Toby's room. It is only shortly after this that the war begins and Toby is killed. The traumas here are therefore compounded: there is the incest itself, the broken trust between close siblings, Toby's death (which is itself the product not merely of the war, but of his sexual indiscretions), and the aspect in which this chapter is interested, Elinor's complicity in the traumatic relationship. The 'treacherous melting' (Barker 2012, p. 12) which Elinor feels as she kisses her brother might be seen to represent the breaking of what Freud calls the 'incest taboo'. Her participation in the incestuous relationship incites a collapse of civilised order comparable to the state of war—that is, a sense that nothing is certain, that all rules have been broken, and that she exists in a state of chaos.

The ironic perception of European cultures as 'civilised' is particularly brought to the fore in the final narrative of Barker's earlier World War One trilogy, *The Ghost Road*. The frequent use of analepsis to Rivers's pre-war role as an anthropologist enables comparisons between the 'civilised' actions of a nation involved in what is increasingly and explicitly referred to as a 'futile' war, and the so-called 'primitivism' of the Melanesian people whom he had studied years before. The head-hunting between local tribes has been stopped by European missionaries, and the community with whom Rivers lives is suffering as a result, 'everywhere apparent in the listlessness and lethargy of the people's lives. Head-hunting was what they had lived for' (Barker 1996, p. 551). And yet, what ultimately strikes Rivers is that the Melanesians have respect for their enemies: the concept of 'deliberate cruelty' is 'foreign' to them (p. 568), and the 'heads' captured on a raid are preserved with spiritual reverence, not because 'the skull was sacred...in or of itself, but because it had contained the spirit' (p. 569). No such respect is apparent in the broader organisational attitudes to the First World War—skulls are forgotten, embedded in trenches, trampled into the ground—although individual soldiers do express pity for their sacrificial counterparts in the trenches only yards away. The soldiers of Barker's *Regeneration* trilogy are therefore subject to the conflict between the individual and the state which Freud describes in 'Timely Reflections on War and Death' (1915):

> In this war the individual member of a people is able to convince himself with horror of what he sometimes found himself thinking even in peacetime, that the state has forbidden the individual to do wrong, not because

it wishes to abolish wrongdoing but because it wishes to monopolise it...
The belligerent state permits itself any injustice, any violence that would
disgrace the individual. (Freud 2005, p. 173)

If civilisation 'has been won', Freud states, 'by the renunciation of drive-
satisfaction' (p. 176), then when 'the community ceases to accuse, the
suppression of evil desires is also abolished' (p. 174), and civilisation
collapses. The characters of Barker's earlier novels escape the narrative's
condemnation because they are able to recognise the conflict between
the individual's consistent moral code and the lapsed morals of the
nation at war. Indeed, they recognise what Freud describes as the fact
that 'there are disproportionately more individuals hypocritically simu-
lating civilisation than there are truly civilised people' (p. 179), so that
the 'enemy' is no longer the German forces, but the 'civilisation' that
demands this behaviour.

In Barker's post-9/11 novels about World War One, however, those
characters—Elinor, above all—who allow their drives to operate free of
any civilising oppression are challenged. Indeed, the art Elinor produces
in the wake of war and incest, then, depicts not only the loss of civilisation, but may be read as a condemnation of her own failure to resist the
absence of state surveillance of drives and desires.

> To be brutally honest, [Paul had] expected nostalgia: scenes from rural life,
> happy children, impossibly long, golden summer days. Instead, he found
> himself looking at a series of winter landscapes, empty of people. Well,
> that was his first impression. When he looked more closely, he realised that
> every painting contained the shadowy figure of a man, always on the edge
> of the composition, facing away from the centre, as if he might be about to
> step outside the frame. (Barker 2012, p. 95)

The characters tend to read these paintings as depicting Toby, suggesting a fairly conventional reading of the way in which trauma and grief
remain as haunting figures or scars in the traumatised psyche, or that 'the
ravaged landscape paintings in war act as a metaphor for the mutilation
of the human body...[while] drawing a mutilated body reflects the rup-
turing of landscape and society that war brings' (Barker 2007b). I suggest, however, that the paintings of the barren landscapes can be seen
to represent the loss of civilisation, and that the shadowy figure is not
Toby, but Elinor. Her haunting presence would in this way depict the

sense in which she at once refuses, and is always already implicated in, the traumatic landscape. Thus, even though Elinor's stated position to the war, as Tolan argues, 'equates to a rejection of a totalitarian vision of collective action and collective ethics; she opposes the utilitarianism of the coerced submission of the individual to the greater good' (2010, p. 380), her paintings suggest the shameful recognition that she has not acted on those beliefs. As much as Elinor might try to erase her presence and abdicate responsibility, the ghostly figure in the paintings suggests that she must necessarily always occupy some position, make some contribution, and hold some responsibility for failing to keep her drives in check, despite the collapse of civilised order. For this reason, 'the failings and ultimate inefficacy of liberal humanism remain evident in a text that cannot in the end accept [Elinor's] position' (p. 391). The impact of 9/11 on Barker's representations of war is to do with the way in which it makes us memorialise war and responsibility in different ways. Even those who think they remain on the fringe, as outsiders or bystanders, become complicit in the traumatic aftermath of 9/11.

All of Barker's novels, John Brannigan notes, 'construct striking analogies that serve to connect individual experiences of trauma to their social and cultural conditions' (2005, p. 4). While her pre-9/11 novels dealing with World War One are confident in their construction of a hero-enemy dichotomy which condemns civilian demand for the combatants' sacrifice, the more recent novels set in the same context are influenced by a twenty-first-century awareness of participation in the traumatic experience. Elinor's response to both individual and collective trauma in which she is complicit therefore contributes to our broader understanding of marginalised or outsider perspectives on war, as well as our interpretations of the ethical memorialisation of war and violence in a media-saturated world.

NOTES

1. Although the trilogy in which *Life Class* and *Toby's Room* appear has recently been concluded by another novel, *Noonday*, this last work deals with the Second World War rather than the First, and as such addresses a different set of concerns about memory and representation, which are beyond the scope of this chapter.

WORKS CITED

Acton, Carol, and Jane Potter. 2012. These Frightful Sights Would Work Havoc with One's Brain: Subjective Experience, Trauma, and Resilience in First World War Writings by Medical Personnel. *Literature and Medicine* 30 (1): 61–85.

Adiseshiah, Siân, and Rupert Hildyard. 2013. Introduction: What Happens Now. In *Twenty-First Century Fiction: What Happens Now*, eds. Siân Adiseshiah and Rupert Hildyard, pp. 1–14. Houndmills: Palgrave Macmillan.

Banita, Georgiana. 2012. *Plotting Justice: Narrative Ethics and Literary Culture after 9/11*. Lincoln, NE:University of Nebraska Press.

Barker, Pat. 2015. *Noonday*. London: Penguin.

———. 2012. *Toby's Room*. London: Penguin.

———. 2007a. *Life Class*. London: Penguin.

———. 2007b. 'Lunch with the *FT*: Pat Barker'. *Financial Times.com*, July 20, 2007.

———. 1996. *The Regeneration Trilogy*. London: Penguin.

Barrett, Michèle. 2012. Pat Barker's *Regeneration* Trilogy and the Freudianisation of Shell Shock. *Contemporary Literature* 53 (2): 237–260.

Bohleber, Werner. 2010. *Destructiveness, Intersubjectivity, and Trauma: The Identity Crisis of Modern Psychoanalysis*. London: Karnac.

Brannigan, John. 2005. Pat Barker. In *Contemporary British Novelists*. Manchester: Manchester University Press.

Caruth, Cathy. 1996. *Unclaimed Experience: Trauma, Narrative, and History*. Baltimore, MD: Johns Hopkins University Press.

Childs, Peter. 2005. *Contemporary Novelists: British Fiction since 1970*. Houndmills: Palgrave Macmillan.

Freud, Sigmund. 2005. Timely Reflections on War and Death (1915). In *On Murder, Mourning and Melancholia*, trans. Shaun Whiteside, 167–194. London: Penguin.

Gilbert, Paul. 1998. What Is Shame? Some Core Issues and Controversies. In *Shame: Interpersonal Behaviour, Psychopathology, and Culture*, eds. Paul Gilbert and Bernice Andrews, 3–38. Oxford: Oxford University Press.

Keniston, Ann, and Jeanne Follansbee Quinn. 2008. Representing 9/11: Literature and Resistance. In *Literature after 9/11*, eds. Ann Keniston and Jeanne Follansbee Quinn, pp. 1–15. New York: Routledge.

Luckhurst, Roger. 2012. In War Times: Fictionalising Iraq. *Contemporary Literature* 53 (4): 713–737.

Pennell, Catriona. 2012. Popular History and Myth-Making: The Role and Responsibility of First World War Historians in the Centenary Commemorations, 2014–2018. *Historically Speaking* 13 (5): 11–14.

Rothberg, Michael. 2008. Seeing Terror, Feeling Art: Public and Private in Post-9/11 Literature. In *Literature after 9/11*, eds. Ann Keniston and Jeanne Follansbee Quinn, pp. 123–142.New York: Routledge.

Smith, Sophie. 2013. Weapons of War: Masculinity and Sexual Violence in Pat Barker's *Double Vision*. In *Men After War*, eds. Stephen McVeigh and Nicola Cooper, pp. 185–200. New York: Routledge.

Tancke, Ulrika. 2009. Uses and Abuses of Trauma in Post-9/11 Fiction and Contemporary Culture. In *From Solidarity to Schisms: 9/11 and After in Fiction and Film from Outside the US*, ed. Cara Cilano, 75–92. Amsterdam: Rodopi.

Tolan, Fiona. 2010. Painting While Rome Burns: Ethics and Aesthetics in Pat Barker's *Life Class* and Zadie Smith's *On Beauty*. *Tulsa Studies in Women's Literature* 29 (2): 375–393.

Author Biography

Jessica Gildersleeve is Senior Lecturer in English Literature at the University of Southern Queensland. She is the author of *Elizabeth Bowen and the Writing of Trauma: The Ethics of Survival* (Brill/Rodopi 2014), as well as essays on other twentieth- and twenty-first-century women writers, including Rosamond Lehmann, Jean Rhys, Agatha Christie, Sarah Waters, and Pat Barker. Her monographs on Christos Tsiolkas and the film *Don't Look Now* will be published later this year.

CHAPTER 7

Novel Wars: David Malouf and the Invention of the *Iliad*

Kezia Whiting

In her essay 'The *Iliad*, or the Poem of Force', Simone Weil suggests that for those 'who perceive force, today as yesterday, at the very centre of human history', the *Iliad* is recognised as 'the purest and the loveliest of mirrors' (Weil 1965, p. 6). Other than this reference to 'force, today', Weil does not mention any contemporary issues. It is the editor's note to the *Chicago Review* version of the essay that tells us it was 'written in the summer and fall of 1940, after the fall of France' and 'may thus be read as an indirect commentary on that tragic event, which signalised the triumph of the most extreme modern expression of force' (p. 5)—providing one example of the mirroring to which Weil refers. If the *Iliad* is the *purest* mirror, this means it is a reflection of whatever is looking at it, not without substance, but in which its substance forms this reflective surface. David Malouf's novel *Ransom* (2009) also engages with this question: what is it in the substance of the *Iliad* that makes it speak to so many entirely different situations of war? Malouf acknowledges the influence of Weil's essay on his own thinking about the *Iliad* in an article published ten months before *Ransom*, in which he begins by claiming

K. Whiting (✉)
State University of New York at Buffalo, New York, USA
e-mail: keziaann@buffalo.edu

© The Author(s) 2017   125
J. Gildersleeve and R. Gehrmann (Eds.), *Memory and the Wars
on Terror*, Palgrave Macmillan Memory Studies,
DOI 10.1007/978-3-319-56976-5_7

that '[t]otal war and genocide are not modern concepts' and ends with Weil's description of the *Iliad* as mirror:

> The *Iliad* reminds us that we inhabit a world of unfinished stories, and echoes, and the repetition of old horrors and miseries. No wonder, when the news is yet again out of Gaza and Ashkelon, that for those, as Weil wrote in 1942, 'who perceive force, today as yesterday, at the centre of human history, the *Iliad* is its most beautiful and purest mirror.' (2009a)

Malouf engages with Weil's figuring of the *Iliad* as a mirror, using his afterword to suggest the ways in which *Ransom*, since it is based on the *Iliad*, is also a pure and lovely mirror, reflecting contemporary issues of war. *Ransom* is not just about these 'old horrors and miseries', but about their repetition and representation in particular forms.

In the Afterword to *Ransom*, Malouf writes about the primary school teacher who first introduced him to the story of the *Iliad*, and what it meant to him in 1943: 'I had immediately connected Miss Finlay's ancient and fictional war with our own. We too were left hanging in the midst of an unfinished war' (Malouf 2009b, p. 222). For Malouf, the poem was also the purest of mirrors. In the novel itself, Malouf makes no mention of contemporary politics or wars, but by relocating this Greek story into another time and place in the Afterword, Malouf prompts the act of transferring it again into our global present, and our own unfinished wars. Although it is set in Ancient Greece during the last days of the Trojan War, *Ransom* is nonetheless an entirely contemporary response to war. If this act of relocation were not already clearly inscribed in Malouf's focus on his experience of the Trojan War through the lens of World War Two in Brisbane (and also of World War Two in Brisbane through the lens of the Trojan War), he goes on to introduce the Vietnam War as another period during which he thought of his first encounter with the stories of the Trojan War by quoting his poem 'Episode from an Early War', which describes his childhood encounter with the Troy story and similarly superimposes the Trojan War and World War Two. Because Malouf highlights the year in which he wrote this poem, 1972, he raises the spectre of the Vietnam War without discussing it explicitly. In indicating that he has twice already considered the Trojan War in the light of wars he was living through, Malouf implies we might do the same with the War on Terror and the many wars that constitute it. By ending his novel with these memories, Malouf retrospectively integrates himself into the story he has finished telling, so that the old-fashioned figure of writer as storyteller is evoked and reworked, linking him to the storyteller figure in the novel, Somax.

Peter Conrad takes up the challenge of the novel's Afterword to consider the novel in terms of contemporary politics. While he recognises that '*Ransom* is a philosophical meditation on Homer's fatalistic universe, not a political allegory', for him it is still 'tempting to see Malouf's Troy, "a city of four square towers topped by untidy storks' nests", as the World Trade Centre arrogantly multiplied' (2009). Indeed, the novel was written in 2002, soon after the September 11, 2001 terrorist attacks in the United States but, in a seminar at the University of New South Wales, Malouf revealed he put it away because he thought people might wonder '[w]hy are we as Australian readers in 2003 (as it might have been) being asked to interest ourselves in the *Iliad*?' (2010) The Troy story meant so much to him as a nine-year-old, he says, because in Brisbane in 1943, 'we were living in a city that was, in which every building was, sandbagged [...] and waiting for the invading army to come with no knowledge then because history hadn't yet happened that we were not going to suffer the same kind of fate the Trojans suffered' (2010). He goes on to consider why what he calls 'the Troy material' is so popular, suggesting that perhaps it is because it 'speaks to people over and over again in different ages about certain kinds of essential and primitive anxieties about the fall of the city. The city is a sacred construct, which represents the best of everything in us in terms of civil behaviour and civil aspirations, and the fall of a city is a terrible, terrible thing' (2010). These anxieties about the fall of a city and all that the city represents would certainly explain why readers in 2003 might be interested in the *Iliad*. Remembering these anxieties opens up ways of considering his novel in light of over a decade of wars, of which the most spectacular image remains the towers collapsing, without forcing it to be the political allegory by which Conrad is tempted.

Malouf's novel forces us to consider anew the way we view images of destruction, and how the fall of a city is represented. In the *Ruins of Modernity* (2010), Julia Hell and Andreas Schönle explore the resonances of the 'images of New York in ruins' with 'other images of destruction', and argue that looking at ruins always entails a rethinking of history:

When history piles wreckage upon wreckage, ruins evoke not only the buildings from which they hail but also a transhistorical iconography of decay and catastrophe, a vast visual archive of ruination. In the era of global media coverage and round-the-clock exposure to visual data, ruins have become ubiquitous. They are images that denote raw reality, yet the way we see them is not raw but framed by a long tradition of ruin gazing. What we see is new, and we might see it in a new way—but not for long. Soon our gaze at the rubble piling up before our eyes is clouded by the iconic wreckage of ages [...]. Ruin gazing always mirrors the terror in the angel's wide-open eyes. It always involves reflections about history: about the nature of the event, the meaning of the past for the present, the nature of history itself as eternal cycle, progress, apocalypse, or murderous dialectic process. (p. 1)

In Malouf's novel, the inevitable ruin and wreckage, the most memorable destruction of a city in the history of Western civilization, is endlessly postponed and recalled: in the present tense of the narration it has not yet happened, but Malouf's readers and characters know what is coming. Part Three is the only part of the novel narrated in the past tense, when Somax, the carter character Malouf invents, takes Priam to Achilles. All other sections are told in the present tense, emphasising the contemporaneity with which Malouf tells these historical events. Thus, the book itself enacts this reflection about history in its form: what does this event mean for us looking back on it, and for those looking forward at it? In Hell and Schönle's account, ruins inevitably blend together, so that we might even see in the wreckage of the Twin Towers a palimpsest of Troy. But Malouf nostalgically brings us back to Troy before its fall, to a city remembered for its destruction, and, following Homer, does not recount that sacking.

Thus, although the ruins of Troy are not made into a voyeuristic spectacle for us, the wreckage already done even before the destruction of the city foreshadows them. Travelling through the land around Troy, Malouf's Priam takes note of the 'utter devastation' the war has enacted upon it:

> The moon was rising fast now. Soon, wafer-like and as if lit from within, it stood high over what had, till the war laid waste to them, been standing wheatfields and groves of ancient olives.

> Priam sat silent. Till now he had seen nothing of this.

The landscape they were entering was one of utter devastation. (Malouf 2009b, p. 155)

The starkness of the narration in describing this landscape, and Priam's reaction to it, echoes Lear's famous 'Oh, I have ta'en too little care of this' (Shakespeare 1997, 3.4.33–3.4.34), the soliloquy in which Lear, stripped of his kingly position and reduced to his human body, recognises the hardships his subjects face daily. The importance of this speech of Lear's for *Ransom* cannot be overlooked, as I will later elaborate. Malouf's archaically inflected negation—'he had seen nothing,' rather than he had not seen anything—suggests that it is not just that Priam has not seen these ruined fields before, but that even if he had looked at them, 'he had seen nothing' of it. Now, having been introduced to new ways of seeing the world through Somax, his eyes are open to the 'utter devastation' of the landscape and the lives that were supported by it. The delicate balance between farming and war, and the damage of war on agriculture, is something Achilles reflects on at the beginning of the novel:

Days, years, season after season; and endless interim of keeping your weapons in good trim and your keener self taut as a bowstring through long stretches of idleness, of restless, patient waiting, and shameful quarrels and unmanly bragging and talk.

Such a life is death to the warrior spirit. Which if it is to endure at the high point needs action—the clash of arms that settles a quarrel quickly, then sends a man back, refreshed in spirit, to being a good farmer again.

War should be practised swiftly, decisively. Thirty days at most, in the weeks between new spring growth and harvest, when the corn is tinder-dry and ripe for the invader's brand, then back to the cattle pace of the farmer's life. (Malouf 2009b, p. 7)

It is not the landscape with which Achilles is concerned, but the 'warrior spirit' that needs the juxtaposition provided by farm life. War, in Achilles' description, should not be separable from agrarian life, but built around it, dependent on the structure it provides. This is not simply a way of limiting war, but of maintaining the true warrior spirit, which also 'refreshes' the farmer. In opposition to this symbiotic relationship is the war being fought in Troy, where the Greeks are far from their farms and the Trojans' wheatfields are destroyed.

But even the devastation the war wreaks on the landscape does not stop life from continuing around it, working over and among the dead. As Priam and Somax drive past barrows of the dead outside the Greek camp,

> Ghostly figures materialise for a moment among them, then dissolve. [...] The women are scavenging for battle relics—a silver pin, the clasp off a pair of greaves. All this part of the plain has been the scene, at one time or another, of skirmishes or pitched battles in which hundreds of men have fallen and been dragged away. The women move close to the earth, their hands turning the clods, breaking them up with practiced fingers. (pp. 205–206)

Malouf describes the life around the battles, giving us only these ordinary traces of the epic battles. The women's hands turning the clods, while not actually working new life into the clay, still seems to be the beginnings of a working-over and through. At present, all that can be taken from the earth are battle relics, but with these hands turning the clods, the earth will return to agriculture and to growth. Already, the ghostly figures are as much the people moving through the landscape as they are dead warriors. These unnamed warriors and the people now are all the ordinary men and women in the background of the *Iliad* whom Malouf materialises for a moment. As he writes in 'Men and Gods Behaving Badly', in the *Iliad* '[t]housands of "average and inferior troops" are slaughtered; their deaths go unrecorded. There are women too, who are traded like cattle or worry and grieve, and if they survive are carried off' (2009a).

It becomes apparent, as Malouf points out in the Afterword, that the novel's 'primary interest is in storytelling itself—why stories are told and why we need to hear them, how stories get changed in the telling' (Malouf 2009b, p. 223), but it is really an even more specific interest in the novel itself as a form of storytelling. Implicit in Malouf's version of the Troy story is the question: what can the novel do that an epic poem cannot? In answering this question, he turns the novel's (his specifically, and the genre's) focus on the everyday and the mundane into an ethical and political response (or non-response) to violence and war. In his review of *Ransom*, Daniel Mendelsohn articulates this decisive shift from epic to novel:

> This is the world of epic, a world governed by conventions that, at the beginning of the novel, neither Priam, in his passive grief, nor Achilles, driving around in circles that symbolise his endless, fruitless rage, knows how to break out of. [...] For Malouf, the solution to this epic problem is, in both senses of the word, the novel—a new way of thinking, and a new form for thinking it. (2009)

In justifying to Hecuba his idea to go to Achilles unadorned and attempt to ransom back Hector's body, Priam emphasises the inventiveness and newness of the idea, using the word 'novel'. This is the only time in the narrative's extensive discussion of newness that the word 'novel' is used: 'The fact that it has never been done, that it is novel, unthinkable—except that I have thought of it—is just what makes me believe it should be attempted. It is possible because it is not possible. And because it is simple' (Malouf 2009b, p. 59).[1] The novel form is what is unthinkable from the position of the epic: as Malouf has said, the novel 'is a form written to take advantage of interesting, appealing, and ultimately wonderful irrelevancies of ordinary life' (2010). Priam's meditation on newness thus becomes a meditation too on the specific newness of the novel form, and the invention by which each novel in itself is characterised.

After listing in the Afterword the 'margins of earlier writers' that he has expanded on in *Ransom*—for example, the 'half a dozen lines in the *Iliad*' devoted to 'how Patroclus came to be the friend and companion of Achilles' (Malouf 2009b, p. 223)—Malouf goes on to say that the story of '[h]ow a simple carter, Somax, for one day became the Trojan herald Idaeus, and Priam's companion on his journey to the Greek camp, appears for the first time in the pages of this book' (p. 224). Malouf separates his text from those which he has retold and adapted, but also ingratiates it at the same level of mythologising as the others, especially through the repetition of 'how' to introduce each of these descriptors of stories. By emphasising the fictionality of the Trojan War, its basis in stories (he calls it 'Miss Finlay's ancient and fictional war' [p. 222]), Malouf positions himself in the tradition of writers creating and expanding on this mythology, making his story no more apocryphal than Homer's or any of the other sources he appropriates. The novel explicitly illustrates invention as working through already existing material when, in thinking

about why Somax's story about his daughter-in-law's pikelets is so interesting and fresh to him, Priam realises:

> It had never occurred to him that the food that came to his table so
> promptly, and in such abundance, might have *ingredients*. [...] Or that
> ingenious arrangements might need to be made before a thing as simple
> as a mere pikelet could make its entry into the world. Or that one of the
> activities a man might give his attention to, and puzzle his wits over, was
> the managing of these arrangements, the putting together, in an experi-
> mental way, of this or that bit of an already existing world to make some-
> thing new. (p. 128; original emphasis)

Invention, in these terms, is not creating something from nothing,
but using the old to make something new, using 'this or that bit of an
already existing world' but seeing and positioning it in a different way.
Malouf's self-reflexivity here and throughout the novel is delicate: he
does not boisterously insert himself and his project into this simple narrative, but makes the two intimately bound together. His adaptation
takes this or that bit of an already existing world (or text) and, in an
experimental way, produces something entirely new. While he is then
commenting on his own project in these lines, this is also just as importantly the realisation that Priam is coming to about new ways of seeing
the world he is in, and about the prospect of seeing the world differently
itself: 'It had had no interest for him. Now it did. And he looked at the
old fellow who had revealed these things to him with growing respect'
(p. 128). Somax shows Priam how to see differently, just as Malouf does
for us.

Through Somax's storytelling, Malouf comments on his own similar
techniques. The third person narration comments on Somax, claiming,
'[t]his old fellow, like most storytellers, is a stealer of other men's tales,
of other men's lives' (Malouf 2009b, p. 218). In extrapolating from
Somax to 'most storytellers', Malouf positions himself as another Somax,
a stealer of other men's tales in his appropriation of Homer's epic. The
significance of Part Three, the journey of Somax and Priam to Achilles'
camp and the only section narrated in the past tense, then, is its association with Somax and with the story of the journey he will tell for years to
come.

Because of its focus on human interests and desires, the gods play a
much more subdued role in Malouf's novel than in Homer's epic, where

they appear almost entirely in control of events. In moving from epic to novel, the role of the gods shifts to the more permeable omniscient narration, blending in and out of the characters' minds. In the *Iliad*, it is Zeus who comes up with what appears as Priam's novel idea in *Ransom*; as he tells the other gods, it is 'a carefully considered solution to suggest, to make Achilles accept a ransom from Priam and release Hector' (Homer 2003, 24.74–24.76) and not a spontaneous and precarious undertaking, as it is in *Ransom*. While the idea is prompted by Priam's vision of Iris, Zeus's messenger, in *Ransom*, it is a much more ambiguous moment of inspiration: 'An old, dreamlike passivity in him that he no longer finds it necessary to resist will dissolve the boundary between what is solid and tangible in the world around him [...] and the weightless medium in which his consciousness is adrift, where the gods, in their bodily presence, have the same consistency as his thoughts' (Malouf 2009b, p. 42). It is not just that the gods know Priam's thoughts, but that they are inextricable from them. There is no clear delineation between the gods' 'bodily presence' and Priam's thoughts, literalising the way the omniscient narration often moves in and out of characters' thoughts, becoming indistinguishable from them. This does not turn the *Iliad* into a tale of modernity and secularity, but it does indicate the pointlessness of designating an idea as belonging solely to the gods and not to humans. This also means that while the gods do have bodily presence, it is not particularly material, as it does often seem to be in Homer, despite their immortality. Iris appears for a moment and then disappears, and while Priam thinks that 'her words continue to drop directly into his thoughts' (p. 46), he has just described the permeability of the boundary between his consciousness and the gods, making the origin of the words indeterminable. When Priam asks, 'where else could such a dangerous suggestion come from if not from an immortal?', he attempts to demarcate his own thoughts from those of the gods, but in fact highlights his uncertainty as to who proposed that the world is 'subject to chance' (p. 46). In contrast, in the *Iliad*, Iris's words to Priam (which do not include any speculation on the nature of the world and why things happen) are almost verbatim from Zeus (see Homer 2003, 24.146–24.188).

In the free indirect discourse of the novel, characters' thoughts often demonstrate these permeable boundaries, with focalisations overlapping and intersecting. After Priam has brought himself to utter the word 'chance' when describing his vision to Hecuba, the focalisation shifts from him to her:

'If I do not succeed in this, and am lost, then all is lost. We must leave that to the gods. Or to chance.'

There!—a little shiver goes through him—he has said it.

Chance?

She looks up quickly. Surely she has misheard. (Malouf 2009b, p. 61)

The word startles both characters. It is repeated here as if in response to Priam's thoughts, but also as segue into Hecuba's, questioning what her husband has just said. If it were purely beginning Hecuba's perspective, there would be no need for the second paragraph break that clearly moves into her focalisation ('She looks up quickly'). Hecuba goes on to describe words as 'the agents of what is new' (p. 61). The word 'agent' can paradoxically indicate both agency and a kind of passivity: it means both acting on behalf of another, but also that which takes an active role. Being the agent of what is new could thus mean either acting on behalf of what is new, or bringing about what is new. Do they work for what is conceivable, or do they create what is conceivable? From this ambiguity, one could ask what it means for humans to be agents of the gods. More to the point, while Priam will go on to discover the delights of minutiae that storytelling creates, Hecuba here already recognises that '[w]ords are powerful', and that they are also agents 'of what is conceivable and can be thought and let loose upon the world' (p. 61). Again, the ambiguity of what being an 'agent' means is central here: are words prior to thoughts, or are they the merely the servants of thoughts?

Part of this power of the words Priam chooses is in renaming fortune or the whim of the gods as chance, which 'offers a kind of opening'. While Priam recognises that he 'cannot stop what may be about to occur,' he does think it might be possible to open a space in the history that he knows is coming to leave a 'living' image of 'something so new' (p. 89). This opportunity to make a kind of opening in the events of history is also what Malouf attempts in *Ransom*. Mendelsohn incisively sees that in 'looking for open spaces in the weave to insert his own design' Malouf finds them

...in the last lines of the poem, where an extraordinary thing happens: one of the characters tries to imagine an alternative to the foreordained narrative. Priam and Achilles have been sketching the details of a truce [...] and decide that eleven days is sufficient. 'On the twelfth,' Homer's Priam says, 'we'll fight again...if fight we must.' That 'if we must'—pregnant with the tantalising, wishful possibility that the two sides might not have to fight anymore, that we can break out of character and create a new history—is the subject of Malouf's subtle and extremely moving novel. (2010)

Mendelsohn's attention to Priam's 'if we must' demonstrates the liberation Priam, but also Achilles, is searching for, and which for a moment, in their meeting one another, they both find. But they cannot create an entirely new history because their stories are written in advance, both by Homer (for Malouf) and by the gods. Another opening such as this is in Book 22, when moments before his death Hector imagines other things he could do instead of fighting Achilles:

> What am I to do? If I retire behind the gate and the wall, Polydamas will be the first to point the finger of blame at me [...]. If I put down my bossed shield and heavy helmet, prop my spear against the wall and approach matchless Achilles myself...if I promise to return Helen and all her property with her...everything in fact that Paris brought away with him to Troy in his hollow ships, which was how this war started...to give it all to Agamemnon and Menelaus to take away, and to divide up everything else with the Greeks as well, everything the town possesses...and then if I take an oath the elders in council on behalf of the Trojans not to hide anything but to divide it all up equally, all the property our lovely town contains...But why talk to myself like this? If I approach Achilles as a supplicant, he'll show me no pity, no respect. (Homer 2003, 22.99–22.123)

Mary McCarthy, in her translation of Simone Weil's essay, produces her own lovely translation of Hector's question at the end of the passage: 'But why spin out these fancies? Why such dreams?' (Weil 1965, p. 17). Here, Hector's attempts to imagine himself out of the desperate situation in which he finds himself is entirely unsuccessful because he realises he can do nothing to change Achilles's mind; however, his speculative 'fancies' develop with so much detail that for a moment we too get caught up in imagining this alternative version of events that would spare the life of Hector, and many others. For a brief moment, the imagination takes over from fate, spinning out other possibilities of events. The repetition of ellipses in E.V. Rieu's translation emphasises hesitation and gaps that make space for other things to happen in Hector's dreams. The 'dangerous' idea of Iris's that Malouf emphasises, but which we now see is indeed in Homer's original too, is thus clearly connected to imagination. When Priam talks of what the gods always intended for him, Iris counters by suggesting that it is in fact 'the way things *are*. Not the way they must be, but the way they have turned out. In a world that is also subject to chance' (Malouf 2009b, p. 46; original emphasis).

While the gods are given much less direct power in Malouf's story, in the end perhaps this is not entirely different from Homer. The focus on the *human*, is, after all, what Edith Hamilton argues is the invention or creation of the Greeks: 'in the earliest Greek poets a new point of view dawned, never dreamed of in the world before them, but never to leave the world after them. With the coming forward of Greece, mankind became the centre of the universe, the most important thing in it. This was a revolution in thought. […] The Greeks made their gods in their own image' (pp. 7–8). While Hamilton notes the humanness of the gods, Malouf details the ordinary humanness of humans. The idea of Greece producing this 'revolution in thought' is central to Malouf's revisiting of this era, and its connection to the contemporary moment. If, as Slavoj Žižek claims, 'on September 11, the USA was given the opportunity to realise what kind of world it was part of' (2002, p. 47), then something of this order—of a new point of view dawning—is also called up by *Ransom*. Of course, according to Žižek the United States did not take this opportunity (or 'chance' to use Priam's word) 'instead it opted to reassert its traditional ideological commitments' (p. 47). Also writing about September 11, Derrida's less authoritarian, more nuanced hope is that

> …there will be, in 'Europe' or in a certain modern tradition of Europe, at the cost of a deconstruction that is still finding its way, the possibility of another discourse and another politics, a way out of this double theologico-political program. 'September 11'—whatever is ultimately put under this title—will thus have been at once a sign and a price to pay, a very high price, to be sure, without any possible redemption or salvation for the victims, but an important stage in the process. (2003, p. 118)

Both Žižek and Derrida see September 11 as an event marking the possibility of a way out of contemporary political ideology, with the potential to instigate an entirely new version of politics—for Derrida, this is the 'democracy to come'—which, among other things, insists upon not

...following, applying, or realising a norm or rule. When there is a determinable rule, I know what must be done, and as soon as such knowledge dictates the law, action follows knowledge as a calculable consequence: one *knows* what path to take, one no longer hesitates; the decision then no longer decides anything but simply gets deployed with the automatism attributed to machines. (p. 134; original emphasis)

Decision can only truly take place when it is unforeseen and unforeseeable, without predetermination, when it is impossible, as Priam's decision to approach Achilles is 'possible because it is not possible' (Malouf 2009b, p. 59). In 'A Certain Impossible Possibility of Saying the Event,' Derrida explores how this construction, 'impossible possibility,' is not a negation: 'To put it otherwise, I will try to explain how I understand the word "possible" in this sentence [the title] in a way that this "possible" is not simply "different from" or "the opposite of" impossible, and why, in this case, "possible" and "impossible" say the same thing' (2007, p. 445). As with Priam's idea, Derrida's impossible possibility describes the structure of invention: 'the only invention possible is the invention of the impossible. The event's eventfulness depends on this experience of the impossible. What comes to pass, as an event, can only come to pass if it's impossible. If it's possible, if it's foreseeable, then it doesn't come to pass' (pp. 450–451). Priam's impossible is also synonymous with something new, with production and not negation of 'the possible': 'the thing that is needed to cut this knot we are all tied in is something that has never before been done or thought of. Something impossible. Something *new*' (Malouf 2009b, p. 58; original emphasis). Here, Priam's desire for something to 'cut this knot' parallels Derrida's desire for 'a way out of this double theologico-political program'. *Ransom*, by skipping over detailed descriptions of the war itself, is not so much focused on violence as event or rupture in itself, but on the possibility of invention in response to it. This is precisely what Derrida calls for when he describes as a kind of autoimmune suicide the way 'defenses, and all the forms of what is called, with two equally problematic words, the "war on terrorism" work to regenerate, in the short or long term, the causes of the evil they claim to eradicate,' reprisals for which he suggests will continue ad infinitum (2003, p. 100). As Priam recognises, the only way out of the 'knot we are all tied in' is something entirely new, not a foreseeable, programmatic response that meets violence with violence.

For Derrida, this kind of escalation, one that involves known responses, cannot bring forth an event.

The uncertainty of the language Priam uses to describe his idea of dressing simply as a man and supplicating himself to Achilles, and his new notion that replaces the whims of the gods with the secular focus on 'chance,' emphasises the contingency of his success as the basis of their possibility at all: '"It seems to me," he says, almost dreamily, "that there might be another way of naming what we call fortune and attribute to the will, or the whim, of the gods. Which offers a kind of opening. The opportunity to act for ourselves. To try something that might force events into a different course"' (Malouf 2009b, p. 61). Priam's repetition of 'might' and his sentence fragments here demonstrate his hesitancy and uncertainty, and the unplanned way these ideas come to him. Yet he is also described as certain, in the first moments after his vision, and even more so as he begins to narrativise it: 'recalling it now, allowing the lines of the picture to grow clear as he adds one detail then the next, makes him more certain than ever that what he intends to do is what he must do' (pp. 54–55). While Priam is certain that this is what he must do, the only chance of success is in not knowing if it is going to succeed because it is something so new, so unprecedented.

Part of what is new and inconceivable in this plan is the movement away from ritual (which is all about precedents and following a clear routine) and the divine image of the king, and toward the freedom involved in being an ordinary man mourning his son. Priam suggests that Achilles too might be longing for this kind of freedom, for 'the chance to break free of the obligation of being always the hero, as I am expected always to be the king. To take on the lighter bond of being simply a man' (pp. 59–60). When Somax describes his son's death to Priam, he is touched by the intimate memories that constitute Somax's mourning and asks 'if the phrase he had taken up so easily, that he knew what it was to lose a son, really did mean the same for him as it did for the driver. Whether what he had felt for the loss of Gorgythion […] and Doryclus and Isus and Troilus and the rest, was in any way comparable to what this man had felt for a boy who was, after all, neither a prince nor a warrior, just a villager like so many more' (p. 136). Priam wonders 'mightn't it be time for me to expose myself at last to what is merely human? To learn a little of what that might be, and what it is to bear it as others do' (p. 85) before he leaves his palace, but it is only through Somax that he accomplishes this exposure to the human.

This is the other moment when I think of those lines of Lear's, when he instructs himself to '[e]xpose thyself to feel what wretches feel' (Shakespeare 1997, 3.4.35). It is perhaps only because of this attempt at sympathetic identification (and the uncertainty of that identification—he is, after all, not at all sure that what he feels is 'in any way comparable' to Somax's grief) that he is able to expose himself to Achilles, and to fall 'to his knees at last and [clasp] Achilles' hand [...] out of instant fellow-feeling' (Malouf 2009b, pp. 186–187). Priam thinks about how much more painful his children's deaths would be if he were to mourn them in this way, as Somax does his children, as individuals:

> When the years arrived in which, one after the other, his sons were brought in from the battlefield and he had twenty times over to stand by a corpse and pour out wine, and give the pierced and bloodless or hacked body a name, wouldn't he have suffered twenty times over if, as he held the brand to the pyre, he had had to remember how this one's sweat, when he crowned him once after a wrestling match, had had an odour of the stable as rank as any grooms; and how that one had had a little spinning top, and had fallen once when he went stumbling after it on the palace floor, and had recognised, with an unexpected onrush of recall, the star-shaped scar that was still visible on the young man's cheek, just inches from where a Greek javelin had shattered the jaw, smashed the teeth and taken a piece the size of his fist out of the back of his skull? Even the ghostly recollection now of what he had never in fact allowed himself to see made his own heart leap and flutter. (p. 139)

As we progress through this passage, it becomes clear that Priam does remember these intimate details of his sons' beings. The detail of the 'star-shaped scar' which could have sparked memories of the boy as a toddler is evidently not hypothetical, but a real detail noticed and remembered on viewing his son's body, and then repressed, 'what he had never in fact allowed himself to see'. Although he does see it now, with that 'unexpected onrush of recall' in identification with Somax's grief, it is not entirely clear if it is Priam who realises 'he had never in fact allowed himself to see' or if he still does not have this degree of self-awareness: again, an omniscient perspective becomes indistinguishable from a character's thoughts. The superimposition of battle wound over childhood scar, and the violence of the damage to Priam's son's skull, again gives us the devastating effects of war without describing the heroics of the battle. Priam moves from duty and the role that he is expected to play toward allowing himself to mourn his son as an individual, and thus as any other father might mourn his son. But removing the ritual and thus the gods from these deaths is, as Hecuba warns, dangerous: 'this idea you're so taken with, of how and why things happen as they do, that is not to be spoken of. Imagine what it would lead to, what would be permitted. The randomness, the violence. Imagine the panic it would spread' (p. 62).

The tension between the gods and the everyday is played out in the episode of Zeus's hawk as the cart is being readied for the journey. The eagle, 'the most perfect of prophetic birds' that Zeus 'instantly' sends in response to Priam's prayer for a bird of omen before his journey in the *Iliad* (Homer 2003, 24.316–24.317) becomes a chickenhawk in *Ransom*: 'Mmm, the carter thinks, a chickenhawk. Riding the updraught and hanging there, on the lookout for a fieldmouse in the furrows below, or a venturesome hamster or vole. But prompted by his mother, the priest Helenus proclaims it an eagle' (Malouf 2009b, p. 101). In metamorphosing what is an eagle in the *Iliad* into a chickenhawk, Malouf undermines Zeus and more particularly the humans' belief in the omnipresence of the gods in their lives, but he can only do this through his use of free indirect discourse, demonstrating an omniscient, god-like knowledge of the characters' thoughts. After describing Somax's perception of the chickenhawk and Helenus's proclamation of it as Zeus's eagle, the narration states that 'the carter is surprised at this though no one else appears to be' (pp. 101–102). The emphasis is on perception over objectivity in that final 'appears to be', but it is not clear from whose perspective this phrase is narrated. We are still with Somax because we know he *is* something whereas the others all only *appear* to be something, but the description of him as 'the carter' marks a distance that is not as evident when the third person singular is used elsewhere to render his thoughts. A perspective outside both Somax and the crowd is implied here, as we move away from the more internal perceptions of Somax to something ('surprised') that could also be seen from the outside. The focus on perception is reiterated when the eagle is described as '[c]lear for all to see, Jove's emblem and messenger is hovering there, holding them, these mighty representatives of Troy, and the many thousands of people outside the palace, in the city and in the villages and provinces beyond, in the quivering net of its celestial attention and concern' (p. 102). The irony of the phrase 'clear for all to see' is truly clear for all to see, coming immediately after Somax's description of the bird as a chickenhawk. The narration now appears to be focalised through the group of onlookers as well as through a distanced and knowing perspective on these people. The omniscience of this passage underlies the implication that there are no gods watching over these events: Zeus has not sent an eagle, but the narration still knows all. Malouf shifts the gods' (or at least Zeus's) omniscience into the very act of narration, a foundational act for the novel form. At the same time, by undercutting the gods, Malouf undercuts the novel's narration, and the idea of omniscience in fiction. By the end of the novel, its focus on the trickeries involved in storytelling will become clear. Omniscience is perhaps the best, most lasting deception of the novel.

One difficulty Malouf faces in working with the Troy myth is that its outcome is indeed inevitable and renowned, just like so many of the characters who foresee their own deaths in Homer's poem. With the events of his story so known, so plotted, how can he introduce an element of chance into it? Malouf makes an opening in the tale, but leaves it looking toward its inevitable, known-in-advance ending, which is of course just what Homer's ending does too, by describing Achilles' and Priam's deaths only in visions of the future. Malouf brings out the uncertainty that threatens destiny in brief flashes throughout Homer's *Iliad*, because this is the effect of storytelling: to spin out new ideas, possibilities, and ways of seeing. While the events of history cannot be 'miraculously suspended,' as 'the end' seems to be for Achilles (p. 211), for just a moment the space of the novel allows this suspension to happen. The narration is quick to undercut Achilles's feeling of freedom from history: 'In the instant warmth and energy that fills him, the end, which is so close now, seems to have been miraculously suspended. It has not' (p. 211), but after describing in gory detail the botched mess Neoptolemus will make of Priam's death, we are consoled with the image of the living Priam: 'But time has not yet reached that point. The blood still warm and ticking in his wrist' (p. 215). But even in this image of Priam alive in the present tense is now tinged with the vision of his death, so that it seems to describe a recently killed man (the man whose violent death has just been described) with blood throbbing out of his body. The 'ticking' of his blood counts us down to the moment of his death that has just been described, but which the narration will not actually take us up to, opening a gap between the present and the future, forestalling it into the space of imagining after the end of the novel.

The novelty of Malouf's novel is the gaps it opens in knowledge. By producing gaps of knowledge in history, Malouf opens space for us to think about what already exists in entirely new ways. In a parallel manner, Malouf opens the space of the form of the novel itself by breaking down the conception of 'omniscient' narration, and the God-like power this implies: instead, we are given flashes of revelation and ambiguous merging between gods and men alike. *Ransom* is not a representation of war, but a shaking of the foundation of how one represents war, and what it means to use particular forms to do so.

NOTES

1. The 'novelty' of the situation is described when Priam gathers his children and councillors to announce his plan (p. 79).

WORKS CITED

Conrad, Peter. 2009. Troy Revisited: Homer's *Iliad* and David Malouf's *Ransom*. *Monthly*, May. Available at: https://www.themonthly.com.au/Homer-Iliad-David-Malouf-Ransom-Peter-Conrad.

Derrida, Jacques. 2003. Autoimmunity: Real and symbolic suicides—A dialogue with Jacques Derrida, trans. Pascale-Anne Brault and Michael Naas. In *Philosophy in a Time of Terror*, ed. Giovanna Borradori, 85–136. Chicago: University of Chicago Press.

——. 2007. A certain impossible possibility of saying the event, trans. Gila Walker. In *Critical Inquiry*, vol. 33, 441–461.

Hamilton, Edith. 1942. *Mythology*. Boston, MA: Little, Brown and Company.

Hell, Julia, and Andreas Schönle. 2010. Introduction, in *Ruins of Modernity*, ed. Julia Hell and Andreas Schönle, 1–15. Durham, NC: Duke University Press.

Homer. 2003. *Iliad*, trans. E.V. Rieu, rev. Peter Jones and D.C.H. Rieu. London: Penguin.

Malouf, David. 2010. UNSWriting Public Seminar. University of New South Wales, Apr 15. Available at: https://thebox.unsw.edu.au/video/unswriting-presents-david-malouf.

———. 2009a. Men and Gods Behaving Badly. *Australian*, Mar 4. Available at: http://www.theaustralian.com.au/arts/men-and-gods-behaving-badly/story-e6frg8px-1111118953999.

———. 2009b. Ransom. Sydney: Vintage.

Mendelsohn, Daniel. 2010. Epic Endeavours. *New York Times*, Apr 5. Available at: http://www.newyorker.com/magazine/2010/04/05/epic-endeavors.

Shakespeare, William. 1997. The Tragedy of King Lear: A Conflated Text. In *The Norton Shakespeare*, ed. Stephen Greenblatt et al, 2,479–2,554. New York: W.W. Norton.

Weil, Simone. 1965 (1939). The Iliad, or the Poem of Force, trans. Mary McCarthy, *Chicago Review*, 18 (2): 5–30.

Žižek, Slavoj. 2002. *Welcome to the Desert of the Real: Five Essays of September 11 and Related Dates*. New York: Verso.

AUTHOR BIOGRAPHY

Kezia Whiting is a Ph.D. student at the University at Buffalo. Her work focuses on narration and subjectivity in modernist literature. Her MPhil, on contemporary literature, was completed at the University of Queensland in 2013.

CHAPTER 8

In Extremis: Apocalyptic Imaginings in Janette Turner Hospital's Post-9/11 Novels

Belinda McKay

In Janette Turner Hospital's *Due Preparations for the Plague* (2003), a young woman who survived an act of terrorism in childhood reflects that

> …we are composed of a frail string of learned sequences (we recognise our own face in a mirror, we know our own name, we can put on our shoes without thinking, we know how to make love, and we know what to do—more or less—when we feel acute physical pain), and these pieces which make up the puzzle of the self are held together by the glue of memory. Certain solvents can dissolve this glue: a stroke, catastrophic events. Then we are forced to become scavengers of our own past, searching, finding, relearning, reassembling the self. (Turner Hospital 2003, p. 47)[1]

The instability of memory has been a constant preoccupation of Turner Hospital's fiction: David Callahan (1996, p. 73) has observed of her earlier work that it 'self-consciously privileges sites and moments of tension in which the operations of memory and its reconstructions are placed in

B. McKay (✉)
Griffith University, Brisbane, QLD, Australia
e-mail: b.mckay@griffith.edu.au

© The Author(s) 2017
J. Gildersleeve and R. Gehrmann (eds.), *Memory and the Wars on Terror*, Palgrave Macmillan Memory Studies,
DOI 10.1007/978-3-319-56976-5_8

question', and Selina Samuels (1996, p. 85) has explored the slippage between past and present in moments of crisis in her short stories. In two post-9/11 novels, terrorism and the Wars on Terror provide Turner Hospital with a new locus for exploring dissolutions and reconstructions of memory. *Due Preparations for the Plague,* which ends apocalyptically on the eve of 9/11, explores the collateral damage to the child survivors and families of victims caused by the hijacking of an Air France flight in 1987. In *Orpheus Lost* (2007), childhood trauma is re-enacted to disastrous effect by three central characters whose lives become entangled with America's Wars on Terror. Through the constant juxtapositioning and interpenetration of the microcosm and the macrocosm in these novels, post-9/11 modernity presents itself as an individual and collective psychopathology generated by living *in extremis.* Turner Hospital's own Pentecostal childhood has given her insight into the disintegrative effects on the psyche of living in the 'end time', but also—paradoxically—a heightened awareness of how that experience can open transformative possibilities for reintegrating the 'puzzle of the self'. In both novels, the creative inner process of 'reassembling the self' brings personal atonement for the central characters, and enables an ethical act of setting the record straight in the wider polity.

LIVING IN THE 'END TIME'

Turner Hospital's distinctive literary imagination, with its interest in the psychology of both the fanatic and the survivor, has been profoundly shaped by her early religious background. Born in Melbourne, Australia in 1942, she moved north to Brisbane at the age of seven with her devoutly Pentecostal family. The gospel church to which the Turners belonged had its immediate origins in the Welsh Revival of 1904–1905, which made 100,000 converts within a year and began a global evangelical outreach of a re-radicalised form of Methodism. Turner Hospital's father converted from Anglicanism to Pentecostalism during World War II: 'my father lonely in Melbourne and in the Air Force, with the war raging, walks into a little gospel church and suddenly feels that his life could be transformed and that he could feel it all had meaning'. Growing up in a Pentecostal household, however, revealed to Turner Hospital 'how quickly things that begin as liberating and empowering turn into their own systems of oppression and rigidity' (McKay 2004, p. 8). In the autobiographical story 'After Long Absence', the narrator recalls that her parents' refusal to allow their children to be vaccinated led her third-grade teacher to accuse her of being a 'religious fanatic' and a 'killer' (Turner Hospital 1995, p. 175) in front of the entire class. Although Turner Hospital chafed against the 'intellectual restrictions' of her Pentecostal upbringing, she recalls that the Bible taught her narrative pacing and that she received excellent training in rhetoric from the church's Welsh 'hellfire and brimstone preachers', who 'really had a sense of art' (Jorgensen 2010). Some reprieve from stultifying theological rigidity also came from other family members. Turner Hospital's maternal Morgan grandfather, who had 'a dramatic conversion on the Western Australian goldfields', was 'a born-again Christian to the core' but paradoxically with a 'pagan, Celtic, Welsh core'. Her paternal Turner grandfather, by contrast, was 'very English and classically trained... an intellectual' who told her stories from Greek and Roman mythology. She was able to study at the University of Queensland with her father's support, despite the opposition of the rest of the congregation, who argued that if young people went to university, they lost their faith. Turner Hospital admits to feeling 'slightly guilty' that they turned out to be right! (McKay 2004, pp. 6, 8, 9). Turner Hospital has spent most of her adult life as a writer and academic in Canada and the United States, and currently lives with her husband, Australian-born theologian Clifford Hospital, in Columbia, South Carolina.

Despite her early loss of faith, Turner Hospital is irritated by the glib dismissal of fundamentalism as a 'totally oppressive system' and keenly aware that initially it provides 'a form of empowerment to marginalised people' (p. 7). A consideration of the ecstatic aspects of religious sects like Pentecostalism, rather than simply their fundamentalism, is useful in the present context as it suggests some practices and features that adherents find particularly empowering and transformative. In addition to elements found broadly across all Protestant churches—including the internalisation of conscience and an emphasis on self-scrutiny—ecstatic versions of Protestantism share an emphasis on an emotional 'heart religion' where the body itself may become a site and sign of transformation through phenomena like quaking, shaking, or falling. The world inhabited by believers is replete with 'signs and wonders' to be interpreted as signifiers of God's plan for the individual or community. God also bestows spiritual gifts, or charisms, such as 'healings, helps, governments, diversities of tongues' (1 Corinthians 12:28). Glossolalia (speaking in tongues) has become central to Pentecostalism, deriving from the first Pentecost as recorded in Acts 2:2–2:4:

> And suddenly there came a sound from heaven as of a rushing mighty wind, and it filled all the house where they were sitting. And there appeared unto them cloven tongues like as of fire, and it sat upon each of them. And they were all filled with the Holy Ghost, and began to speak with other tongues, as the Spirit gave them utterance.

David Martin argues that for Pentecostalists, 'signs form part of a complete "field" which is integrated around the key notion of transformation' (1990, p. 163). Transformation occurs most dramatically in the conversion experience, the New Testament model for which is St Paul's conversion on the road to Damascus, as recorded in Acts 9.

In *The Rise of the Novel*, Ian Watt has demonstrated the extent to which the subjective, individualist, and introspective qualities of Protestantism contributed to the rise of the novel in the eighteenth century. His work also suggests that elements of Protestant belief and practice tend to migrate into new cultural domains, detaching themselves from the spiritual domain: 'we can say of [Defoe]', he writes, 'as of later novelists in the same tradition, such as Samuel Richardson, George Eliot or D.H. Lawrence, that they have inherited of Puritanism everything except its religious faith' (1957, p. 85). As a young adult, Turner Hospital distanced herself from the religious context of her childhood: she has not incorporated any conventional religious belief or practice into her adult life, and her physical migrations—to North America, but with periods in other countries, including India—have reinforced the inner movement from a somewhat circumscribed faith to broader spiritual and intellectual horizons. Nonetheless, following Watt, I suggest that *as a writer* she has inherited from her Protestant background everything except the religious faith. Like Defoe, Richardson, Blake, Eliot, and Lawrence—and, as I have argued elsewhere, the American modernist H.D. (McKay 2010)—Turner Hospital transposes key elements of her formative Protestant identity from the spiritual domain to the domain of the literary imagination. As she herself has observed (McKay 2004), her writing is about exploring 'transformative moments' and the role of the ecstatic impulse of her childhood religious experience lurks behind these literary moments.

However ambiguous and deceptive they may be, signs and wonders are the stuff of Turner Hospital's fiction, and are intimately linked to her vocation as a writer. This is perhaps most clearly articulated in the autobiographical short story 'Morgan Morgan'. Grandpa Morgan, a breeder of dahlias, is a Welshman and a Pentecostal convert. He introduces his granddaughter to a world of signs and wonders, promiscuously blurring the distinction between the worldly and the spiritual, and causing Grandma Morgan to observe that the child will 'never know the difference between truth and lies' (Turner Hospital 1995, p. 167). Reminiscing about his experiences on the goldfields before his conversion, he recounts his blinding Pauline vision of finding a nugget as big as a man's fist and tells his granddaughter: 'I...put it right back down where I found it, inside the vision' (p. 164). Like Paul, who was blinded for three days after his vision of Christ (Acts 9), Morgan Morgan is nearly blinded when sunlight strikes the nugget. By such signs he has come to see himself as a man of destiny, and he tells his granddaughter that the Morgan nugget is waiting 'for one of us to find it again' (Turner Hospital 1995, p. 165). In the story, he passes on this sense of destiny or spiritual giftedness to his granddaughter, who will find the nugget again through writing. On Sundays in the gospel church, the Spirit is a wind which '[blusters] and [rushes] through' Grandpa Morgan, causing him to shout '*hallelujah*' and sending 'seismic' shocks through the man in the pew in front of him:

> The shock waves hit Mr. Peabody sharply in the nape of his neck and travelled down his spine with such force that he would rise an inch or two from the pew. Most of his body would go rigid, but his head and his hands would quiver for seconds at a time, Glory, glory he would murmur in a terror-stricken prayerful voice.

Not surprisingly, it is here in the chapel that the narrator has her first ecstatic experience:

> But then came the day that a shaft of sunlight fell from a high amberglass window in the church and placed a crown of gold on Mr. Peabody's head. 'Oh!', I gasped aloud. '*Look!*' And Grandpa shouted *Hallelujah!* And Mr. Peabody rose up into his corona like a skyrocket and I saw a million doves and the gilded petals of all the dahlias in the world rising up into the pointed arch in which God lived. (pp. 169–170; original emphases)

Initially the pastor is convinced that the young girl has seen the Holy Spirit, but not everybody is so sure: "'She makes things up", my Sunday School teacher insisted. "She handles the truth very carelessly. She believes her own lies"' (p. 170).

The scepticism of the Sunday School teacher destabilises the narrator's belief in her vision, despite Grandpa Morgan's reassurance that she did indeed see doves with gold wings. He also reassures her that the story of the Morgan nugget is true, but the narrator has been awakened not simply to the power of transformation but also to the ambiguity and deceptiveness of signs: an irrevocable break in faith accompanies the awareness that not all ecstatic visions originate from God. In 'Morgan Morgan', Turner Hospital reveals to her readers the moment at which signs and wonders become dislocated from the Pentecostal spiritual context, and spill into the secular domain of the creative imagination. The consolation implicit in the story is that an ecstatic revelation can be experienced by 'making things up'. 'Morgan Morgan' is a parable of how Turner Hospital became a writer. Indeed, she has revealed that in 'the dramatic and intense moment of conception of my novels...I feel a bit like Saint Paul being blinded and stunned on the road to Damascus' ('A Conversation').

A second area where Turner Hospital reveals her debt to the ecstatic dimension of Protestantism is in her literary response to the problem of living in apocalyptic times. Pentecostalism promotes a sense that believers are living in the 'last days': in other words, that they occupy a liminal space of heightened awareness, and exist in a state of 'becoming'. In an interview, Turner Hospital recalls her childhood experience of living in the end time:

> When you grow up in a fundamentalist world you actually grow up in a mythic narrative space because everything in the Old Testament has immediate relevance and you read it at the dinner table, so in a way you grow up in timeless space. You grow up with a 'God's eye' view of time because you always know that the Second Coming could be tomorrow or next week. Every Sunday you are told that you are living in the end time. There's always this feeling that at any moment God is going to put mankind to account.... (cited in McKay 2004, p. 7)

Living in the end time, or *in extremis*, is an experience to which she returns frequently in her writing. In her story 'After Long Absence', the protagonist/narrator gives a powerful impression of what it is like to live in a house where 'nothing has ever been secular': as the mother washes the dishes in 'water just on the leeside of boiling', the narrator glances at the Biblical text in needlepoint on the wall, '*He shall try you in a refiner's fire*' (McKay 1995, pp. 172, 173; original emphasis). This allusion to Malachi 3:1–3:3 reminds us of the need to be prepared for the arrival of the 'messenger of the covenant': 'But who may abide the day of his coming? and who shall stand when he appeareth? for he is like a refiner's fire, and like fullers' soap'. The New Testament version of the Second Coming, however, emphasises the spiritual gifts that will be bestowed on believers:

> And it shall come to pass in the last days, saith God, I will pour out of my Spirit upon all flesh: and your sons and your daughters shall prophesy, and your young men shall see visions, and your old men shall dream dreams.... (Acts 2:17)

Prophesies, visions, and dreams—the stuff of ecstatic Protestantism—are equally the stuff of literature. As Callahan has argued, Janette Turner Hospital's work exemplifies existence as interpretation: 'From family history and academic training, Hospital has been exposed to a view of reality as having been written by God, in which nothing and no possible connection can be without significance, for how could God create anything that was meaningless or insignificant?' (2009, p. 10) When contemplating how the human spirit can survive cataclysmic events, Janette Turner Hospital returns to hermeneutic habits acquired in her childhood of scrutinising the self and the world, interpreting the signs, preparing oneself, seeing visions, and prophesying.

DUE PREPARATIONS FOR THE PLAGUE

Due Preparations for the Plague, which traces the effects on survivors of an act of terrorism, was begun before September 11, 2001, but completed after. The title of the novel is borrowed from that earlier Protestant writer and plague survivor, Daniel Defoe, whose treatise *Due Preparations for the Plague, As Well for Soul As Body* (1722) has been described by Turner Hospital as 'a how-to-survive manual for use if the plague reached English shores again…a kind of Red Alert of the kind now issued by the Department of Homeland Security' (Turner Hospital

2004, P.S. p. 8). Drawing on this treatise and a prophetic literary tradition that deals with human beings confronting almost certain death—the Essene Gospels, Defoe's *A Journal of the Plague Year*, Boccaccio's *Decameron*, and Camus's *The Plague*—Turner Hospital is exploring whether it is possible to make 'due preparations' for a cataclysmic event such as an act of terrorism.

Powerful invisible forces shape human lives in *Due Preparations for the Plague*. Two intelligence agents, an Arab and an American, both have codenames beginning with 'S'. Sirocco and Salamander—'split selves, Siamesed' (Turner Hospital 2003, p. 219)—epitomise the labile, deceptive quality of signs in Turner Hospital's fictional world: while their code names and attributes suggest that they are spirit messengers in some sense, it is unclear whether the destruction that they wreak in any way serves to purify their victims into an 'offering in righteousness' (Malachi 3:3), or whether, in the (post)modern world, all messengers are fallen angels. Sirocco is 'the desert wind that scorches where it blows' (Turner Hospital 2003, p. 301)—an equivocal association with the Pentecostal 'rushing mighty wind' which brings 'cloven tongues like as of fire' (Acts 2:2–2:3). The American agent Salamander, named for the mythical Luciferian creature who can survive flames, attempts to channel the 'madness of true believers' such as Sirocco 'in the interests of global stability for the greater good of all' (Turner Hospital 2003, p. 226). Ironically, it is Salamander, through a counter-terrorist initiative code-named 'Operation Black Death', who unwittingly sets in motion the chain of events that leads to the hijacking in 1987 of Air France flight 64 and the killing of all passengers except the children. American intelligence services initiate a cover-up to obliterate the evidence of their involvement, and in the process further traumatise the children by denying them the truth of their own past.

Thirteen years after the hijacking, fragmentary pieces of evidence about Operation Black Death begin to resurface. Making contact with each other via the Web, the child survivors—whose psychological instability and addiction to risk are manifestations of survivor syndrome—form the Phoenix Club to share shards of memory and other information about the catastrophe which destabilized their very identities. At least two child survivors and Salamander himself die in mysterious circumstances, and Salamander's widow disappears, but as the name 'Phoenix Club' suggests, the survivors seek to be reborn out of the ashes of AF 64. Gradually, with the help of Salamander's American son and illegitimate French daughter, 19-year-old Samantha Raleigh pieces together the mystery of AF 64 from intelligence files, recollections, phone transcripts, newscasts, video-tapes, and an encrypted journal—the process she describes as 'becoming scavengers of our own past, searching, finding, relearning, reassembling the self'. Since there are gaps in the record, the reassembly of the self is an active and creative process, in which Samantha becomes, to borrow from psychoanalyst Adam Phillips (1996, p. 12), 'the artist of [her] own life'. Just as, according to Phillips, the dream functions in psychoanalysis 'more as a hint than an instruction, setting the dreamer and the child off on the work of inner transformation', Samantha achieves that inner transformation by her imaginative reconstruction of memory—picking up on hints, making associations, filling in gaps, and reading beyond the letter to the spirit.

The Pentecostal habit of reading the signs written onto the world is brought here into a contemporary context where surveillance is ubiquitous, but generates only fragmented and deceptive information that eludes meaning. The novel also intersects with contemporary concerns in its interest in the use of sub-rational ways of knowing and of responding to crises in espionage. The CIA agent Salamander recommends the deliberate cultivation of a practice that induces the radiant calm of religious believers in the face of death:

Do with this secret what you will. When *in extremis,* close eyes, open mind, step out into uncharted abysses of your own memory and imagination, open parachute, create a floating world, explore in tunnels and byways, stay there until All Clear sounds. (Turner Hospital 2003, p. 262)

One of the most chilling and disturbing aspects of the novel is Turner Hospital's insight into the ways in which spiritual exercises developed in various traditions are taken up by CIA agents and terrorists alike, and prove to be remarkably effective in empowering them to carry out ruthless acts of destruction.

In *Due Preparations for the Plague,* Turner Hospital turns to the past as a way of understanding catastrophic events, and of preparing oneself—to the extent that preparation is possible—for the next crisis. The epigraph to the novel, taken from Defoe's treatise of the same title, alerts the reader that 'preparations for the plague are preparations for death', and the novel ends apocalyptically in a stroke of dramatic irony. Samantha Raleigh has released to the press the dossier that exposes the lies and reveals the truth about the Air France hijacking, and now the final piece of the puzzle of her personal history (that her aunt is actually her mother) is revealed in the safe haven of the graveyard behind St Paul's Chapel, the oldest extant church in Manhattan. Located opposite the eastern side of the World Trade Center, the Chapel will in a few days' time survive the attack on the Twin Towers without so much as a broken window—just as St Paul's Cathedral in London famously survived the World War II German air attack. The reader's knowledge of the future renders Samantha's questions, which conclude the novel, especially poignant: '[H]ow do we ready ourselves for what might happen tomorrow? What possible preparations can be made?' (p. 390) The novel's response is that although each crisis is different, and individual survival cannot be ensured, a prophetic literary tradition born of earlier cataclysms in human history ensures that the truth will endure. Salamander in his civilian identity as Mather Lowell Hawthorne (whose overdetermined name itself points to the American Protestant literary tradition) tells his son:

> Think of it, Lowell...a message sent through twenty centuries of time. What does that tell us about the desperation and faith of the Essenes?...It tells us that the truth will endure, Lowell. Even if you kill the messenger, it tells us, a dangerous message can hide and bide its time until the message can safely be read. (p. 175)

Although Samantha's documentation of the true story of the hijacking is dismissed in the United States as 'just another crackpot conspiracy theory thing', she takes comfort in the fact that the truth '*is* out there now' on the Web, and in the British and French press.

For Turner Hospital, the 'burning question' that generated *Due Preparations* was: 'how do we protect ourselves against terrorism? And also, why terrorism? Why is it so inevitable that foreign policy makes these decisions in the short term that mean that far greater problems will come and haunt you?' (Sullivan 2003) In interviews, she has deplored the short-term expediency of American foreign policy which is exemplified by the support initially given to Osama bin Laden and Saddam Hussein (see, for example, Hall 2003), but in the fictional world the stakes are raised by drawing parallels with past civilizations. In coming to terms with his role in Operation Black Death, Salamander identifies with Scipio Aemilianus, who—invoking Hector's prophecy for Troy in

The Iliad—foresaw that one day Rome would suffer the same fate he was inflicting on Carthage: 'And so I too, Salamander—like Scipio—came by degrees to Carthage, burning, burning, burning…and night after night from the middle of the furnace of Carthage and of Flight 64, Scipio turns to me and cries: O Salamander, how do we tell a glorious victory from horror?' (Turner Hospital 2003, p. 244)

Orpheus Lost

Turner Hospital's second post-9/11 novel, *Orpheus Lost,* takes the reader into the Wars on Terror and back to Vietnam and the Holocaust through the framework of a Greek myth with a long literary pedigree— the descent of Orpheus into the Underworld. The novel shifts focus from the psychological fallout of an act of terrorism to the ways in which three survivors of childhood domestic trauma find themselves re-enacting past traumas during the Wars on Terror, when surveillance produces misunderstandings that have disastrous outcomes. Leela Moore, Cobb Slaughter, and Mishka Bartok have all lost a parent, and are formed psychologically in a 'timeless space' reminiscent of Turner Hospital's Pentecostalist childhood. Leela grows up in the Pentecostal Church Triumphal of Tongues of Fire; in the 'Slaughter house', Cobb lives in constant terror of the 'werewolf moment' which will unleash the violence of his Vietnam veteran father; a poignant family deception consigns Mishka to live in the 'not-here and not-now', so that 'it might never be possible for him to be certain of what was real and what was not' (Turner Hospital 2007, p. 182). The intersection of the three lives in Boston during the Wars on Terror sets up a 'strange loop' in which the past and the present become entangled in a form of static that can only be unscrambled by returning to, and reinterpreting, the original layer or starting point (pp. 63, 303).

A profoundly traumatising event plays a crucial role in the psychosexual development of each of these three characters, signalling the irrevocable loss of prelapsarian innocence. As a five-year-old, Leela watches a primal scene of tender lovemaking between her father and heavily pregnant mother. She becomes 'strangely excited and frightened'; touching herself, she 'imagine[s] Cobb kissing her there' (pp. 346, 347). When her mother dies in childbirth shortly afterwards, Leela blames her act of voyeurism. Increasingly alienated from her father Gideon, who is *'held together with duct tape and the Bible and magic numbers and us* [his daughters]' (p. 131; original emphasis), Leela becomes addicted to indiscriminate promiscuity as a means of reliving this volatile mix of loss, guilt, and desire: 'She wanted Cobb, but would settle for almost any boy. She always pulled them down. She always had a mad itch between her legs and she always wanted someone's mouth or someone's prick to ease it' (p. 347).

Seven-year-old Cobb finds his mother's body hanging by a sheet from a ceiling fan 'like a fish on a hook' (p. 102), and is left to face his father's violence alone. The loss of dignity that he experiences when Leela sees him cry for his mother is reactivated on his twelfth birthday when Leela watches Calhoun Cobb break his son's thumb, leaving him with a cleft nail: '*Mark of the Beast*, ran the schoolyard murmur. Cobb's got a cloven paw'. When Leela sends him a sand dollar as a protective charm, Cobb is simultaneously 'ridiculously comforted' and 'ashamed', and his love-hate is intensified later by having to share Leela with other boys. (pp. 48–49) In his adult sex life, the sand dollar becomes a fetish in a sexual ritual which memorialises his mother's suicide, his father's violence, and his love-hate for Leela. He places the sand dollar under the pillow while having 'acrobatic and slightly violent' sex with women (preferably black) that he carefully selects from the clientele of dark bars, then before leaving requests 'something personal, a little kinky, a little odd' in return for a doubling of the fee:

> The role-playing involved a chair, a sheet, and the ceiling fan. Part of the task belonged to Cobb. He would twist the sheet into a rope and sling it over a blade of the fan. He would knot the rope around the woman's neck. She was then required to stand on the chair. 'I'll leave the money on the bed,' he would say. He was generous. 'Best if you don't move,' he would say, 'until someone comes. I'll send the manager up.' He would exit the room and leave the woman standing naked on the chair. (p. 231)

Violinist Mishka Bartok grows up with his Jewish mother, Auschwitz-survivor grandparents, and reclusive great-uncle Otto—a violin virtuoso of the 1930s—in the North Queensland rainforest in a house 'with turrets and minarets and gables', which is mockingly dubbed Chateau Daintree or Reffo Castle by the locals (p. 22). Like the rainforest that buffers them from the outside world, the family is saturated with loss so painful that it can only be expressed in music, never in words. At one with nature and nurtured musically by his grandfather, Mishka lives in 'paradise' until at school he learns that other children have fathers (pp. 24, 174). Unable to express in words 'the great bruise inside him, the hole where his father should have been', he adopts Orpheus's lament from Gluck's *Orpheus and Eurydice* as his musical code for loss. The words 'Che farò senza Euridice?' (What shall I do without Eurydice?) speak to him as '*What shall I do without my father?*' (p. 175; original emphasis). Sublimating loss into music is a coping mechanism that Mishka has imbibed from birth. Every night, the family listens with rapt attention to Uncle Otto giving an after-dinner violin recital from behind his closed bedroom door until one day Mishka's schoolmate Tony Cavalari opens Uncle Otto's door and reveals a room empty of everything but photographs. That night, Mishka 'listened to the loudest silence he had ever heard' (p. 178): 'He had a sensation of falling the way a shot parrot falls, falling into the river and on down through the river bed and down and down below it to where a vast underground cavern opened up and he felt that his falling would go on and on without end' (p. 179). Not until Mishka is 18 years old does Devorah Bartok explain that her father was never able to speak about his brother's death in a concentration camp: 'It seemed to get more and more painful over time, and then one day he simply un-made the past' (p. 180). Devorah, who has attempted to un-make her own painful past, also reveals that Mishka's father was a Lebanese Muslim oud player, Marwan Rahal Abukir, whom she believes to be dead.

When these survivors of turbulent childhoods are brought together in Boston during the Wars on Terror, the outcome is inexorably predetermined. The novel opens *in media res* with a hermeneutical conundrum:

> Afterwards, Leela realized, everything could have been predicted from the beginning. Every clue was there, the ending inevitable and curled up inside the first encounter like a tree inside a seed. The trouble was that the interpretation was obvious only in retrospect. (p. 3)

Leela—a post-doc researching the mathematics of music—hears composition student Mishka playing Gluck's lament in the subway, and instantly falls in love with the intense young man who reminds her of Cobb (pp. 7–8). Despite their passionate and apparently committed relationship, the enigmatic Mishka Bartok disappears after every terrorist attack in Boston, and it transpires that he lives a parallel life as Mikael Abukir, an oud player who is a member of a Muslim Youth Association and frequents a local mosque. Searching for 'nuggets of his father', Mishka is befriended by a fanatical fellow student, Jamil Haddad, and is drawn 'like an addict' into a circle of jihadists who reveal that his father (whom he believes to be dead) has become 'a fanatic and a terrorist' (p. 217). When Jamil carries out a suicide bombing on the Boston subway, Leela is illegally abducted and subjected to a chilling off-the-record interrogation by Cobb Slaughter. Formerly a code-breaker with the rank of Major in the US Special Forces but now running a private security force, Cobb has had Leela under close surveillance for years and her relationship with Mishka now provides him with the opportunity to make her 'know fear the way he did' (p. 38). Cobb's pretext for the interrogation is that Leela's mathematical transcriptions of Mishka's musical compositions might be coded terrorist messages, but he is also punishing Leela for childhood crimes by using her to feed his addiction to 'switch-flow', an adrenalin rush in which there is a reverse flow of energies: he chalks up a victory—and ejaculates—when he becomes 'soaked with her power' and she becomes 'flooded with his anxiety' (p. 59).

With each of the main characters re-enacting raw childhood trauma in a climate of paranoia about homeland security, the catastrophic entanglement of their personal lives with the Wars on Terror is inevitable. Because Leela fails to warn her lover that he is under surveillance, Mishka becomes the unwitting 'bait' to catch a whale when he travels to Lebanon on a false passport to meet his father. Cobb—with the mixed motives of 'forestalling acts of mayhem' but also of 'making Leela understand the gross errors in the choices she had made'—arranges for the kidnapping and detention of both men in Beirut, then their extraordinary rendition to Baghdad (p. 239). As a known terrorist, Marwan Rahal Abukir is to be transferred to US Military Intelligence, while Cobb himself intends to interrogate the enigmatic Mishka. Cobb's plans go awry when both men are seized and 'ghosted' by American Special Forces. Mishka is outsourced to Iraqi militia and subjected to torture by the strappado: hooded and hanged behind his back by his wrists, 'he felt his wing tendons giving way' (p. 254). In the underworld of a ghost prison, his pain-induced hallucinatory 'confessions' scramble memory and myth until he breaks through into a state of psychotic euphoria where 'he was in the absolute radiant embrace of the sun and the music of the spheres was all around him and he felt no pain at all' (p. 257).

Leela and Devorah Bartok's failure to rescue Mishka through diplomatic and human rights channels underlines the novel's preoccupation with war as a problem of masculinity that must in the end be solved by men. Leela makes Cobb aware that he is the only person who can right the personal wrong that he set in motion, but he can only do that by undergoing an inner transformation: 'Atonement. That was what he was hungry for' (p. 345). At the site of the original trauma, Promised Land, his understanding of what happened in his childhood is reshaped by new information from his father. Although Calhoun Slaughter was wrongly accused of committing a war crime in Vietnam, he has been hiding a 'fuckin' great boulder of guilt' because on a separate occasion he was unintentionally responsible for the deaths of thirteen Vietnamese children (p. 326). Cobb's birth intensified Calhoun's guilt and self-loathing, and later he drove his wife to suicide by demanding that she abort the second child she was carrying. Intuiting that Cobb too is burdened by unspoken guilt, Calhoun encourages him to 'fix it' rather than do nothing. In an allusion to the 2003 Abu Ghraib scandal, Cobb clears his conscience by sending photographs of Iraqi prisoners being tortured to the press before flying to Baghdad to rescue Mishka on what he knows is a suicide mission. Operation Underworld is Cobb's final act of atonement: in rescuing Mishka, he symbolically revisits his discovery of his mother's hanged body, and at the same time exposes to the world the existence of a secret torture centre used by rogue Iraqi militia groups. In a final token of reconciliation and love, he bequeaths the sand dollar to Leela.

The trichotomous structure of *Orpheus Lost* (three protagonists, three fathers, three Abrahamic religious traditions) effects a triangulation of psychological coordinates to suggest that loss and trauma operate in similar ways across cultures and generations to create misunderstandings which have tragic consequences for individuals and societies. Turner Hospital continues her longstanding reticence about speaking for 'someone quite "other"' (Baker 1987, p. 257) in her contained depiction of Marwan Rahal Abukir. Nonetheless, Abukir's triangulation with Gideon Moore and Calhoun Slaughter suggests that the trauma of being forced by his family to abandon Devorah and her unborn child triggers his transition from musician and lover to recruiter of suicide bombers. Like Gideon and Calhoun, he retreats from unbearable emotion into absolute certainties which obliterate historical contingency and the memory of loss. Music, Marwan tells Mishka, 'is like the sexual power of a woman. It is evil because man has no resistance against it. It must be crushed before it destroys' (Turner Hospital 2007, p. 256). Ironically, it is an America intelligence officer's misreading of music as a terrorist code that nearly crushes Mishka/Orpheus. The novel offers a prophetic warning that the threat from within lies less with terrorism itself than with flawed responses like ubiquitous surveillance and brutalizing practices which dehumanize both victim and perpetrator.

'Do with this Secret What You Will'

Turner Hospital's two novels about terrorism and the Wars on Terror are densely allusive, syncretistic, and self-referential works which forge links between different times and places through palimpsest and myth, drawing on extant traces of past prophecy to renew prophecy in the post-9/11 world. In a world more than ever filled with misinformation and disinformation, the writer-prophet turns to history and myth to provide orientation for individuals living through cataclysmic upheaval. In *Due Preparations for the Plague*, the past—as both individual memory and collective history—holds messages for us, if only we are capable of interpreting them. In *Orpheus Lost*, Turner Hospital explores the post-9/11 American experience of prosecuting wars abroad while—for the first time—being simultaneously under attack from within. Living *in extremis* reactivates unresolved personal and historical traumas, setting up a 'strange loop' in which the characters endlessly repeat the past like a form of static. A hermeneutical conundrum lies at the heart both novels: surveillance and recording are ubiquitous in the modern world, but asking the wrong questions produces only false answers. Only the individual with a conscience can challenge this self-replicating machine. Always at risk of psychological disintegration, Turner Hospital's protagonists must effect an inner transformation by scavenging for the truth, reassembling the self and taking responsibility for interpretation: only then can they have an ethical engagement with each other and the wider polity. Following Defoe (1895, p. 19), Turner Hospital's post-9/11 novels are a call to a world confronting terrorism to make preparations 'as well for soul as body' and avoid 'shedding innocent blood, which is a kind of evil not to be done that good may come'.

Note

1. Parts of this chapter were originally published in Belinda McKay (2010), 'Living in the End Time: Ecstasy and Apocalypse in the Work of H.D. and Janette Turner Hospital', *Queensland Review*, vol. 17, no. 2, pp. 75–87.

WORKS CITED

A Conversation with Janette Turner Hospital. nd, *W.W. Norton Reading Group Guide to* Due Preparations for the Plague. Available from: http://books. wwnorton.com/books/readingguidesdetail.aspx?id=13698. 13 Jan 2016.

Baker, Candida. 1987. *Yacker 2: Australian Writers Talk About Their Work.* Sydney: Picador.

Callahan, David. 1996. Acting in the Public Sphere and the Politics of Memory in Janette Turner Hospital. *Tulsa Studies in Women's Literature* 15 (1): 73–81.

———. 2009. *Rainforest Narratives: The Work of Janette Turner Hospital.* St Lucia: University of Queensland Press.

Defoe, Daniel. 1895 [1722]. *Due Preparations for the Plague, As Well for Soul as Body,* ed. George Atherton Aitken. London: Dent. Available at: http://hdl. handle.net/2027/hvd.hwpwiu.

Hall, Eleanor. 2003. Book *Due Preparation* [sic] *for the Plague* Explores Death, Terrorism, *The World Today,* 21 May 2003. Available from: http://www.abc. net.au/worldtoday/content/2003/s860328.htm.

Jorgensen, Cheryl. 2010. Interview with Janette Turner Hospital. *Hecate* 36 (1/2): 186–196.

Martin, David. 1990. *Tongues of Fire: The Explosion of Protestantism in Latin America.* Cambridge: MA, Blackwell.

McKay, Belinda. 2004. Transformative Moments: An Interview with Janette Turner Hospital. *Queensland Review* 11 (2): 1–10.

———. 2010. Living in the End Time: Ecstasy and Apocalypse in the Work of H.D. and Janette Turner Hospital. *Queensland Review* 17 (2): 75–87.

Phillips, Adam. 1996. On Interest. *London Review of Books* 18 (12): 12–14.

Samuels, Selina. 1996. Dislocation and Memory in the Short Stories of Janette Turner Hospital. *Journal of Modern Literature* 20 (1): 85–95.

Sullivan, Jane. 2003. The Thrills in Turner Hospital. *The Age,* May 31: 3.

Turner Hospital, Janette. 1995. *Collected Stories: 1970–1995.* St Lucia: University of Queensland Press.

———. 2003. *Due Preparations for the Plague.* Pymble: Fourth Estate.

———. 2004. *Due Preparations for the Plague.* Pymble: Harper Perennial.

———. 2007. *Orpheus Lost.* New York: W.W. Norton.

Watt, Ian. 1957. *The Rise of the Novel: Studies in Defoe, Richardson and Fielding.* Berkeley: University of California Press.

AUTHOR BIOGRAPHY

Belinda McKay publishes in the fields of Australian literary and cultural history and Anglo-American modernism. She was a founding co-editor of *Queensland Review*, and with Patrick Buckridge, she co-edited *By the Book: A Literary History of Queensland*, which was published by the University of Queensland Press in 2007. After teaching literary studies for 25 years, she is now a research fellow in the School of Humanities, Languages and Social Science at Griffith University in Brisbane, Australia.

CHAPTER 9

'Shock and Awe': The Memory of Trauma in Post-9/11 Artworks

Denise N. Rall

Artists have memorialised war since 'time immemorial' but the collisions between artists and war did not begin with the modern era. This chapter reconsiders the various ways that anti-war artists have reframed public conceptions of war, heroism, loss, and pain. War memorials and protest artworks in Australia and the United States are reevaluated here through an exploration of how the evocation of trauma is activated within public and private memories. The mechanisms of trauma, including post-traumatic stress disorder (PTSD), are often considered a private concern. A better understanding of how trauma works in public or collective memory will elucidate how a few anti-war artists have found traction for eliciting protest in their post-9/11 artworks. Anne Bogart suggests that 'it is only in a crisis that art is found', and cites novelist Toni Morrison, who explains that 'the best art [is] political and [is] revolutionary. It doesn't mean that art has an agenda or a politics to argue; it means the questions being raised were explorations into kinds of anarchy, kinds of change, identifying errors, flaws, vulnerabilities in systems' (2007, p. 1). The ongoing commemorations of 9/11 anniversary events in the US and

D.N. Rall (✉)
Southern Cross University, Lismore, Australia
e-mail: denise.rall@scu.edu.au

© The Author(s) 2017
J. Gildersleeve and R. Gehrmann (eds.), *Memory and the Wars on Terror*, Palgrave Macmillan Memory Studies,
DOI 10.1007/978-3-319-56976-5_9

throughout the world will continue to challenge artists to reconceptualise issues that arise from the Wars on Terror, including social injustice, the powerlessness of women and children, the world's refugee crises, and the difficulties of all civilians residing in war zones. This chapter argues that artists need to continue their work and reclaim public memories against the dominance of the media conglomerates during these anniversary events.

Societies both ancient and modern created artefacts to record the events of war (the exceptions are those whose religious practices forbid the depiction of human figures). Images of warfare include historical records that range from Egyptian hieroglyphics, to the battles in the carvings at Angkor Watt, to Greek and Roman vases, and the Bayeux Tapestry. Further, glorification of military heroes are found in centrally located statuary in most European cities (and elsewhere). Artists illustrated the themes of war through sumptuous uniforms or references to mythical warriors (such as Mars or Hercules) in portraitures of noble figures in the eighteenth and nineteenth centuries. In the First and Second World Wars, images of troops and their battles flooded the public arena through newspaper, photography, and film, where heroic aspects were freely added as propaganda in newsreels and posters. In the twentieth century, post-war monolithic statues from Lenin to Saddam Hussein joined past military heroes to feature prominently in civic centres. The symbolism attached to the heroic solder has continued into the twenty-first century through the exaggerated shape of buffed male soldiers' bodies (Smith and Gehrmann 2014). It is evident that these public images have shaped both individual and public memories regarding heroism and war.

Notions of heroism changed during the Vietnam War era as shocked public reactions to images from photography, television, and newspapers integrated with international counterculture movements in the 1960s, and artists often joined anti-war protests (Arlen 1997). Later, anti-war protests were seen as unpatriotic after the 9/11 attacks in the United States. This chapter offers a few modalities for artists who engaged in social activism and shows how the mechanisms of post-traumatic stress disorder evoke various disruptions and fragmentations of memories as artists locate their works as 'sites of trauma' (Adamson 2013, p. 226). This new aesthetic, as exemplified in the Vietnam War memorial in Washington, D.C., has developed 'a contested form of remembrance' (Sturken 2002, p. 356). Several post-9/11 artists in Australia and in the US have taken up the mechanisms associated with trauma in various modes of expression outside previous engagement with social activism. These artworks evoke trauma, both privately and publicly, as a route to challenge the mainstream collective memory of war in order to nurture the possibilities of broader public anti-war engagement.

MEMORIES OF THE PAST, REACTIVATED

In the battle for 'public hearts and minds' during the Iraq War campaign, Pablo Picasso's famous painting of the village of Guernica came alive again. Picasso (1881–1973) is remembered as the master of cubism and an innovator who changed the very vernacular of painting through his prodigious and inventive artworks. He also produced one of the world's most famous anti-war paintings, *Guernica* (1937). Rather than a military battle, *Guernica* is a gruesome depiction of a small Basque village after aerial bombardment by German forces during the Spanish Civil War. These hapless civilians and the tortured head of a horse are betrayed by their presence in a global conflict in which they played no part. *Guernica* becomes linked to the Iraq War following the 9/11 bombings because a tapestry reproduction of the original painting hangs in the United Nations building in New York City (see Fig. 1.1).

However, when the Secretary of State, Colin Powell, presented his case for the declaration of war against Iraq, the anti-war tapestry was covered (see Walsh 2003). While the UN official policy responded that the tapestry was often covered by a plain wall hanging to facilitate television coverage during some events, the fact remains that this particular piece of art, with its graphic depictions of screaming bodies of men, women, and children, and centrally, an enormous gored horse, could not be considered a 'good look' as a backdrop for Powell's call to war on Iraq. Further, images from *Guernica* remain in the canon of protest: Richard Notkin includes, in a small ceramic tile, Picasso's grimacing horse's head within a larger piece of work (2007, p. 27). In this way, images from the past become recirculated in the public's memory as undercurrents to present-day anti-war artworks.

Fig. 1.1   *Guernica.* Pablo Picasso. 1937. Oil on canvas. Held in the Museo Reina Sofia, Madrid, Spain. Wikipedia Commons: https://en.wikipedia.org/wiki/File:PicassoGuernica.jpg. A woven reproduction of the painting, *The Rockefeller Guernica*, hangs in the United Nations building in New York City. The hanging is dated 1937 for Picasso's original painting in addition to the tapestry date of 1955. The mark of the weavers' studio is detailed on the *left*—a C (Cavalaire) with an A (Atelier). At the *bottom* of the label is the name of the lead weaver, J. de la Baume Durrbach (Ashmore 2016)

THE SOCIAL TURN, SOCIAL ACTIVISM IN THREE MODALITIES

From the 1990s onwards, the Wars on Terror took centre stage in the media. As Toni Morrison stated, contemporary artworks often contain a critical core even if not overtly part of an anti-war protest, such those with environmental and human rights concerns. Social critique through critical and participatory artworks is part of a process called the 'social turn' that many critics date from the protests of the Vietnam War era, but could equally find its roots in Dadaism and elsewhere. The sociologist Claire Bishop explains how the 'social turn' raises the tension between 'truth-content of images and the purposes to which they are put—in other words, their effects and means' (2012, pp. 28–29). However, rather than re-cloaking anti-war artworks as allied to propaganda, Bishop takes this dichotomy as a positive contradiction in 'art's relationship to social change': art is considered simultaneously autonomous and yet bound to the 'promise of a better world to come' (p. 29). The 'social turn' is first employed here to explore the connection between artists, workers and political protest.

Art on Strike: Workers Unite

All artwork indicates something, whether discursive or conceptual, through an 'active exploration' of the artist's world that can be expressed in poetic, psychological, or political terms (Adamson 2013, p. 163). Anti-war art, or protest art, falls largely into the category of the political. The Vietnam War era, along with the global protest movements of Paris in 1968, offered the modality of expression as that of 'students and workers united'. In this environment, if artworks did not function as works of protest, they were classed as illegitimate or co-opted by 'dominant paradigm' of the military-industrial complex.

The 1960s anti-war protest movement, while sincere in its efforts to end the war in Vietnam, also served as a smokescreen that masked the oncoming global 'industrial revolution' which moved manufacturing into the developing world, leaving unemployed factory workers in the former industrial centres (Klein 2001). This second revolution deconstructed the industrial core and subsequent economies of the ore-based industries of both the US and the UK and gave rise to the policies of deregulation associated with Ronald Reagan and Margaret Thatcher (Klein 2001). Often, 1960s protest commentary has emphasised the 'outlaw' role of the various protest movements, from the music of Woodstock to Hell's Angels bikers in San Francisco, forming an alliance of 'drugs, sex, and rock 'n roll'. Workers and students did not agree on the role the revolution would take against the 'military-industrial complex' as globalised trade agreements came into force and trade unions continued to be marginalised (Maddison 2001). Student protest was also powerless against changes in the education system, represented by the storming of X Nantere and the Sorbonne in Paris 1968 after free tertiary education for students was replaced with capitalist models (see Kurlansky 2005).

Therefore, the underlying connections between student protest against the Vietnam War and the eroding industrial base of manufacturing in the developed world have not been taken up as relevant. Indeed, Julia Bryan-Wilson points out that

> In the late 1960s and early 1970s, the concept of 'art worker' provided a flexible, if unstable and frequently contradictory, identity for artists and critics...[I]t furnished artists a framework in which to understand their production as politically meaningful, even vital, during a time in which the

meanings and values of '*work*' and who counted as '*workers*' were undergoing massive transformations. (2009, p. 217; emphasis added)

The model of trade unionism became important for a group of the most radical artists of the day, and coalesced into a political movement in New York City. In 1970, the New York Art Strike galvanized 500 artists to leaflet the city with their protests and to go on strike until their claims to 'free artistic expression' (more specifically, the desire to be freed from capitalist interventions) were met. Only nine years later there was a second call for New York artists to resist oppression, provoking criticism from one of the early loyalists: 'From whom would artists be withholding their art if they did go on strike? Alas, from no one but themselves' (cited in Dordević 1979).

While this is not an exhaustive survey of the potential for a 'strike mentality' among artists who protest war and other issues of social unrest (for example, the treatment of asylum seekers), it brings forward a modality for protest that today's artworks have largely ignored. Rather, artists and workers appear widely divided in their public expressions but strangely united in their goals of better pay from industry for workers and more government funding for artists (see recent conflicts over funding allocated by the Australian Arts Council [Eltham 2015]).

Art and Protest: The Dada Manifesto

Claire Bishop also included the Dada movement in her discussion of the social turn (2012, p. 29). The Dada movement is rife with contradictions, but is generally considered to be a movement of 'anti-art' first conceptualised by Marcel Duchamp and represented in his ready-made art, such as his infamous 1917 piece, 'Fountain' (a urinal). They formed a critical movement responding to World War I as well as anti-capitalist and anti-bourgeois sentiments. This is clear in their adoption of the word 'manifesto' from the 1848 Communist Manifesto of Marx and Engels. The first Dada Manifesto was written by Hugo Ball in 1916, but the more famous Second Manifesto was published by Tristan Tzara in 1918. However, the core of Dadaism as a theory insisted that 'Dada meant nothing' and they retreated from the core of optimism inherent in social activism, instead pursuing a generalised anti-polemic which involved, for example, a complete break with contemporary artists and their work, a disavowal of the public of so-called 'art lovers', and the view of war as a by-product of a capitalist regime. In Mark Hutchinson's terms, 'the Dadas were explicit time and again that Dada was not an art movement nor literary school...as one Dada pamphlet put it [in 1921]: "Imitators of Dada want to present Dada in an artistic form it never had"' (2011, p. 122). A portion of Tzara's manifesto (1918) makes this clear:

> I write a manifesto and I want nothing, yet I say certain things, and in principle I am against manifestoes, as I am also against principles (half-pints to measure the moral value of every phrase too too convenient; approximation was invented by the impressionists). I write this manifesto to show that people can perform contrary actions together while taking one fresh gulp of air; I am against action; for continuous contradiction, for affirmation too, I am neither for nor against and I do not explain because I hate common sense.[1]

The Dadas or Dadaists represent a complete disillusionment with critical social movements alongside the ineffectiveness of art to address any issues. As Hutchinson explains, 'Dada's violent intrusions into the public sphere were part of the radical attempt to destroy art and its public... through symbolic violence against the everyday habits and practices of art and culture' (2011, p. 124). They pointed to complete destruction of the artistic sphere in order to refresh artists, their work, and the public sense of what art means. They postulated total revolution, but are usually remembered as nihilists. As Dave Beech and John Roberts conclude, then, 'anti-art...drains art of its artistic qualities so as to expose the trauma of art's self-formation' (2002, p. 293). It is this core of trauma as a mechanism of production that aligns the Dadaist stance with some post-9/11 artworks.

Art and Craft: Craftivism and Communitarian Protest

A third mode of protest art could be considered a form of outsider art, but is better known by the moniker *craftivism*. This form of public activism through amateur craftwork began with the AIDS Memorial Quilt project in the US in 1987 (Rall and Costello 2010, p. 89). Since the Iraq War, specific craftwork tailored to anti-war campaigns has appeared: for example, the Melbourne Craft Collective (MCC) contributed to the Australian Broadcasting Corporation's Sunday *Arts* program offering community workshops called 'Bang! Knit! Purl! KaPOW!' for men and women to learn how to knit or crochet explosives. The MCC's website also offered instructions alongside the proposed deployment of textile weapons, along with encouragement for advanced crafters to undertake 'the more challenging' full-body explosive pack.[2]

The Melbourne Craft Collective is not alone. Rather, the first decade of the 2000s has delivered a groundswell of (mostly) women who craft in protest. The term *craftivism* was coined in 2003 by Betsy Greer in order to join the separate spheres of craft and activism. In her definition, 'craftivism is a way of looking at life where voicing opinions through creativity makes your voice stronger, your compassion deeper and your quest for justice more infinite' (2007, p. 401). Previous conceptions of protest craftwork, such as the AIDS quilt, depended on public marches to garner publicity. Today, craftivism is often organised via the Internet and facilitated through online communication. It is this connection between craft and creativity that allows the employment of craft as a protest against social injustice, environmental degradation, and war. Craftivists turn to craftwork as a meaningful exercise in a world overwhelmed by cheaply manufactured goods. A similar movement exists in the protest against the unsustainable practices of the fashion industry (see Brown 2013).

So far, this discussion has flagged several modalities for protest artworks: social activism, disillusionment and meaninglessness, and craftivism. The argument presented here is that post-9/11 artists have enlarged the repertoire of anti-war imagery through modes of memory, specifically the mechanisms of trauma. Trauma, as a psychological response to loss and pain, evokes a disturbed pattern of memory that plays out in post-9/11 artworks.

THE LOSS OF CRAFT AND THE RISE OF TRAUMA

In *The Invention of Craft*, Glen Adamson offers a detailed scenario of how Freudian conceptions of trauma were evoked in response to broadscale social changes following industrialisation in Great Britain (2013, pp. 185–191). Adamson tracks both real and imaginary configurations of trauma suffered by the British Arts and Crafts movement following the perceived loss of craft. The antecedents of craft and protest stem from the British Arts and Crafts movement of the early twentieth century, promulgated through two of its most famous spokesmen, William Morris and John Ruskin. They conceived of craft, in community, as the ultimate means of protest; for them, 'craft was valued for its anti-capitalist and expressive potential [as well as] its capability to support an imaginary continuity, a line of invented tradition cast backward into history' (p. 209). Further, craftwork was foundational to the establishment of Morris's Arcadian community in the UK. The focus, like today's craftivism, became less an expression of individual skill than an exercise in communitarian values. As Adamson explains, it is this 'casting back' that affords craftwork its power to process the present:

> [M]odern craft is potent not in spite of its temporal impurity [its 'casting back'], but because of it. Its dynamic relation to memory provides a framework in which traumatic experiences can be processed, forms from the past renewed, questions of agency brought to the fore, and new possibilities explored, all at once. (p. 210)

This concept of trauma as being 'processed' or 'worked through', as well as the ways in which it disrupts memory, is central to Sigmund Freud's understanding of it. For him, 'trauma was an experience that immersed the victim in the traumatic scene so profoundly that it precluded the kind of [distance] necessary for cognitive knowledge of what had happened' (Leys 2000, p. 9). The result is a distortion in memory that becomes a wound, or as Adamson puts it, 'a fragmentation of the subject, an inability to grasp the traumatic scene in its totality' (2013, p. 185). For this reason, '[i]t can only be dealt with piecemeal, in ways the patient is unaware of, treating the psychic wound without ever fully healing it. Such traumatic response provides a degree of comfort, but it also shields the subject from ever confronting the underlying, unresolved conflict' (p. 185). Here, one need only replace the word 'patient' with 'viewer' to see where trauma plays out in relation to artworks following the Twin Tower attacks. In classic Freudian interpretation, Adamson explains that trauma is activated through three main mechanisms: repetitive behaviour, false memories, and flashbacks (2013, p. 185). We can see these mechanisms at work in the visual records of the destruction of New York City's Twin Towers on September 11, 2001.

PTSD AND THE FALLING OF THE TWIN TOWERS

Repetition

The video of the Twin Towers falling ran 'as a continual loop' following the September 11 attacks, and on every anniversary of the date since. It has shaped the public memory of the Wars on Terror. It reminds viewers that this is an unprovoked attack on American soil, thus justifying any response taken by the US government and military. However, the replayed recording has been reduced in order to remove the image of the incoming airplanes. This assures Americans, as well as those in other countries, that air travel remains safe. At the same time, this repetitive image draws attention away from potentially more disturbing images, such as those of the planes hitting the Pentagon, the central organisation of the US military. This replay reinforces the relocation of the site of the terrorist airstrikes from military targets to buildings full of innocent civilians; although the plight of United Flight 93 is not replayed, as no video recording exists, recordings of the poignant phone calls to loved ones have served as the backdrop for movies screened on cinema as well as television (Markle 2006).

False Memory and Propaganda

The 'false memory' mechanism was skilfully executed by the US and British governments in seeking 'weapons of mass destruction' to justify the Iraq War. The strength of the falsehoods generated by the Twin Towers on constant replay distracted from the military campaign to pursue a false target. Many scientists felt that Saddam Hussein's so-called program for 'weapons for mass destruction' was inaccurate, and after David Kelly, a top British scientist, was outed by the BBC, he committed suicide; questions remain about his death (Cassidy 2003). The operation of flashbacks are evident in the Twin Towers video, and are often augmented by extremely brief video clips of other terrorist bombings, most often including the aftermath of the London Underground strikes. Another popular repetitive video clip is the toppling of Saddam Hussein's statue in Baghdad (Maas 2011). The repetitive falling of tall buildings has also become a common theme in cinema, as post-apocalyptic films show the collapse of skyscrapers falling in large city centres (Hartman-Warren 2014, p. 51).

Flashbacks

The mechanisms of trauma are repetitive and compulsive, but with a purpose: to distract. Thus, the video replay of the demolition of the Twin Towers

> ...affords a constant distraction that prevents the subject [the viewers] from having to encounter the memory of the trauma, which is too disturbing to fully integrate back into consciousness. The traumatic event might return in fragments—the particular actions repeated may be telltale clues to the source of the trauma, in fact—but never as a whole. (Saigh and Bremner 1999, p. 9)

As such, the trauma evoked by the falling of the Twin Towers stands in sharp contrast to that which is called up by Picasso's *Guernica*. Since, while the former seeks to distract, hide, and repress, the latter provides an immediate, even uncomplicated, sensation of the horror of war, as innocent villagers and even their animals are torn apart. Here, the fact of slaughter in war is non-negotiable and must be confronted.

Post-9/11 artworks cannot provide such assurances to viewers, as any opportunity for psychic integration has been contaminated by operations of trauma. Indeed, I want to suggest that the repetition via video replay of the Twin Towers in particular, as well as subsequent terrorist strikes, has contaminated both individual and collective memory (see Hodgkin and Radstone 2003). The falling of the Twin Towers has become a traumatised memory, and remains in conflict between the repetition of media replay of the event, the falsehoods evoked to provide a rationale for the Iraq War (and subsequent invasion of Afghanistan), and the rebranding of 'heroism' in the US that served to mask anti-war protests in America and elsewhere. A concerted hunt for Osama bin Laden, the acknowledged planner of the 9/11 attacks, was taken up only after President Barack Obama came into office. The falling of the Twin Towers on video replay served as both distraction and continual reminder, providing a convenient outlet for the public's indignation that continued during the prolonged reconstruction of a suitable memorial (Doss 2010).

REVIEWING POST-9/11 ARTWORKS THROUGH THE LENS OF TRAUMA

The operation of these modes of trauma have influenced anti-war artists in the post-9/11 era. Peter Mateer has argued that

> [t]he intense anxiety created by the War on Terror during the past decade has meant that the small number of international artists directly concerned with images of war, the understanding of how art might critique politics and its extension into warfare resides not solely in what they depict but also in the nature of representation. (2014, p. 398)

Since war induces trauma and interacts with memory and visualisation to produce fragmentation, repetition, false memories, and flashbacks, it must affect the representations of war offered by post-9/11 artists and anti-war protestors. While there is no single way to evaluate all post-9/11 artworks for their employment of traumatic themes and structures, now I want to examine a range of artworks from the Anglophone world that use techniques of shock, distraction, repetition, fragmentation, violence, war, and false memory in order to suggest a post-trauma perspective.

SHOCK, AND THE ARTIST'S REALIGNMENT OF SELF

Trauma can induce fragmentary recollections and the need for 'wholeness' in experience maintains a psychic struggle: the goal is to reintegrate the traumatic experience into the 'whole' consciousness. In the months following the September 11 attacks, a local free news magazine in the 'anti-war' town of Madison, Wisconsin (see Silber 1979), published a striking article addressing the relationship between art and terrorism. The piece began with reports from the *New York Times* immediately following the attacks, such as Stephen King's assertion that 'what I do has absolutely no significance [now]', and Cynthia Ozick's similar sentiment, 'I could not do my daily nibbling on my novel. It seemed so irrelevant' (cited in Darlington 2002, p. 13). The article juxtaposes these attitudes with those of a local artist, Bird Ross, who found instead that she wanted to express her shock in some meaningful activity that would assist her and other artists in constructing a memorial project:

I just kept hearing the number 6000 [the estimated number of people who died in the event]...I sat glued to the radio, and I just started counting out 6000 lentils...next I began tying 6000 knots...I collected 6000 leaves...I used a world map to punch 6000 holes....(p. 13)

Ross notes that she felt she had to reconcile the falling of the towers in order to maintain a sense of self: 'I had to somehow manipulate what had happened—physically, tactilely—for me. There wasn't any way around it' (p. 13). Tenaya Darlington's article also summarises the responses of many other artists, intellectuals, and poets who each responded to the 9/11 attacks in their own way, and concludes:

We need artistic expression during times of crisis. Despite living a thousand miles away from ground zero, we all continue to internalize the tragedy. Through creative endeavours, we make a step towards understanding the world beyond the *constant media blitz.* (p. 14; emphasis added)

The response to trauma recorded here and its expression in a craft form with objects to hand presages Greer's craftivism. However, it also memorialises a personal sense of shock. These artists recognised that a tear had opened up their artistic firmament, the 'bubble' that had cushioned artists in their political convictions in this Midwestern town since the end of the Vietnam War. They sought a personal realignment with the reality of the Twin Towers (and other) attacks, and however they fashioned their response, Darlington notes, 'expressing oneself seems more necessary than ever' (p. 13).

Their work recalls that of British artist Aya Haidar, who has taken craft into war zones and uses craft workshops to assist traumatised children in Somalia. Haidar locates craft as a feminist way to 'create a new normal' (Adamson 2013, p. 225). In her artwork *Recollections* (Seamstress series) VII (2011), unidentified bombed ruins in Beirut are printed on linen, and the pockmarks in the buildings are marked by 'a tight clutch of brightly coloured stitches' (p. 225). For Adamson, the stitches are brilliantly 'coloured bandages' which both highlight and stitch up the wounds of the war: 'if the building is anthropomorphised into a traumatised body, then craft also acts in a double capacity, both as a forensic description of violence and as the means of working though it' (p. 227). In the most basic sense, stitching is linked to repair (Rall

2015). Like the artists in Madison, Haidar's artworks in her *Recollections* series both address the damage of war and attempt to repair it.

F.E.A.R. (FALSE EVIDENCE APPEARING REAL) AND FALSE MEMORY SYNDROME

In other ways, images can work to disguise 'the real'. In 'Good and Evil: At Home and Abroad', Diane Bell describes her personal encounter with a clerk shortly after the 9/11 attacks:

> My car has been serviced. I am signing my credit card slip. The young man...slams down a sticker on the counter and says with real menace in his voice, 'Put this on your car, lady.' It is an American flag [imprinted with] God Bless America. I don't want this on my car...but I bite my tongue. He knows where I live. He has access to my car. I am momentarily silenced. (2002, p. 432)

Bell continues, 'one must be loyal, and the flag says, "I am a patriot"... One's patriotism cannot be assumed or tweaked. Even more important is to fly the flag—that way there is no question' (p. 433). She contends that asking questions about September 11 is perilous, but 'that is exactly where feminists excel. We ask the awkward questions' (p. 436). At a time when the American flag literally papered the landscape in the United States, Bell and other feminist writers chose to speak out against the dominant paradigm and against the false memories constructed by the image.

DISRUPTION AND FRAGMENTATION: CAMOUFLAGE

Craftwork can take on a number of roles in relationship to protest (see Rall and Costello 2010). Not only is craftwork available as a site for public protest, or a finely tuned response to war, it can also act out a role of disruption via piecework. The artist Annabelle Collett took on the military's 'disruptive pattern' as the central concept in her Far North Queensland exhibition, *Disruptive Pattern Syndrome* (Naylor 2007). The Pinnacle Gallery, which hosted the exhibition, is near the Lavarack Military Base (between Thuringowa and Townsville, Queensland), and the relevance to military organisation is made clear in the exhibition title: 'disruptive patterning' is the term for camouflage. The purpose of

camouflage is to disrupt the viewer's ability to distinguish a meaningful pattern that would potentially identify an object, depending on its
background. In other words, 'camouflage works well in a natural environment, but attracts attention at the supermarket', providing a disruption to the normal or non-military state of affairs in a local community
(Naylor 2007, p. 40). It is the nearly ubiquitous overlay of the military
via 'camo' (camouflage-patterned clothing) that shows its penetration
not just in the fashion industry, but also in popular youth clothing.

Collett's use of disruptive pattern is displayed through a variety of
objects, and she 'picks up on the visual confusion generated by irregular
patterning as it affects concealment' (p. 40). In 'Knitted Forms', strands
of brightly coloured wool are intertwined, twisted, stretched, and penetrated by sharp knitting needles. 'Commando Wear' includes transparent camouflage-patterned lingerie as well as a collection of books with
similarly patterned covers, including embroidered fictional titles such
as, 'Women in War: From Bearing Children to Bearing Arms' and 'The
Guide to Ethnic Cleansing' (p. 41). While these objects present obvious anti-war protests, another series of works in the exhibition, 'Broken
Colour 2007', includes works of laser-cut textiles with intermingled patterns, so that the 'shapes create disruptive effects as the eye hovers over
the almost imperceptible joins' (p. 40). Collett's 'strategic assaults on
visual literacy' thus form the core of the exhibition (p. 40). In Collett's
work, pattern disruption works directly through piecework, including cut
textiles, embroidery, stitching, and knitting to confuse the viewer. Just as
there is no opportunity given to 'heal' from the visual disruption, so too
civilians are damaged by the Wars on Terror.

Pattern disruption and piecework, especially through the use of camouflage, are also present in the recent work of Aboriginal artist Jemima
Wyman:

When you look at some of the first investigations into camouflage in the
early 1900s, military units were enlisting artists, zoologists and magicians
to help...even Pablo Picasso suggest[ed] that soldiers should be wearing
'harlequin' garments as they do the same thing as camouflage. (cited in
Cull 2014, p. 35)

Wyman locates the problem of integration between the disruptive patterning of the military and problems of disruption in everyday life, especially during protests. For Wyman, only after unifying these disparate

pieces of the pattern could one generate a 'collective voice of protest' (p. 36). As in Haidar's work, then, Wyman suggests her use of military patterning in craftwork could take it from the war zones to a place of healing. Importantly, although the keffiyeh, symbol of Palestinian resistance, is used by protestors for peace, in the iconography of post-9/11 popular culture, the keffiyeh is more strongly linked with the attire of movie celebrities than of activism. As such, even though her disparate patterns, including 'the Arabian keffiyeh pattern, a boldly tessellated black and white...tie-dye, op-art, camouflage and paisley materials' may produce 'discordancy...they have each been used to unify and protect people in protest' (p. 40).

BEN QUILTY, THE AUSTRALIAN WAR ARTIST

Ben Quilty rose to national prominence after he went to Afghanistan in 2011 as an official war artist commissioned by the Australian War Memorial and attached to the Australian Defence Force. This position makes it difficult to see Quilty as an anti-war artist. However, Quilty's work is characterised by a tension between violence and vulnerability, as in his project, *After Afghanistan*.

> Keen to capture their sheer physicality, Quilty asked the soldiers to sit for their portraits naked...[H]e needed to see the body after its protective layers of uniform and body armour had been stripped away. For him, their nakedness expressed both the strength and the frailty of the human condition in time of war. Each soldier was asked to select a pose that reflected an aspect of his or her experience. Some of them drew on an actual event from their deployment, others on the tiredness or the emotions they felt after their return to Australia. (Australian War Memorial n.d.)

The soldier's vulnerability is underscored by his nudity, as well as the expression of emotion. Although he is not taking a clear social activist stance, therefore, Quilty's work is determined to speak to the 'truth' of wartime activity. In contrast to the 'buffed' images of masculinity typical of the contemporary war hero (see Smith and Gehrmann 2014), Quilty offers a 'naked' heroism in his soldiers' portraits, recalling the Dadaist disillusionment in response to the threat of the First World War.

CONCLUSION

This chapter has outlined various ways that memorials, commemoration, and remembrance all challenge the mechanisms of human memory in its response to trauma. The ongoing commemorations of 9/11 anniversary events in the US and throughout the world will continue to challenge artists to reconceptualise issues that arise from the Wars on Terror, including social injustice, the powerlessness of women and children, the world's refugee crises, and the difficulties of all civilians residing in war zones. These reframings will need to work against the dominance of the media conglomerates during these anniversary events. As David Reiff puts it, such anniversary events come at the cost of exciting partisanship:

> But in affirming that remembrance is humanly necessary, we must not pretend that it is ever completely innocent, or, to put it more bluntly still, that it has no moral downside...what will remain then *is not memory but remembrance*, which again, may be many things, positive as well as negative, but is always a form of politics. (2011, pp. 47–49; emphasis added)

As contemporary artists continue to 'push back' against the realities of war, they are 'mindful of the tension between their own image-making and that of the media through which "visions" of conflicts are circulated' (Mateer 2014, p. 398). It is left to each individual artist to meaningfully re-process the constant recirculation of the video replays of terrorist strikes, such as the apparently continual falling of the Twin Towers in New York. The modalities of social activism, disillusionment, craftivism, and feminist theory each offer a possibility for expression in a world now dominated by the Wars on Terror, where memory is compromised.

NOTES

1. The '1' replacing 'I' is part of the Second Manifesto.
2. At the time of writing, the Craft Cartel website is no longer active.

WORKS CITED

Adamson, Glenn. 2013. *The Invention of Craft*. London: Bloomsbury Academic.
Arlen, Michael J. 1997 [1966–1967]. *Living-Room War*. New York: Syracuse University Press.

Ashmore, Nicola. 2016. Travels to America, September 2015. *Guernica Remakings*, 10 Aug. Available from: http://guernicaremakings.com/travels-to-america-september-2015/.

Australian War Memorial. n.d., *Ben Quilty: After Afghanistan*. Australian War Memorial, Canberra. Available from: https://www.awm.gov.au/exhibitions/quilty/portraits/.

Beech, Dave, and John Roberts. 2002. *The Philistine Controversy*. London: Verso.

Bell, Diane. 2002. Good and Evil: At Home and Abroad. In *September 11, 2001: Feminist Perspectives*, ed. Susan Hawthorne and Bronwyn Winter, 432–449. North Melbourne: Spinifex.

Bishop, Claire. 2012. *Artificial Hells: Participatory Art and the Politics of Spectatorship*. London: Verso.

Bogart, Anne. 2007. *And Then, You Act: Making Art in an Unpredictable World*. New York: Routledge.

Brown, Sass. 2013. *Refashioned: Cutting-Edge Clothing from Upcycled Materials*. London: Lawrence King.

Bryan-Wilson, Julia. 2009. *Art Workers: Radical Practice in the Vietnam War Era*. Berkeley: University of California Press.

Cassidy, John. 2003. The David Kelly Affair. *New Yorker*, 8 Dec. Available from: http://www.newyorker.com/magazine/2003/12/08/the-david-kelly-affair.

Cull, T. 2014. The Power of Patterns. *Artlines*, Spr., 34–37.

Darlington, Tenaya. 2002. In Response to Sept. 11, Madisonians Create Art Against Terrorism. *Isthmus*, 11 Jan. 13–14.

Dordević, Goran. 1979. *International Strike of Artists?* Museum fur [Sub] Kultur. Berlin.

Doss, Erika. 2010. *Memorial Mania: Public Feeling in America*. Chicago: University of Chicago Press.

Eltham Ben. 2015. Budget 2015: George Brandis' Extraordinary Raid of the Australia Council. *ABC News*, 13 May. Available from: http://www.abc.net.au/news/2015-05-13/eltham-brandis-extraordinary-raid-of-the-australia-council/6467534.

Greer, Betsy. 2007. Craftivism. In *Encyclopedia of Activism and Social Justice*, ed. Gary L. Jackson and Kathryn G. Herr, 401. Thousand Oaks, CA: Sage.

Hartman-Warren, Kylee M. 2014. Fashionable Fascism: Cinematic Images of the Nazi Before and After 9/11, in Rall. *Fashion and War in Popular Culture*, 35–51.

Hodgkin, Katherine, and Susannah Radstone (eds.). 2003. *Contested Pasts: The Politics of Memory*. London: Routledge.

Hutchinson, Mark. 2011. Anti-Public: Dada, Negation and Universality. *Art & the Public Sphere* 1 (2): 121–137.

Klein, Naomi. 2001. *No Logo*. London: Flamingo.

Kurlansky, Mark. 2005. *1968: The Year that Rocked the World*. New York: Random House.

Leys, Ruth. 2000. *Trauma: A Genealogy*. Chicago: University of Chicago Press.

Maas, Peter. 2011. The Toppling: How the Media Inflated a Minor Moment in a Long War. *New Yorker*, 10 Jan. Available from: http://www.newyorker.com/magazine/2011/01/10/the-toppling.

Maddison, Angus. 2001. *The World Economy: A Millennial Perspective*. Paris: OECD.

Markle, Peter dir. 2006. *Flight 93*. A&E Network.

Mateer, John. 2014. War's Unquiet Eyes: A Brief Disquisition on Contemporary Art and Conflict. *Art and Australia* 51 (3): 397–401.

Naylor, Stephen. 2007. Disruptive Pattern Syndrome. *Textile Fibre Forum: The Australian Magazine for the Textile Arts* 88: 40–41.

Notkin, Richard. 2007. All Nations Have Their Moment of Foolishness. *Ceramics: Art and Perception* 68: 26–29.

———. 2015. Can we "Repair" Repair? *Minor Cultures*. Cultural Studies Association of Australia. Melbourne, 1 Dec.

Rall, Denise N., and Moya Costello. 2010. Women, Craft and Protest—Yesterday and Today. *Australian Folklore: A Yearly Journal of Folklore Studies* 25: 79–96.

Reiff, David. 2011. After 9/11: The Limits of Remembrance. *Harper's Magazine*, Aug., 47–50.

Saigh, Philip A., and Douglas Bremner. 1999. *Posttraumatic Stress Disorder: A Comprehensive Text*. Boston, MA: Allyn and Bacon.

Silber, Glenn dir. 1979. *The War at Home*. New Front Films.

Smith, Heather, and Richard Gehrmann. 2014. Branding the Muscled Male Body as Military Costume, in Rall. *Fashion and War in Popular Culture*, 57–74.

Sturken, Marita. 2002. The Wall, the Screen and the Image: The Vietnam Veterans Memorial. In *The Visual Culture Reader*, 2nd ed, ed. Nicholas Mirzoeff, 357–370. London: Routledge.

Tzara, Tristan. 1918. *Dada Manifesto 1918*. Available from: http://writing.upenn.edu/library/Tzara_Dada-Manifesto_1918.pdf.

Walsh, David. 2003. UN Conceals Picasso's "Guernica". *World Socialist Web Site*, 8 Feb. Available from: https://www.wsws.org/en/articles/2003/02/guer-f08.html.

AUTHOR BIOGRAPHY

Denise N. Rall is an Adjunct Research Fellow in the School of Arts and Social Sciences. She publishes on the social, political and military significance of fashion. Her recent edited collection is entitled *Fashion and War in Popular Culture* (2014).

CHAPTER 10

Bearing Witness to Injustice: Latin America, Refugees, and Memorialisation in Australia

Robert Mason

For Latin Americans, September 11 is significant for the *coup d'état* that occurred in 1973. Every September in Sydney, a group of Latin American Australians meet quietly with left-wing activists at a statue of the former Chilean president, Salvador Allende. The bronze and marble statue sits in suburban parkland in the western suburb of Fairfield, and serves as a focal point for the community and visitors to pause and reflect on the violence that the President's forced removal precipitated. It is also a site of contested memory, and has been extensively damaged in acts of aggravated vandalism that outraged many in the Chilean community. The memorial to Allende is not unique, and similar sites and ceremonies exist in cities across Australia every September 11 to commemorate the overthrow of Allende's government by a military coup.

Left-wing attitudes to Latin America were crystallised globally by the events in Chile on September 11, 1973. The coup by General Augusto Pinochet sparked decades of repression, violence, and death in that country. It was part of a pattern of similar actions in Latin America during the 1970s and 1980s that were supported by the United States of

R. Mason (✉)
Griffith University, Brisbane, Australia
e-mail: r.mason@griffith.edu.au

© The Author(s) 2017
J. Gildersleeve and R. Gehrmann (eds.), *Memory and the Wars on Terror*, Palgrave Macmillan Memory Studies,
DOI 10.1007/978-3-319-56976-5_10

America (USA), and hundreds of thousands fled the subsequent violence as political refugees (Hirsch 2016). Latin Americans moved throughout the states of the global north to seek resettlement, and a large number settled in Australia. Once in Australia, they were especially welcomed by left-wing Australians, who remained enamoured with stories of Fidel Castro and Che Guevara, and who were enervated in their anti-Americanism by the still-vivid legacies of the Vietnam War. Over time, these refugee groups reforged their identities in multicultural Australia.

This chapter explores the impact on former refugees from Latin America of another occurrence on the date of September 11, namely the attacks on the Twin Towers in New York on September 11, 2001. It assesses how unresolved historical injustice was reconceptualised by refugees when their former adversary, the USA, asserted itself in the aftermath of a second 9/11. Through the prism of memory studies, it analyses online blogs, activist websites, and interviews with former refugees in the decade that followed the New York attacks. The USA's so-called Wars on Terror echoed the Dirty Wars that followed the events of September 11, 1973, and reactivated the Latin American Australian's status as a 'community communicating injustice' to wider Australian society. At the same time, the events re-inscribed the refugee's historical experience in Latin America within a universal narrative of anti-imperialism and support for human rights. The result of the attacks, paradoxically, was to deepen their sense of social connectedness and inclusion within their new homes.

MULTICULTURAL MEMORIES AFTER 9/11

The attacks on the Twin Towers in New York had profound implications across an array of international arenas. They transformed domestic politics in regions from the Middle East to East Asia as security paradigms shifted, and the relationship between sovereignty and human rights altered dramatically. Within the multicultural nations of the global north, the attacks defined civilian's experience of national belonging. As Amanda Laugesen examines in this collection, the rise of exclusionary language resonated throughout society as political rhetoric fuelled domestic moral panic towards both terrorists and migrants. The chronic violence popularly associated with overseas regions, such as the Middle East or Africa, now seemed to threaten communities in the global north directly. In this context, many came to view nation's migration intakes as dangerous experiments in cultural diversity that now risked national cohesion. Establishment politicians sought to neuter the appeal of demagogues on both the left and right of the electorate by appropriating aspects of their language of fear in order to reassert 'western' values. The result, for many in the country, was to position visibly different and non-European Others in an apparently precarious relationship to core aspects of the national identity.

One consequence of the increased discussion of national identity was a heightened focus on national security and sovereignty. While troops fought overseas, politicians reasserted border controls to reassure populations that they retained control of domestic safety. Combined with acts of terrorism and an increasing language of fear in the media, the result was an escalating sense of alienation for a number of minority groups in society (Aly 2012). Rather than a hoped-for increase in social cohesion, it instead appeared that vulnerable groups experienced a heightened sense of insecurity. Few governments investigated this systematically. Until 2001, for example, Australia had no national survey for measuring social cohesion across key indicators such as belonging or migrant's sense of personal worth. In fact, and in contrast to both the preceding decade and popular perception, most migrant's sense of belonging increased consistently from the 2001 onwards (Markus 2013). Far less clear is how this was experienced according to different social contexts and ethnic groups and in light of particular historical experiences.

In many ways, Australia acts as an exemplar of cultural diversity in the global north. In the 50 years following the end of the Second World War, millions of migrants settled in the country and transformed its demography. Well over 100,000 new arrivals were refugees sponsored by the International Refugee Organisation, with many more arriving unsponsored or by intergovernmental agreement. It was increasingly clear by the late 1960s and 1970s that new approaches to government services were required to ensure new arrivals had appropriate access to welfare services. The resultant multicultural policy was focussed initially on preventing structural poverty in suburbs dominated by newly arrived populations, but gradually evolved into a broader attempt to reimagine an ethnically diverse Australian nation. Conservatives' wariness at the pace of cultural change coalesced with populist concerns from the mid-1990s. From that time, Prime Minister John Howard used the language of border control and nationalism to marginalise multiculturalism in favour of a re-emphasis on citizenship and British heritage. The country retained its strong commitment to the settlement of asylum seekers through the United Nations High Commission for Refugees, but their arrival was increasingly framed as a potential risk to national unity that had to be controlled and monitored.

The public framing of refugees as a potential threat to Australian security had a powerful impact on their social inclusion in the years following September 11, 2001, and particularly affected their ability to articulate memories of their lives prior to settlement. Australians had long been highly sensitive to any risk that new arrivals imported past prejudices and conflicts to their new homes. Throughout the twentieth century, there had been an expectation that migrants assimilate by assuming the characteristics of Anglo-Australians; projecting a relaxed disinterest in distant conflicts in favour of assisting friends and neighbours in need locally. This had remained true in the years following the Second World War, as fears simmered that Displaced Persons might retain sympathy for Nazism or Communism. Refugees fleeing Vietnam and arriving unbidden in Australia accelerated changes to the country's migration policies in 1976. They did not shift expectations that refugees would conform to Anglo-Australian ideals, nor did they alter the strong denial of public space to discuss the legacies of their former conflicts. Australians would not bear witness to new arrivals' violent pasts, and would not affirm that such violence had a legitimate presence within Australia.

Clearly this silence did not erase memories of violence, nor did it substantially aid in forgetting traumatic events. It did, however, frame those memories in the new social context. Victims and perpetrators found themselves observers of reconciliation from afar; morally bound into the networks of violence but unable to find resolution other than as an observer. The cultural meaning of violent experiences was fluid, but remained foundational to why the refugees were in Australia. While communities continued to sustain narratives regarding violent displacement, the performance and inscription of these legacies in the Australian cultural landscape remained publicly silenced. The implications of this shifted on September 11, 2001, when Latin American Australians' discourses of historical acts of violence and injustice resonated so directly in the contemporary moment. It demonstrated how the particular construct of Australian multiculturalism and neo-liberalism provided new ways to contextualise and, ultimately, publicly delegitimise acts of historical injustice.

9/11 IN AUSTRALIA

The first significant influx of Latin Americans to Australia was the Chileans, who fled General Pinochet from 1973 onwards. The coup had been widely reported in Australia, and Australian trade unionists had been among the first to travel to Chile to assess the implications for fellow unionists in the confused months following the coup (Jones 2007). The Chileans' settlement in Australia was popularly viewed as a success, buoyed by their social connections with the unions. More broadly, their arrival offered the government an opportunity to broaden Australia's intake of nominally 'European' migrants, as arrivals from Europe declined. Over the next fifteen years, the numbers of Latin American refugees and migrants continued to rise as military repression in the region increased. While allied to the USA, Australia was not directly involved in supporting military dictatorships in the region. As a consequence, it was markedly more willing to offer assistance to those who had been displaced and offered refugee status to nationalities denied by the USA. Most notably, this included the offer of refugee status to 10,000 Salvadorans fleeing civil war, who were only permitted to enter the USA as economic migrants.

There are currently over 100,000 Latin American Australians, but terminology and self-identification is highly contextual. On arrival in Australia, most identify primarily by nationality rather than as Latin American. In part, this can be attributed to the low number of Latin American Australians, which is in sharp contrast to the high-density concentrations of particular 'Hispanic' nationalities in the USA. It is also connected to Anglophone Australians' limited capacity to recognise differences between countries in the region, and tendency to focus on a hyper-sexualised image of tropical dance and Mexican food that resonated with Australian's own culture (Cohen 2005; Zevallos 2003, 2005). Yet, every one of the countries from which the migrants arrived had experienced military dictatorship, one party rule, or civil war in the preceding three decades.

While refugees comprise the core of Latin American Australians, most new arrivals since the 1990s have been economic migrants or international students. The legacies of previous violence on this diverse contemporary community are not well understood, and the limited research to date has focussed on their immediate welfare needs (Refuge of Hope 2015). Many nationals retain ongoing border disputes in their former homes, as well as endemic conflicts between government and non-government forces. Nonetheless, there is a strong sense of pan-Americanism that continues to energise emigrants from the continent. Although its influences are culturally diverse, the pan-Americanism has been articulated most ardently by Venezuela in the decades following September 11,

2001, to oppose American involvement in the continent. This Bolivarian pan-Americanism draws on the nineteenth-century liberator Simon Bolivar, and offers one widely recognised context in which the continent's nationalities can be conflated and associated with resistance to imperialism.

The attacks in New York on September 11, 2001, directly recalled the horror of September 11, 1973. The effect of the New York attacks was to resignify the date '9/11' and, by extension, to write over established community narratives of their own day of commemoration. The USA had routinely denied groups such as Salvadorans or Chileans official refugee status, and there was very limited recognition of the group's political status in the Australian public imagination. Yet, the events in 2001 repositioned the USA from imperial aggressor to victim, and appeared to challenge the refugees' own sense of victimhood in the popular imagination. Over time, however, particular groups associated the two attacks together within a structure of violent imperialism.

Direct references to September 11, 2001, were often silenced in refugee and activist literature as a means to keep alive the memories of those who had died in Chile. The 1973 coup, and repression that followed, operated as a synecdoche for all USA involvement in Latin America. This attitude is presented most clearly in a regular circular sent to supporters from an umbrella group comprising Chilean, Bolivarian, and left-wing Australians. The darkness referred to in the email is in clear juxtaposition to the light shed by their own acts of remembrance:

> The CIA backed military coup against the elected government of Salvador Allende plunged Chile into a darkness that still clouds our country and our people. We consider it especially appropriate to mark this day now that the dictator that so symbolised both Chile's burden and the neoliberal experiment our country was the laboratory for, has died...even if his legacy is yet to be buried.

> We want to remember the thousands of Chileans who were tortured, imprisoned, killed and disappeared at the hands of the military regime. Our commemoration is an important event of remembrance but also a chance to reflect on the history and lessons of struggle written with so much sacrifice by the people of Chile. (Bolivarian Circle 2007a)

To acknowledge the presence of alternative victims on 9/11 was to challenge those Latin Americans whose remembered sacrifice struggled to exist. In sharp contrast to those killed in the omnipresent imaginary of New York's skyline, the Chileans had been hidden from the Australian gaze in secret tortured prisons in Latin America. In this sense, and drawing on Judith Butler's (2009) work, they could not be counted as a subject in the political life of Australians. This lack of subjectivity in effect rendered them unable to be grieved in the lives of the majority (Lawson 2014). For most Australians in the neo-liberal state, the shadowy and morally dubious nature of anti-capitalist protesters, such as the Chilean victims, was implicit but clearly positioned them on the borders of criminality. For Latin American Australians, this conflation had to be contested if their identities and experiences were to be recognised as legitimate within their new homes.

The years following the 9/11 attacks witnessed a shift to the Left among governments throughout Latin America. The decision by American President George W. Bush to extend the Wars on Terror paradigm to Latin America was viewed with great concern in the continent. Many states had unresolved border issues, and a number had active insurgencies that crossed international borders. The application of the doctrine of pre-emptive action by Colombia to kill a guerrilla leader within Ecuadorian territory in 2008 set a precedent that revealed the paradigm's potentially destabilising influence throughout the region. Leftist governments, especially those associated with Venezuela, led the criticism of a policy that appeared to ignore the lived experiences of citizens and which viewed dissent as criminal and synonymous with support for terrorism.

Within Australia, the extension of the Wars on Terror into Latin America was seen as one reason for the escalation of citizen activism in that region. Popular Australian journalist John Pilger's film *War on Democracy* (2007) was widely circulated within the refugee community, and was praised for its support for 'those who suffered under dictatorships tolerated and encouraged by the US and the West'. According to activists, his film revealed 'that what happened in Latin America in the 1980s is a metaphor for how the rest of the world is being "ordered" today, with the Middle East as its epicentre' (Bolivarian Circle 2007b). For those in Australia, Latin American struggles were now clearly positioned within the same structures of violence that operated globally as part of the post-2001 Wars on Terror.

Large numbers of left-leaning Australian organisations reached out to the Latin Americans, seeing in the refugees' actions a reflection of their own struggle. Many of these groups had originated in the community organisations that had supported Latin Americans' struggle against the USA in the 1980s (Mason 2013). The new organisations occasionally included those whose task was overtly political and who aimed to remember those who had suffered through a continuation of their struggle.

Other contact took forms that were more tangible. The Australia-Cuba Friendship Society (ACFS) was a longstanding network of local groups, often based in universities, which organised social and cultural events in Australia that culminated with a working holiday to Cuba. These physical trips to Latin America expanded in the decade following September 11, 2001. Regular visits by Latin American and left-leaning Australians to see the changes occurring in President Hugo Chavez's Venezuela were one manifestation of how these connections fostered a renewed emphasis on social transformation and anti-Americanism. They were not the only example, and Latin American and left-leaning Australians also acted as observers in a number of Central and South American elections.

These visits to Latin America were matched by organised tours of speakers from the continent. Groups such as the Australia Venezuela Solidarity Network (AVSN) invited speakers from that country to talk at venues such as Victoria Trades Hall, where they put forward 'Latin America as alternative [that offered] new models of economic, social and political power'. The words of one visiting Venezuelan activist carefully situated the struggles of his audience members within a broader universal context when he asserted that 'we are here in Australia as community activists but also as working-class activists'. One tour included visits to multiple trade unions, but also talks to students, Spanish-language media, Green Party councillors, library talks, and an Indigenous education forum in which they were welcomed 'as brother and sister, [who] extend our solidarity to your struggle, as I know you do to ours' (AVSN 2009). The event mirrored that of visiting Salvadoran politicians, who fostered connections and solidarity across similar groups in 2009 (Mason 2012).

In contrast to the social groups driven by a moral imperative grounded in their personal experience, interventions by the USA in Latin America were condemned as serving a realist imperial agenda. Cuba and Venezuela exemplify this narrative in particular. Cuba had existed as an exemplar of Latin American defiance for decades. The hardship and sanctions imposed by the USA were directly connected to the period of intense suffering Cuba had undergone in the 1990s, after the collapse of its ally the Soviet Union. During the decade following September 11, 2001, Venezuela occupied the position of leadership that Cuba was no longer able to hold. Buoyed by wealth in resources, Chavez garnered widespread plaudits among migrants for his efforts to create an economic and social alternative to neo-liberalism (Chodor 2013). Despite Venezuela's important role in developing anti-imperial pan-American sentiment, Cuba's example retained its emotional resonance for Latin American Australians, many of whom had fled their homes at a time when Cuba offered one of the few bastions of resistance to pro-American governments.

Throughout the global community of Latin American radicals, the case of the Cuban Five acts as an example of American perfidy and pursuit of its own interest. The USA arrested the men on suspicion of espionage on behalf of Cuba. After a number of court challenges and disputed rulings, the men were sentenced to long terms of imprisonment for conspiring to commit acts of espionage. For those in Australia, the men were symbols of a corrupt judicial system. They claimed the men had been 'detained in Miami for fighting against terrorism organised, financed and carried out [by Cuban exiles in Miami] from US soil' (ACFS 2011a). Citing the extrajudicial processes at Guantanamo Bay, the group referred to the Cuban Five and demanded 'will the real terrorist please stand up' (ACFS 2011b). Others sold T-shirts imploring 'Stop US Terrorism: Free the Cuban 5'. The groups sought to use the Cuban example to reveal the hypocrisy of the USA and its apparent manipulation of the events of September 11, 2001. The ACFS asserted that 'Cuba's right to self-determination has been undermined by the actions of these terrorist groups who are tolerated on US soil. These terrorist acts included the bombing mid-air of Cubana 455 Flight that killed 73 people in 1976' (ACFS 2011a). Throughout the Australian community, the treatment of the Cuban Five provided a case study that was believed to prove the hypocritical nature of USA rhetoric regarding the Wars on Terror.

Concern at events in Cuba was not the only reason for increased mobilisation among Latin American Australians. They increasingly viewed the extension of the Wars on Terror to Latin America as a concerted attempt to reinstate the USA's interference and Dirty Wars of the 1970–1980s. Commentators accused Washington of 'massacres' and 'alarming interventionism' in language echoing the contemporary events in Iraq and Afghanistan (Marchetti 2011). The apparent reassertion of

USA imperialism drew attention to the structures of violence that had caused the refugees' own displacement decades prior, and they saw clear parallels in contemporary events. The wave of coups against the newly elected left-wing governments appeared to presage another era of repression against activists. One circular protested the 'shamefully long list of recent coup attempts':

> ...there was a failed coup against Chavez in Venezuela in 2002, defeated by mass protests and loyal soldiers. In 2004, Haitian president Jean-Bertrand Aristide was overthrown in a coup backed by the military forces of Canada, the United States and France. In 2008, right-wing Bolivian forces used fascist gangs against President Evo Morales stopped by mass mobilisations and loyal sections of military. And in 2009, Honduran President Manuel Zelaya was overthrown by the military. All but Haiti were ALBA members [an international organisation cofounded by Venezuela to counter USA dominance in the region] and one of the main acts of the coup regime in Honduras was to withdraw from ALBA. (Kellog 2010)

Activists did not suggest that the Australian residents should engage directly in opposing these events, given the threat of being seen to aid foreign terrorist organisations. The refugees' 'job is to build solidarity with the ALBA countries against attacks from the US' (Kellog 2010). Echoing the language from Venezuela and its allies in the region, refugees saw this military involvement as directly recalling earlier imperialist interference in democracy. Chavez and Morales' joint address following unrest in Bolivia was widely supported, when it stated defiantly that:

> ...as thousands remembered the military coup in Chile of September 11,1973 only a few days ago, once again we are reminded of the lengths that the United States will go to make sure that it controls the destiny of people around the world. (Bolivarian Circles 2007c)

This evocation was not only due to Australian material being reproduced from left-leaning Latin American media outlets. Such views were, if anything, stronger in Australia, where the foundational mythology of September 11, 1973 was crucial to Latin Americans' community identity. In 2003, a prolific local blogger commented on the visit of a Venezuelan community activist to Australia. He focussed particularly on the recent instability in Venezuela, and the alleged attempt to remove Chavez from power. The reporter agreed that 'that the revolution in Venezuela should not be seen in isolation from the political developments that are unfolding throughout the continent'. He continued to note ominously that 'September 11, 2003, marked the 30th anniversary of the military coup that ousted left-wing Chilean president Salvador Allende. In April 2002, a similar coup was organised against President Chavez, but was defeated through a massive uprising of Venezuela's workers and urban poor'. To the second-generation refugee, the epoch-defining nature of the Chilean coup appeared transferrable to the Venezuelan coup, which had similarly sought to halt the redistribution of resources to the landless. In a statement of affirmation, and a call to arms for activists in Australia, the blogger felt the coup 'in Venezuela was a textbook copy of the coup that happened in Chile. In other words, it is as if the coup plotters in Venezuela studied the coup in Chile' (Jorquera 2003).

> The situation existed in Venezuela [in April 2002] for it to end the same way it did in Chile. In Venezuela there are plots against the president many of which have been stopped thanks to the security services. We are organising to make sure that the same thing that occurred in Chile 30 years ago does not occur in Venezuela. (Jorquera 2003)

The military intervention that had halted Allende's own redistribution of land for the peasants in 1973 appeared to be repeating itself. The moral imperative that had demanded the refugees leave their countries was reinvoked; the obligation to act and remember those who died was clear. This extended beyond individual acts of solidarity; if the second War on Terror was a continuation of the first, then activists were obligated to act if they were to sustain the memory of those who had died during conflicts and dictatorships.

In many ways, the characterisation of the USA as a rapacious presence is clearest in its promotion of neo-liberalism and capitalism. The international alliance Bolivarian Alliance of the Peoples of Our America (ALBA) was launched by Cuba and Venezuela with 11 further countries joining (and one other membership pending at time of press). One Australian journalist described it approvingly as 'a united organisation that reflects and fights for the needs of the people the 99%—against the greed and destructiveness of the corporations [that are] changing the shape of politics across that continent' (AVSN 2011). Rather than the neo-liberal interests of the USA, this approach emphasised the state as a vehicle to enable local community organisations. In contrast, the Australian Federico Fuentes endorsed the view that 'the United States appears as one of the last defenders of the ancien regime, that of pacted democracy and neoliberal reforms' (Sivak 2011).

Awareness of the USA's efforts to advance its trade interests was widespread in Australia, and focussed on Venezuela as an emerging alternative model. For one Australian trade unionist, 'the Venezuelan revolution is totally opposed to the neoliberal capitalism which rules most of the planet today' (McIlroy 2011). In this context, Venezuela again became 'a reference point, not only for Latin America but the whole world' (AVSN 2009). Australian events, such as the Latin America and Asia Pacific International Solidarity Forum, attracted over 400 participants and focussed on workshops that discussed how to extend the Venezuelan example to Australia. In the words of one speaker at the conference, 'there is not only one road to socialism, each country will build its own path. But to do so, we must accept socialism as a valid alternative to capitalism, and not utopian' (AVSN 2009). For Latin American Australians, the growth in global critiques regarding neo-liberalism offered a bridge to extend their experiences in Latin America to similar struggles in Australia.

This anger at the neo-liberal imperialism of the USA offered opportunities for deep connections in Australia between various members of the traditional Australian Left, including anarchist and Marxist protesters, environmentalists, and Indigenous activities. Within Australia, much commentary focussed on control of natural resources in countries such as Bolivia. While there are relatively few Bolivians in Australia, activists widely condemned what they perceived to be the USA's intervention to destabilise the government of the Indigenous President Morales, and viewed this as emblematic of the dispossession and historic imperialism endured by Indigenous Latin Americans.

The experiences of violence could only be rendered logical through a focus on the structures that sustained them. Any focus on the personal or individual experience risked appearing nonsensical in its viciousness. This focus created a context in which the Wars on Terror sustained a series of slippages, or 'infinite justice'. There could be no extralegality, hypocrisy, unjustifiable human rights abuse, or legitimate political refugee, because the USA's need for justice in the wake of September 11, 2001, justified all means. In the words of Sivak, the USA's 'grand narrative framed Washington-La Paz relations as part of the U.S. agenda particularly the

War against Communism, War on Drugs and Wars on Terror' (2011). For the Latin American Australians whose families had been displaced, this infinite justice enabled a concomitant space of infinite injustice. Not only were historical injustices unresolved, but they were amplified by ongoing USA actions that were seen to continue the conflicts of the 1970s and 1980s.

CONCLUSIONS

Latin America has been at the centre of international research in memory studies for two decades, as its governments established sustained attempts to come to terms with the social and political legacies of military violence and dictatorship. Truth and reconciliation commissions were established in many of the states, and have served as international benchmarks for processes elsewhere in the world. Similarly, extensive research has been conducted into how social memories functioned during the democratic transitions, as people sought to rearticulate silenced narratives and make meaning from their experiences of violence (Bickford 2000; Stern 2006). There has only been a limited potential for migrants in countries such as Australia to contribute their stories to these processes. As a consequence, the forgiveness that lies at the heart of these reconciliation initiatives can feel unattainable to many emigrants (Lacroix and Fiddian-Qasmiyeh 2013). Engagement can occur, often through contacts with visiting politicians from former insurgent groups (Mason 2012), but the experience is limited in its everyday impact. In effect, a double silence surrounds their prior exposure to violence. Migrants are unable to engage fully with the changing context in their former homes, and lack broader social recognition to articulate their experience in Australia.

Despite the difficulty with finding sustained or concrete support, Australians from a variety of cultural and linguistic backgrounds formed many hundreds of organisations to express solidarity with Latin America (Austin and Ramirez 2012). For many activists, the events in Latin America were a microcosm of events and moral debates in Australia and worldwide. Relatively few of these groups formed lasting bonds with the Latin American community, but the expression of solidarity gradually extended across a limited number of national groups (Marrow 2013). Solidarity to oppose the USA's perceived interference in Latin America frequently had an online presence in the decade following 9/11. Yet, the spaces for public expression and recognition of past injustice remained constrained (Mason 2014). In the decade following September 11, 2001, these limitations continued to be in marked contrast to public debates regarding the victimhood of those who died in the Twin Towers. This raises questions beyond the specific experiences of Latin American Australians, regarding the experiences of those who survive violence but who are disconnected from their former homes and who are denied the ability to articulate their suffering within local communities. While individuals rarely made sense of traumatic experiences at a personal level, the structural conditions that caused the violence were easier to understand as in some way logical. Violence continued to haunt community members for decades as they sought a sense of coherent life narrative in their new country. When those accused of being complicit in *tortured* were found to be living in the community, as occurred in Sydney during 2014, such haunting ceased to be figurative. Similarly, when the statue of Allende was severely vandalised in July 2014, outrage was fierce. The legacies of violence also served to bind community members together in grief in less tangible ways, constantly reiterating the foundational narratives of their displacement. The obligation to remember renewed social bonds and reconnected with the past, but also defined the community in the present. The acts of remembrance reaffirmed that there was indeed an 'us' and 'them', a universal 'Good' and 'Evil', that would continue to give meaning to the future. As Carolyn Nordstrom (2004) writes, 'violence becomes a determining fact in shaping reality as people *will* know it, in the future' as well as looking backwards to the past (226; original emphasis). The experience of violence became the basis through which the community renewed its bonds.

The Wars on Terror following September 11, 2001, was not understood as a singular event. Rather it was situated in social memories that emphasised the USA's interventions of the 1970s and 1980s as foundational mythologies for the Latin American Australian community. As such, the renewed rhetoric against terrorism, and the infinite justice that castigated those who opposed USA actions in the region, were perceived as a continuation of earlier imperialism and violence. Within the context of a refugee community, this continuation demanded they take action to bear witness and recall fallen comrades. It was not simply that the date of the attacks challenged their commemorative practices, but that it evoked a process of haunting that reconnected them with those who died. Refugees continued to complain of the 'virtual blanket of silence around the enormous movements against imperialism across Latin America and the Caribbean' (Kellog 2010). The Wars on Terror enabled a space in which the silenced suffering of those who had died could again be recognised as worthy, and part of an ongoing struggle.

The wider social activism prompted by the Wars on Terror enabled Latin American Australians to become a community that communicated injustice to a large subsection of the population (Alexander 2004). With the recognition of their suffering, they were able to form bridges and bonds with other groups outside their particular community. The results were meaningful connections with an array of civic organisations that embedded communities in both Australian and Latin American contexts. These collaborations recognised the refugees' legitimate knowledge of alternative models to neo-liberalism (not just recognition of having previously been victims of USA's imperialism). This relied on the neo-liberal construct of Australian multiculturalism. Without this, the Latin American Australian's experiences would have remained distant and unrelatable to activist Australians. As neo-liberalism was perceived to be increasingly overt in Australia, Latin American Australians were brought from the perpetually disempowered spaces of 'multiculturals' to become subjects within the Australian polity themselves.

Previous literature has focussed on how the Wars on Terror changed mainstream political discourse, and on the socially exclusionary effects of this on vulnerable social groups in society. This chapter does not dispute these findings. However, it argues that the neo-liberal multicultural state also created spaces for solidarity between migrant and non-migrant groups who shared political aspirations. For Latin American Australians, this relied on their sense of unresolved historical injustice that propelled them to bear witness to past experience of conflict. Their memories of violence, both structural and personal, recast September 11, 2001, as a moment that recalled the epoch-changing events of September 11, 1973. It was not a date that stood alone, but one understood through a long history of infinite injustice in the pursuit of American imperialism.

WORKS CITED

Alexander, Jeffrey. 2004. Toward a Theory of Cultural Trauma. In *Cultural Trauma and Collective Identity*, ed. Jeffrey Alexander, Ron Eyerman, Bernard Giesen, Neil J. Smelser, and Piotr Sztompka, 1–30. Berkeley: University of California Press.

Aly, Anne. 2012. Fear Online: Seeking Sanctuary in Online Forums. In *Cultures in Refuge: Seeking Sanctuary in Modern Australia*, ed. Anna Hayes and Robert Mason, 163–178. Farnham: Ashgate.

Austin, Robert, and Viviana Ramírez. 2012. The People United? Australian Solidarity with Latin America since Allende. *Jornadas de Trabajo: Exilios Politicos del Cono Sur en el siglo XX* 1: 1–37.

Australia-Cuba Friendship Society Perth. 2011a. ACFS Perth Calls on President Obama to Release the Cuban Five! *ACFS Perth*, Sept 11. Available from: http://www.acfs-perth.blogspot.com.

———. 2011b. Will the Real Terrorist Please Stand Up! *ACFS Perth*, Oct 14. Available from: http://www.acfs-perth.blogspot.com.

Australia Venezuela Solidarity Network. 2009. *Report on 'People's Power' Speaking Tour by Daniel Sanchez and Yoly Fernandez*. Available from: http://www.venezuelasolidarity.org/?q=node/413?q=week/2011/06/05.

———. 2011. *Public Forum with Ruben Pereira: For the 99%—Social Movements and Political Change*. Available from: http://venezuelasolidarity.org/?q=node/508?q=week/2011/06/05.

Bickford, Louis. 2000. Human Rights Archives and Research on Historical Memory: Argentina, Chile, and Uruguay. *Latin American Research Review* 35 (2): 160–182.

Bolivarian Circle. 2007a. Bolivarian Circle Weekly Newsletter September 9: Chile—Commemoration of September 11, Sept 9.

———. 2007b. Bolivarian Circle Weekly Newsletter September 10: Tickets to John Pilger's the War on Democracy, Sept 10.

———. 2007c. Bolivarian Circle Weekly Newsletter September 26: Solidarity Message with Bolivia, Sept 26.

Butler, Judith. 2009. *Frames of War: When Is Life Grievable?* London: Verso.

Chodor, Tom, and Anthea McCarthy-Jones. 2013. Post-liberal Regionalism in Latin America and the Influence of Hugo Chavez. *Journal of Iberian and Latin American Research* 19 (2): 211–223.

Cohen, Erez. 2005. Here/There: Cultural Performances and the Construction of a Latino Locality at the Communal Fiestas in Adelaide. *Journal of Iberian and Latin American Research* 11 (1): 113–122.

Hirsch, Shirin. 2016. Chilean Exiles Reconciliation and Return: An Alternative View from Below. *Journal of Refugee Studies* 29: 1–16.

Jones, Ann. 2007. "Sindicalistas Australianos": A Case Study of International Trade Unionism. *Labour History* 93: 197–211.

Jorquera, Roberto. 2003. Bolivarianism Is an Inclusive Democracy. *Green Left Weekly*, vol. 554, Sept 17.

Kellog, Paul. 2010. Latin America: Their Struggle Is Ours. *Green Left Weekly*, vol. 859, Oct 31.

Lacroix, Thomas, and Elena Fiddian-Qasmiyeh. 2013. Refugee and Diaspora Memories: The Politics of Remembering and Forgetting. *Journal of Intercultural Studies* 34 (6): 684–696.

Lawson, Erica. 2014. Disenfranchised Grief and Social Inequality: Bereaved African Canadians and Oppositional Narratives about the Violent Deaths of Friends and Family Members. *Ethnic and Racial Studies* 37 (11): 2092–2109.

Marchetti, Zambrana, and Juan Carlos. 2011. Bolivia-USA: Morbid Relations Beyond Diplomacy. *Bolivia Rising*, Oct 28. Available from: http://boliviarising.blogspot.com.au/2011/11/bolivia-usa-morbid-relations-beyond.html.

Markus, Andrew. 2013. *The Scanlon Foundation Surveys—Mapping Social Cohesion National Report*. Available from: http://scanlonfoundation.org.au/wp-content/uploads/2014/07/mapping-social-cohesion-national-report-2013.pdf.

Marrow, Helen B. 2013. In Ireland "Latin Americans Are Kind of Cool": Evaluating a National Context of Reception with a Transnational Lens. *Ethnicities* 13 (5): 645–666.

Mason, Robert. 2012. Translocality and Coalitions of Justice: Locating Sites of Democratic Transition in the Australian Salvadoran Community. In *Seeking Sanctuary*, ed. Hayes and Mason, 95–112.

———. 2013. Hispanics and Human Rights in Queensland's Public Spaces. *Queensland Historical Atlas*, vol. 3, Jan. Available from: http://www.qhatlas.com.au/hispanics-and-human-rights-queensland-public-spaces.

———. 2014. Incorporating Injustice: Immigrant Vulnerability and Latin Americans in Multicultural Australia. *Journal of Intercultural Studies* 35 (2): 549–562.

McIroy, Jim. 2011. Venezuela, Bolivia Brigade reported on Sunday, September 25, 2011. *Green Left Weekly*, vol. 897.

Nordstrom, Carolyn. 2004. The Tomorrow of Violence. In *Violence*, ed. Neil Whitehead, 223–242. Santa Fe: School of American Research Press.

Refuge of Hope. 2015. *Significant Needs within the Latin-American Community of Melbourne*. Available from: http://www.refugeofhope.org.au/wp-content/uploads/2015/09/ROH-Survey-Report-August-2015.pdf.

Sivak, Martin. 2011. Evo Morales Through the Prism of Wikileaks. *Bolivia Rising*, Oct 7. Available from: http://boliviarising.blogspot.com.au/2011/10/evo-morales-through-prism-of-wikileaks.html.

Stern, Steve. 2006. *Battling for Hearts and Minds: Memory Struggles in Pinochet's Chile, 1973–1988*. Raleigh, NC: Duke University Press.

Zevallos, Zuleyka. 2003. "That's My Australian Side": The Ethnicity, Gender and Sexuality of Young Australian Women of South and Central American Origin. *Journal of Sociology* 39 (1): 81–98.

———. 2005. "It's like we're their Culture": Second-Generation Migrant Women Discuss Australian Culture. *People and Place* 13 (2): 41–48.

AUTHOR BIOGRAPHY

Robert Mason is a lecturer in Migration and Security Studies at Griffith University in Brisbane, Australia. His research focuses on violence, memory, and emotion in both heritage and migration. He has a particular interest in the Spanish- and Portuguese-speaking communities in the Pacific Rim.

CHAPTER 11

A Sense of Embattlement: Australian Jewish Community Leadership's Response to 9/11

Dashiel Lawrence

In 2003, a disquieting story about Australia's Jewish community screened on the popular current affairs television program, *Sunday*. It told of the heightened concerns of terrorist attacks being plotted against the community and its institutions. The program's sources alleged that in the wake of September 11, Australian Jewry had become a prime target of Al-Qaeda terror cells. Reporter John Lyons explained to viewers: 'What we can reveal today is that the Jewish community in Australia is now officially regarded as a category one target. That means of all the people in this country, they are the most likely to be the subject of any terrorist action' (2003). Several other Jewish community figures interviewed in the program suggested that an attack could be imminent. Stephen Rothman, Chairman of the New South Wales Jewish Board of Deputies (NSW JBD), warned: 'we have been told of attacks on Jewish institutions or/and Jewish communal leaders...the mere fact that they haven't yet occurred doesn't mean they won't' (Lyons 2003).

The program's revelations would have shocked and surprised many Australians. For Jewish community leaders in Australia, the story

D. Lawrence (✉)
University of Melbourne, Melbourne, VIC, Australia
e-mail: dashiellawrence@gmail.com

© The Author(s) 2017
J. Gildersleeve and R. Gehrmann (eds.), *Memory and the Wars on Terror*, Palgrave Macmillan Memory Studies,
DOI 10.1007/978-3-319-56976-5_11

201

reaffirmed what they already believed: Jews were seriously vulnerable to violence—not just low-level anti-Semitism, but targeted terrorist attacks. In the wake of the Second Intifada (beginning in October 2000), the events of September 11 a year later, and the subsequent Wars on Terror, the threat was deemed to have dramatically increased. Synagogues, community halls, and even Jewish sporting groups were identified by Australia's security agencies as possible targets. However, it was the spectre of an attack on Jewish day schools that drew most concern. One Jewish parent featured in the *Sunday* story explained that when he dropped his children off at school, thoughts of a terror attack were never far from his mind: 'I genuinely wonder whether I'm leaving them in safe custody, whether in fact when I'm saying goodbye, I'm really saying goodbye' (Lyons 2003). It was a view reflected several years later by Sydney-based Jewish community leader Jeremy Jones: 'after that day (9/11) there was enormous fear within the community. Nobody knew what was happening next. I can tell you, in the Jewish community many people rang me and said "am I sending my children to school?" because they were scared' (cited in Kohn 2011).

Jones and others painted a picture of a vulnerable community on a heightened state of alert. Other discussions on the effects of 9/11 on Australian Jewry, however, have sometimes drawn different conclusions. Dan Goldberg has written of a people 'affluent', 'ensconced in their community', 'segregated', 'wrapped in cotton wool', and largely divorced from the Wars on Terror and the insecurity of the West post-9/11 (2006). He has argued that Prime Minister John Howard's alliance with the United States and longstanding support and sympathy towards the state of Israel contributed to the Jewish community feeling 'robust, strong and confident' at a time of global upheaval (2006, 148). Similarly, in 2004 one community leader argued that to suggest Australian Jewry was living in fear in the wake of 9/11 was 'arrant nonsense' (Lipschutz cited in Goldberg 2006, p. 143).

This chapter does not seek to empirically prove or disprove that Australian Jewry experienced the events of 9/11 and the Wars on Terror with more fear and anxiety than non-Jewish Australians. Instead, I draw attention to how Jewish community leadership in Australia, or as I refer to them, the *established leadership*, responded to these attacks, represented them to Jewish communities across Australia, and ultimately discursively linked them to the wider context of the Israel-Palestine conflict to argue for the emergence of a perceived 'new anti-Semitism'.[1]

I interrogate the legacy of these events on the memory of Australian Jewry, whose experience of trauma has been informed by the large number of Holocaust survivors who settled in Melbourne and Sydney in the middle of the twentieth century.

First, the chapter explores how terror attacks in New York (2001) and Bali (2002) and the Wars on Terror (2001) were discussed and constructed publicly. Second, I explore how community leaders, commentators and other influential participants in the Jewish public sphere employed specific narratives emphasising insecurity and vulnerability. Third, I analyse how these voices lobbied federal government and mobilised Australian Jewry financially to assist with a wave of new expenditures on security in the wake of these events. Finally, the chapter considers the legacy of these responses on Jewish community life in Australia, many years on from 9/11 and the Wars on Terror.

THE AUSTRALIAN JEWISH DIASPORA AND SECURITY

There are approximately 115,000 Jews in Australia (Goldlust 2008, p. 12). Although they only account for a small percentage of the overall population (around 0.5%) the Australian Jewish diaspora is a well-established one. Jews have lived in Australia since the arrival of the First Fleet in 1788 (Rutland 2001, p. 8). Despite periodic declines in religious affiliation, community activity, and demography, since the post-war period the Australian Jewish diaspora has enjoyed an enviable position among global Jewry. Between its two major centres, Sydney and Melbourne, the diaspora boasts an outstanding network of Jewish day schools, well-resourced communal organisations, welfare services, a diversity of synagogues, and cultural and social outlets. For the better part of the last six decades, Jews have enjoyed a comparatively secure and stable place in Australia. They have been free from the kind of anti-Semitism that has stalked diaspora Jewry for centuries. Today, Jews are leaders in commerce, industry, and the arts. They represent on most counts a diaspora community that is 'thriving' (see Markus et al. 2011).

For a community that has carved out a secure place in Australia, a collective sense of vulnerability has persisted for the Australian Jewish diaspora over the last three decades. This insecurity can be identified in physical and symbolic ways (overtly and covertly), it can be heard in community discussions and debates, read in commentary and community media, and visualised in community buildings and spaces.

Many prominent Jewish halls and communal offices in Australia are equipped with formidable security infrastructure including CCTV, high-scale fencing, metal detectors, and bomb-proof glassed windows and exteriors. Jewish schools, museums, synagogues, and community offices are fronted by teams of security guards. Community security and major, and even comparatively minor, incidents of anti-Semitism dominate the pages of the community's newspaper, the *Australian Jews News* (AJN).

There are two compelling reasons for this focus on security. In December 1982, Australian Jewry was confronted by an act of terror when the Israeli Consulate in Sydney's CBD and a popular Jewish social club in neighbouring Bondi were bombed within five hours of each other. Although no one was killed in the attacks, injuries were sustained in the bomb blast at the consulate. Despite the efforts of Jewish community organisations and the New South Wales Police, the attackers have never been apprehended, although members of an Iraqi-based terror organisation remain the primary suspects ('Police Reopen Probe' 2012). The attacks shocked Jewish communities across Australia into action and precipitated a strengthening of security capabilities during the 1990s. A network of security volunteers trained and coordinated to conduct security checks and feed information to authorities within the Jewish communities in Melbourne and Sydney was established and basic security infrastructure was installed. These measures, as I will demonstrate later, were significantly tightened in the wake of 9/11.

The memory of Jewish persecution and vulnerability remains omnipotent. Familial connections, communal spaces, and commemorative events combine to ensure the Holocaust casts a shadow over Australian Jewish communal life. It is often remarked that the Australian Jewish diaspora is home to the largest number (per capita) of Holocaust survivors and their descendants across the global Jewish diaspora (Rutland 2001, p. 256). The Melbourne and Sydney Jewish communities each have their own prominent Holocaust museums as well as a number of public commemorative events throughout the year. Holocaust education is a major component of the Jewish day school experience, as is the popular 'March of the Living tour'.[2] The Jewish memory of persecution, anti-Semitism, and violence that culminated in the largest modern genocide remains an abiding feature of Jewish private and community life. For these reasons the established leadership, as representatives of Australia Jewry, has long committed itself to engineering a sense of security in what has remained a largely safe and harmonious place of Jewish domicile.

THE SECOND INTIFADA, 9/11, THE STATE OF ISRAEL, AND JEWISH DIASPORAS

The beginning of the twenty-first century is likely to be remembered by historians as a major turning point in the life of the State of Israel and Jewish diasporas globally. Several years of fruitless Middle East peace process negotiations and the failed Camp David Summit led to a renewal of violence between Israelis and Palestinians in late 2000. The Second Intifada, a popular uprising across the Palestinian territories, inspired an unprecedented series of terrorist attacks by Palestinian militants (in the cities of Israel; in cafes, shopping malls, on buses and at checkpoints). When retribution came from the Israeli Defence Force (IDF), it was swift and often crushing. The IDF's campaigns into the West Bank inspired a wave of revenge attacks on Jewish institutions across much of Europe. From London to Antwerp, synagogues were firebombed, cemeteries were desecrated, and Orthodox Jews were attacked in the streets (Bergmann and Wetzel 2003).

Yossi Shain has argued the outbreak of the Second Intifada deeply affected the thinking and organisational efforts of the Jewish diaspora and its relations with Israel (2007, p. 61). It gave rise to a new-found unity across Jewish diasporas and Israel; this unity manifested in the political mobilisation of diaspora groups (in support of Israel) and an Israeli government that focused on the core issue of anti-Semitism (p. 61). Israel's bid to bring international attention to the notion of a 'new anti-Semitism' was given greater credence when Israel came under heavy criticism at the UN World Conference against Racism, Racial Discrimination, Xenophobia and Related Intolerance in Durban in August of 2001. In response, Israel's Deputy Foreign Affairs Minister Rabbi Michael Melchior described the anti-Zionist attacks launched against his country at the conference as anti-Semitic, deliberately propagated, and manipulated for political ends (2001). Similarly, Jewish commentators used the moment to decry the emergence of a new anti-Semitism (Bayefsky 2001) that was manifested politically (via discrimination against Israel) and violently through attacks on Jews in the diaspora. This new anti-Semitism was regarded as qualitatively different to previous forms of anti-Semitism. It was motivated by an opposition to Zionism, a hatred of Israel, and a belief that the Jewish state must be destroyed.

The calamitous events of 9/11 did little to allay fears in Israel and Jewish diasporas globally of a new anti-Semitism. The attacks may have been primarily directed at the United States, but they came to be described by diasporic Jewish leaders and figures in Israel as further evidence of a global campaign in which the West, Israel, and Jews were the primary targets of terror. As Gregg Rickman surmised several years later, 'with the attack on the United States came the War on Terror and Terror's war on the West, a war directed as much against Israel and Jews as against the West' (2012, p. 25). Commentators both inside and outside Jewish diasporas created a chorus that suggested these were 'dangerous times to be a Jew'. In Britain, Simon Sebag Montefiore argued September 11 marked a 'sea-change' for British Jewry and that 'in the mythical scale of 9/11, al-Qaeda had unlocked a forgotten cultural capsule of anti-Semitic myths, sealed and forgotten since the Nazis, the Black Hundreds and the medieval blood libels' (2004). Similarly Petronella Wyatt claimed in *The Spectator* that in the wake of 9/11, anti-Semitism and its open expression had become respectable at London dinner tables (2001), while in the United States, Abe Foxman, the Chairman of the US Anti-Defamation League, became convinced after 9/11 that 'we (Jewish people) are facing a threat as great if not greater to the safety and security of the Jewish people than we faced in the 30s' (Foxman 2002).

Jewish diaspora leaders, commentators, Israeli politicians, and other prominent figures all contributed to this discourse. It was a discourse that emphasised Jewish insecurity and vulnerability, while simultaneously aligning the fate of Jews in the diaspora with Jews in Israel. As Australian Jewish commentator and prominent community figure Sam Lipski pronounced: 'the gathering storm of anti-Semitism has forced us to face some bitter truths, and to relearn the core truth: the interwoven nature of our destinies as Jews in distant Australia—or Argentina, France, Canada—with those of the Jews of Israel' (2002a). In this new vision, Jewish solidarity and Jewish security were completely intertwined with Israeli security (Shain and Bristman 2002, p. 77). While it was a discourse designed to mobilise Jewish diaspora organisations and diaspora Jews into a pact of unity, in the case of the British Jewish diaspora, it also 'generated a kind of "gallery of others" threatening Jewry today and a discursive equivalence between each of them' (Kahn-Harris and Gidley 2010, p. 137). Thousands of kilometres away, this discourse also began to frame the thinking of the Australian Jewish diaspora, with tangible consequences.

'THE COMMUNITY'S FIRST PRIORITY': SECURITISATION OF JEWISH COMMUNITIES

In the wake of the Second Intifada, 9/11, and a rise in anti-Semitic attacks internationally, the established leadership embarked on a dramatic process of securitisation. Their campaign was manifested in two different ways. First, Jewish community finances and resources were injected into securing the institutions and assets, its spaces and people. Second, community leaders began to lobby government for financial support to assist with the ongoing security costs Jewish communities were expected to face. Community leadership used the threat of the aforementioned events, particularly a documented rise in anti-Semitic attacks in Australia, to argue this expenditure was warranted and necessary. In addition, at a state level, Jewish representative organisations increased expenditure on security funding and resources. Executive Council of Australian Jewry (ECAJ) began to lobby the federal government in earnest to broker government support for the expenditure outlays in infrastructure. Between 2001 and 2003, the Jewish Community Council of Victoria (JCCV) committed itself to a significant increase in annual security expenditure. Expenditure on security for the Council increased by 185% (Jewish Community Council of Victoria 2001–2003, p. 27). By the end of the 2003 financial year, approximately $250,000 was being allocated to security costs annually by the JCCV (p. 27).

A key element in the JCCV's security plan revolved around the deployment of the Community Security Group (CSG), a volunteer organisation providing security services and support to community organisations, events, and institutions. The JCCV placed a short-term security levy on all Jewish community organisations who accessed the services of the CSG. The group's funding requirements grew significantly during the period of 2001–2003. Funds were primarily used on equipping, training, and insuring new guards as well as funding paid personnel (p. 21). For its part, CSG pressed the JCCV to increase funding and resources by pointing out the dangers to Jewish diasporas around the world. In its 2001–2003 report to Council, the organisation warned that as US, British, and Australian governments better protected their facilities, Jewish communities were more vulnerable to terror attacks (p. 44). CSG leader Gavin Quielt argued that the security lesson of 'recent terrorist activity in US, Bali, Kenya and Europe' impressed the need to expand and hone security during quiet times, 'in order to prepare for the inevitable busy times'. The group took on an additional 250 guards at this point and received a significant expansion to its budget (p. 44).

A secondary element in the securitisation campaign undertaken by the established leadership was the effort to lobby government for financial assistance. As expenditure in communal security increased, ECAJ began to lobby federal government to provide financial support and relief to Jewish communities across Australia for their security expenses. The organisation highlighted the security work and cost carried out, coupled with the international and domestic evidence that the Jewish community was a target for terrorists. Initially these efforts went unsupported with requests 'shuffled from Minister to Minister' with no one prepared to make a contribution (Executive Council of Australian Jewry 2005, p. 44). ECAJ criticised this decision internally in their annual report stating that 'it would make a significant mental difference knowing the government is treating the protection to Jews as equal to the threat against them' (p. 44). The organisation declared they would continue to push, until the weight and cogency of their arguments became too powerful to put off.

ECAJ's lobbying campaign ultimately proved fruitful. During the 2007 federal election campaign, then Opposition Leader Kevin Rudd announced that, if elected, a Labor government would make $16 million dollars available for Jewish and other schools facing security risks to fund security upgrades (Coorey 2007). At the announcement, Rudd emphasised the funding program (later called the Secure Schools Program) would predominantly be for Jewish schools because 'we are very conscious of the particular needs of the Jewish community in regard to security' (cited in Levin and Levi 2007).

The Secure Schools Program would prove to be the most significant legacy of the post-9/11 period for the Australian Jewish community. Between 2009 and 2012, more than $20 million in federal government funding was awarded to Jewish schools and kindergartens across Australia to assist with security upgrades. The money was primarily spent on improvements to existing CCTV, security fencing and lighting, and reinforced windows. In some cases it contributed towards bomb-proof walls and windows and security bollards (Zwartz 2012). Jewish schools accounted for around 60% of the total funding made available under the Program ('Secure Schools Program' 'Secure Schools Program Funded Projects' 2008). The rest was directed towards Islamic and Christian schools and other state schools with students vulnerable to racially-, religious-, or ethnically-motivated violence.

During the 2013 federal election, both the incumbent Labor government and the Liberal Opposition announced that if elected they would continue to fund the program to the tune of $18 million over three years. The election of a Liberal government soon after ensured the money could be used for the employment of private security guards (Hall 2014)—an expenditure that was previously prohibited under the program. Now called the Schools Security Programme, the program has awarded nearly $30 million in funding to Australian Jewish schools since first established in 2007.

'PALESTINIAN TERROR INC AND ISLAMIC TERROR INC': A PROBLEMATIC DISCOURSE

In the wake of 9/11 and the Wars on Terror, Jewish community leaders and Israeli politicians made a clear discursive link between the Second Intifada, terrorist activity in Israel, and terrorist attacks launched against the West. This narrative aligned suicide bombings committed by Palestinians on Israeli civilian and military targets as indistinguishable from acts of mass terror directed against Americans in New York and Washington. In the weeks that followed the 9/11 attacks, then Israeli Prime Minister Benjamin Netanyahu gave voice to this in a speech to the United States Congress in Washington:

> Today, we are all Americans—in grief, as in defiance. In grief, because my people have faced the agonizing horrors of terror for many decades, and we feel an instant kinship with both the victims of this tragedy and the great nation that mourns its fallen brothers and sisters. In defiance, because just as my country continues to fight terrorism in our battle for survival, I know that America will not cower before this challenge. (2001, p. xii)

Gargi Bhattacharyya argues that Netanyahu's statement acts to build an underlying kinship linking America and Israel as victims of international terrorism and members of the same civilisational family, a family facing an attack its very being (2008, p. 51). Thus, 9/11 and the Wars on Terror enabled Israel to present its interests as coterminous with others fighting the forces of international terrorism (p. 51). On one hand, suicide bombings in Israel and the hijacking of airliners in the US did share some core elements: both acts were targeted at civilians and were intended to inflict fear and terror on a population and a state. On the other, Netanyahu's narrative was problematic. Although flawed and profoundly reductive, there can be no doubt it carried deep resonance in Israel and across Jewish diasporas.

In time, the link between Israel's war against Palestinian terrorism and global Wars on Terror was also publicly echoed throughout the Australian Jewish diaspora. By 2002, with Israelis and Palestinians deadlocked in a confrontation, and the United States having declared the Wars on Terror, this discourse began to emerge in subtle and sometimes not so subtle ways. The established leadership, Jewish commentators and other prominent communal figures engaged in discussions via opinion articles in the *AJN*, speeches at rallies, and other communal events in support of Israel. For its part, the paper also contributed to the proliferation of these ideas. Sam Lipski, a long-time community commentator and former editor of the *AJN* was one of the most significant contributors to this discourse. In an article that argued security needed to be the community's greatest priority, Lipski connected the upsurge in violence in the Second Intifada, including suicide bombings in Israel, with the global phenomenon of terrorism that emerged in 9/11: 'Palestinian terror groups, their religious leaders and their supporters in the Middle East and around the world don't 'distinguish' between Israeli and diaspora Jews'. On the contrary, Lipski argued, 'Palestinian Terror Inc and its allies in Islamic Terror Inc spell out their hatred for Jews and Judaism everywhere and have declared us to be "legitimate" targets' (2002c). It was a theme Lipski would return to over the next few years. In prominent articles featured within the *AJN*, he continued to stress the inextricable link between Israel's conflict with Palestinian terror and the Wars on Terror being fought by the United States. To his mind, the success of both 'wars' was dependent on the other: 'the future of America's war against terror, and particularly its plans to attack Iraq, are in turn tied to Israel's war against terror within the Palestinian camp' (2002b).

Other prominent figures in the Australian Jewish diaspora were keen to promote the connection between violence in Israel and the Wars on Terror. Making such an equivalence enabled the Labor member for the electorate of Melbourne Ports, Michael Danby, to promote his security credentials through an advertisement in the lead-up to the November 2001 federal election. His advertisement read: 'There is only one parliamentarian who can convey the connection between the terrorist attacks on the United States and the suicide bombings in Israel' (2001). The implication made to readers of the *AJN* was that only Danby, a Jewish politician and one-time Zionist activist, could advocate on Israel's behalf in Australia's federal parliament.

Drawing a link between the two conflicts was not only left to Lipski and other prominent members of the Australian Jewish community. Rather, it was a view variously promoted in the editorials of the *AJN*. As the first anniversary of 9/11 and the second anniversary of the Second Intifada approached, the paper reflected that 'for all their nuances, the two anniversaries we mark this week are interrelated; Israel's war on Palestinian terror is not wholly removed from America's war on militant Islam' (5763' '2002). In the same edition, Rabbi Raymond Apple of Sydney's Central Synagogue warned that as long as Palestinians continued to commit suicide bombings, a September-11-style attack could occur in the West again. According to Rabbi Apple, the international community and media pandered to terrorists and peddled apologies for suicide bombers in Israel and 'those acts of intolerance elsewhere, especially towards Jews and Jewish institutions' (2002). Rabbi Apple's damning assessment placed Jews as inherently vulnerable and insecure. He suggested how Jews in the diaspora and Israel were treated would prove to be a measure for the West. This was a theme pursued by others, including the *AJN* who editorialised in 2001 that it was a historical pattern that Jews acted as a barometer for civilisations. As the paper evocatively stated: 'we have been the canaries in the goldmine of public decency, when the air gets thin, it seems we are the first to feel it' ('The Cost of Security' 2001).

CONCLUSION: LEGACIES OF WAR

This chapter has illuminated the response of Australian Jewish community leaders, commentators, and other significant communal figures to the events of 9/11 and the Wars on Terror. The post-9/11 period made a profound physical and discursive impact on Australian Jewish life and community. Tens of millions of dollars were invested in upscaling security at Jewish institutions, schools, and communal spaces across

Australia. Community security organisations and community emergency plans were bolstered. Fifteen years on and this focus on security shows no sign of dissipating. Funding for security measures at Jewish institutions and spaces continues to be announced annually by both the NSW and the Victoria state governments. The Secure School Program—now under a new name—continues to invest heavily in Jewish schools nationally. During the funding round of 2015, 17 Jewish day schools across Australia shared in $7.5 million of the $18 million dollars made available nation-wide. The vast majority of that money would be spent on employing security guards.

I do not argue that the allocation of this funding has been unnecessary or unwarranted. Clearly Australian Jews, as with other Jewish diasporas globally, have been and continue to be exposed to a particularly virulent and persistent form of hatred: anti-Semitism.[3] It is often expressed in threatening and violent ways. Expenditure on security infrastructure and protection is one way to respond to the threats faced by Jewish communities. The established leadership will do what it can to protect its constituents from violence. That is to be expected. However, if such expenditures have been made on the basis of the threat of a 'spectacular' or catastrophic terrorist attack, then the grounds are becoming less comprehensible.[4]

In recent years, some Australian Jews have publicly questioned the community focus on security.[5] These concerns represent an emerging reassessment of communal priorities and identity. Grahame Leonard, a community leader who played a key role in lobbying for the Secure Schools Program, remains convinced the leadership pursued the correct policy in the wake of 9/11. However, he too is troubled by the consequence of the security outlay: 'it's very sad I think, that young Jewish Australians grow up thinking that it's normal to have to have security on where they go to school or where they go to synagogue.'[6]

The second key outcome of 9/11 and the Wars on Terror was the shift in communal discourse within Australian Jewry's public forums. In the period that followed 9/11, Australian Jews were told they were vulnerable to attack and violence from a radical Islamic terror threat. Similarly, Israel was continually positioned in Jewish and non-Jewish community media as a key player in the global Wars on Terror. The implication was that while Jews in Israel confronted a Palestinian terror machine, Jews in Australia were vulnerable to similar attacks. The logic followed that no matter where Jews were in the world, they represented a target for terrorists.

This calibre of discourse had multiple effects. It legitimised the re-securitisation campaign that the established leadership undertook and it encouraged a greater intensity of support for Israel in Australia. Scott Burchill has argued that after 9/11 any pretence of even-handedness by the Howard government towards the Israeli-Palestinian conflict was abandoned. In its place came a policy that was virtually indistinguishable from Washington's (2006, p. 123). In addition, I argue the discourse developed by the established leadership and community commentators had the effect of obfuscating three complex geopolitical conflicts and phenomena—namely, the Israel-Palestine conflict, the global Wars on Terror, and contemporary anti-Semitism.

In the years since 9/11 and the start of the Wars on Terror, 35 prosecutions and 26 convictions for terror-related offences were recorded in Australia.[7] A large-scale terror attack has yet to materialise on Australian soil, although the Commonwealth's review into Australia's Counter Terrorism Machinery concludes: 'many plots— some quite major—have been disrupted' (2015, p. iv). Once regarded as 'target no.1 by Al-Qaeda', Jewish community sites and institutions remain untouched. In 2010, Christopher Michaelsen argued that neither Al-Qaeda nor Jemaah Islamiyah posed any significant threat to Australia (2010, p. 250). However, the international and domestic context vis-à-vis terror networks has changed significantly since 2010. 'Australian Jihadism' is now said to have shifted away from externally guided terror plots to self-starting plots (Zammit 2013). The emergence of ISIL's sophisticated propaganda campaign positions it as a powerful source of inspiration for young radicalised Australians to commit a self-starting terrorist plot.

As the security paradigm shifts, the challenge for Jewish community leaders in Australia will be this: to distinguish between violence committed by Palestinians against Israelis in the course of the Israel-Palestine conflict, large scale acts of terror committed against Western targets (be they American, English, or French) and the persistent phenomenon of anti-Semitism, borne out in Australia usually through spontaneous acts of vandalism and assault. Conflating the three has, in the years that followed 9/11, created a problematic binary of 'us and them', of 'our friends' and 'our enemies'. Above all, it has contributed to a 'sense of embattlement' (Rutland 2006, p. 24). This is a sense that will not abate.

Notes

1. By "established leadership", I refer to the major communal and Zionist organisations that claim to represent the interests of Australian Jewish diaspora at a state and federal level. They include the Executive Council of Australian Jewry (ECAJ), and their state affiliates, the New South Wales Jewish Board of Deputies (NSW JBD), and Jewish Community Council of Victoria (JCCV), Zionist organisation, the Zionist Federation of Australia (ZFA), and their respective state councils of NSW and Victoria. Though not a representative body, I also include the Australia Israel Jewish Affairs Council (AIJAC), who play an important and influential role in lobbying at a federal level on behalf of Jewish communal interests and the state of Israel.

2. A tour program that takes Australian Jewish school students on tours of Auschwitz-Birkenau with Jewish students around the world, it is accompanied by a commemorative event to mark international Holocaust Remembrance Day.

3. According to the Executive Council of Australian Jewry's annual report on anti-Semitic incidents, the total number of reported anti-Semitic incidents in Australia in 2012 was the second highest on record (Goldberg 2013).

4. ASIO's 2001–2002 report to Federal Parliament stated that while incidents of anti-Jewish harassment had increased, the harassment and attacks were not regarded as part of an organised campaign. ASIO's next report in 2002–2003 indicated there had been a small increase in the number of reported anti-Jewish incidents, however there were fewer and less severe violent attacks than in the previous year. The report revealed the organisation had issued a Threat Assessment relating to 'Israeli and Jewish interests in Australia'. In recent years the organisation has not reported any major Threat Assessments relating to Israeli or Jewish interests in Australia.

5. *Galus Australis*, a popular online website and blog in Melbourne's Jewish community, contained several commentary articles that criticized CSG, the funding, and focus it receives. These articles were predictably met with outrage from the supporters of the security group.

6. Author interview with Grahame Leonard, 18 Feb. 2014.

7. In recent years two separate incidents have raised the spectre of terrorism in the public consciousness. In December 2014, a lone man, with a history of erratic and violent behaviour, laid siege to a popular café in the heart of Sydney before displaying a black Jihadist flag and killing a hostage. There remains a lack of consensus on whether this constituted an act of terror or had more to do with the mental health issues of the attacker. In October of 2015, a radicalised young man in Sydney's West shot dead a NSW Police employee in an incident described by New South Wales Police

Commissioner Andrew Scipione as a 'politically motivated act of terrorism' ('Parramatta Shooting' 2015). The young man was later shot dead by police. However, as of January 2016, three men facing charges over the murder of the police employee have also been charged with being members of a terrorist organisation.

Works Cited

5763. 2002. *Australian Jewish News*, Sept. 6.

Apple, Raymond. 2002. September 11 Can Happen Again. *Australian Jewish News*, Sept. 6.

Bayefsky, Anne F. 2001. Terrorism and Racism: The Aftermath of Durban. *Jerusalem Centre for Public Affairs*, 468, Dec 16.

Bergmann, Werner, and Juliane Wetzel. 2003. Manifestations of Anti-Semitism in the European Union. *European Monitoring Centre on Racism and Xenophobia, Vienna.*

Bhattacharyya, Gargi. 2008. Globalising Racism and Myths of the Other in the "Wars on Terror". In *Thinking Palestine*, ed. Ronit Lentin, 43–62. London: Zed Books.

Burchill, Scott. 2006. The Israel-Palestine Conflict Since 9/11. In *Australia and the Middle East: A Front-Line Relationship*, 123–133. London: Tauris Academic Studies.

Coorey, Phillip. 2007. Labor to Fund Schools with Security Needs. *Sydney Morning Herald*, Aug 11.

Danby, Michael. 2001. Advertisement. *Australian Jewish News*, Oct. 19.

Executive Council of Australian Jewry. 2005. Security Costs. *Annual Report.*

Foxman, Abraham H. 2002. New Excuses, Old Hatred: Worldwide Anti-Semitism in the Wake of 9/11, speech to *Anti-Defamation League*, Feb 8.

Goldberg. 2006. After 9/11: The Psyche of Australian Jews. In *New Under the Sun: Jewish Australians on Religion, Politics and Culture*, eds. Michael Fagenblat, Melanie Landau, and Nathan Wolski, 140–152. Melbourne: Black Inc.

Goldberg, Dan. 2013. Anti-Semitic Incidents on the Rise in Australia, Report Shows. *Haaretz*, Nov 26.

Goldlust, John. 2008. Jews in Australia—A Demographic Profile. In *Jews and Australian Politics*, ed. Geoffrey Brahm Levey and Philip Mendes, 11–43. Brighton: Sussex Academic Press.

Hall, Bianca. 2014. Private School Security Guards Are Provided by the Tax Payer. *Sydney Morning Herald*, Feb 16.

Jewish Community Council of Victoria. 2001–2003. Report of the Community Security Group. *Biennial Report.*

Kahn-Harris, Keith, and Ben Gidley. 2010. *Turbulent Times: The British Jewish Community Today*. London: Continuum.

Kohn, Rachael. 2011. God After Ground Zero. *ABC Radio National*, Sept. 11. Available from: http://www.abc.net.au/radionational/programs/spiritofthings/god-after-ground-zero/2938718.

Levin, Naomi and Joshua Levi. 2007. Rudd's $20 m Security for Jewish Schools. *Australian Jewish News*, Aug 10.

Lipski, Sam. 2002a. Antisemitism's Bitter Truths. *Australian Jewish News*, May 10.

Lipski, Sam. 2002b. Why the Worst of Times in Israel May Also Be the Best of Times. *Australian Jewish News*, July 26.

Lipski, Sam. 2002c. Security Must Be Community's Top Priority. *Australian Jewish News*, Dec 6.

Lyons, John. 2003. Terror Target No. 1: The Jewish Community. *Channel Nine Sunday Program*, Sept 7.

Markus, Andrew et al. 2011. *Jewish Continuity: Report 2*, Australian Centre for Jewish Civilisation, Melbourne.

Melchior, Michael. 2001. Statement to the Durban Conference, Sept. 3. Available from: http://mfa.gov.il/MFA/PressRoom/2001/.

Michaelsen, Christopher. 2010. Australia and the Threat of Terrorism in the Decade after 9/11. *Asian Journal of Political Science* 18 (3): 248–268.

Montefiore, Simon Sebag. 2004. A Dangerous Time to Be a Jew. *New Statesman*, June 28.

Netanyahu, Benjamin. 2001. *Fighting Terrorism: How Democracies Can Defeat the International Terrorist Network*. New York: Farrar, Straus and Giroux.

Parramatta Shooting: "The Shooters Actions Were Politically Motivated and Linked to Terrorism" 2015. *Daily Telegraph*, Oct 3.

Police Reopen Probe into 1982 Bombings. 2012. *Sydney Morning Herald*, Aug 26.

Rickman, Gregg. 2012. *Hating the Jews: The Rise of Antisemitism in the 21st Century*. Brighton: Academic Studies Press.

Rutland, Suzanne. 2006. Negotiating Religious Dialogue: A Response to the Recent Increase of Anti-Semitism in Australia. In *Negotiating the Sacred: Blasphemy and Sacrilege in a Multicultural Society*, eds. Elizabeth Burns Coleman and Kevin White, 17–30. ANU ePress.

Rutland. 2001. *Edge of the Diaspora*. New York: Holmes and Meier.

Secure Schools Program Funded Projects. 2008. *Attorney-General's Department*. Available from: https://www.ag.gov.au/CrimeAndCorruption/CrimePrevention/Pages/SchoolsSecurityProgramme.aspx.

Shain, Yossi. 2007. *Kinship and Diasporas in International Affairs*. Ann Arbor: University of Michigan Press.

Shain, Yossi, and Barry Bristman. 2002. Diaspora, Kinship and Loyalty: The Renewal of Jewish National Security. *International Affairs* 78 (1): 69–96.
The Cost of Security. 2001. *Australian Jewish News*, Nov 2.
Wyatt, Petronella. 2001. Poisonous Prejudice. *Spectator*, Dec 8.
Zammit, Andrew. 2013. Explaining a Turning Point in Australian Jihadism. *Studies in Conflict & Terrorism* 36 (9): 739–755.
Zwartz, Barney. 2012. Safety at all Costs. *Age*, Jan 31.

AUTHOR BIOGRAPHY

Dashiel Lawrence is a doctoral graduate from the Jewish Studies program at the University of Melbourne. He is the co-editor of two books: *Australia and Israel: A Diasporic, Political and Cultural Relationship* (Sussex Academic Press 2015), and a forthcoming collection about Australian Jews and sport.

CHAPTER 12

Violent Femmes: Collective Memory After 9/11 and Women on the Front Line of Journalism

Rebecca Te'o

In 2001, a global audience watched the fall of 2WTC, the south tower of the Twin Towers in Manhattan's World Trade Center. Although it was the first to fall, it was the second tower to be hit that morning by Al Qaeda-backed radicals in a jet aircraft packed with passengers. This is significant because the global audience, which had tuned into rolling TV coverage after the surprise strike on 1WTC (the north tower), watched both the subsequent attack on and the disintegration of the south tower *as it happened*, making its attack a template in terror propaganda now reflected in modern terror campaigns, most notably that of the media campaigns of the Islamic State (IS) (Kellner 2004).[1] Its 'live unfolding' and the ensuing weeks of extensive coverage etched the events of September 11 into public memory in a way that had never occurred in any other conflict and prompted debate, at least in academic circles, about 'visual agenda-setting' (Fahmy et al. 2006). The collapse of 2WTC, followed a half hour later by that of 1WTC, permanently altered

R. Te'o (✉)
University of Southern Queensland, Queensland, Australia
e-mail: rebecca.teo@usq.edu.au

© The Author(s) 2017
J. Gildersleeve and R. Gehrmann (eds.), *Memory and the Wars on Terror*, Palgrave Macmillan Memory Studies,
DOI 10.1007/978-3-319-56976-5_12

219

lower Manhattan's financial district, but it also significantly modified the global landscape in which the media operates by transforming the expectations of audiences and news providers, and impacting the way many journalists practice their profession (Carey 2002).

Scholars and practitioners have already written much about the effects of September 11 on journalism. There has also been much examination of related issues, such as the violence associated with conflicts arising from the 'Wars on Terror', the increasing need for safety and risk training for journalists, media agenda setting and framing of biases, the influence of political power, the proliferation of anti-terror legislation, transparency in journalistic practice, the growth of 'terror PR' and propaganda, and the increasing public distrust of mainstream media and subsequent rise of citizen-based media. By no means is this chapter meant to be an exhaustive examination of influences on post-9/11 journalism (that requires an entire text of its own); rather, the investigations within are meant as a reference point regarding how the aftermath of September 11 has specifically affected female journalists who have traditionally grappled with journalism's many pre-existing challenges, some of which are gender-related and affect women's career goals and achievements (Poindexter et al. 2008). It acknowledges the effects of September 11 have spread throughout the entire industry rather than just those sectors dealing with high-risk reportage, but will provide a snapshot of how female journalists have responded to these challenges. It will explore women's experiences in relation to how hyper-masculinity helps establish a myth (the 'hard-bitten journalist') which in turn creates and sustains journalists' collective memory about their profession, and will also examine the argument that female journalists, like their male counterparts, may be at risk because of the rigours of post-9/11 reporting.

In addressing the stated objectives, this chapter will consider some of the gender issues in journalism prior to the September 11 attacks on the US and the Wars on Terror, and examine whether the events of September 11 affected the culture and practice of women journalists afterwards. It will also consider the interaction between the ways in which journalists both shape and are shaped by their experiences of trauma post-9/11. Three journalists have been chosen as case studies for this chapter:

- *Lara Logan*: A South African journalist with extensive front line experience in the wars in Iraq and Afghanistan;

- *Kate Adie*: A British journalist who has decades of experience covering conflict and war in China, Rwanda, Bosnia, and Iraq;
- *Marie Colvin*: A US journalist who was killed covering the civil war in Syria in 2012.

Each journalist has covered events of significant conflict and/or trauma as a requirement of their profession, and each is considered a veteran of this type of high-risk reporting. These case studies help provide an overview of the implications of the Wars on Terror on reporting practice, and greater contextualisation of the subject matter within journalism. This contextualisation is an essential component of understanding the individual experiences of the subjects (Niglas 2004). Specific primary evidence, including transcripts of video and audio recordings, have been analysed, as well as the case study subject's own work in the form of personal essays and various articles for media publication. Secondary data in the form of published, peer-reviewed academic research in the areas of journalism, trauma, and memory have also been investigated. Each case study was analysed using the same questions to elicit specific information on the same types of themes relevant to the overarching key questions of the chapter: did the journalist cover an event of trauma, conflict, or confrontation, or endanger their mental or physical health in the practice of their reporting? Did they identify any issues related to post-9/11 reporting practice? Did they exhibit compliance with and acknowledgement of the 'hard-bitten journalist' myth during or after covering the news event?

While this inductive approach does not necessarily mean findings can be extrapolated to a broader context, it does mean that a theory could be developed for future investigation (George and Bennett 2004). Therefore, while the findings of this chapter are largely relevant to the selected case studies examined in the chapter, it provides a basis from which to explore the issues surrounding myth and memory in journalism, and could be used in a much larger context.

For ease of reading, this chapter uses the term *collective memory* to refer to the collective identity of journalists, while the term *public memory* refers to the way in which the audience views journalism and the broader media landscape.

Women on the Front Line: Pre-2001

Journalism is often referred to as 'the front line of history': it captures events as they happen to provide information and analysis for their audiences and helps people make sense of the world around them (Scheufele and Tewksbury 2007). In the longer term, journalism becomes a key material in the patchwork of human experience investigated by the social sciences and humanities, and because of this, journalism is not merely a conduit of public memory, it is also a primary *constructor* or agent of memory (Kitch 2008; Zelizer 2008). The 'serious' side of the profession—hard news reporting beats, political analysis, and war and conflict reporting—were traditionally considered male-dominated fields (Djerf-Pierre 2007). However, the history of women reporting in these fields is as diverse as it is interesting. While the popular image of the war reporter is a hard-bitten, risk-taking man, women have often been on the front line, recording events, living rough, and risking—and losing—their lives. High-profile women in 'serious' journalism include Helen Thomas, who pioneered the role from the 1950s, eventually becoming the first female officer of the US National Press Club and the first female member and president of the White House Correspondent's Association; and Marguerite Higgens, who covered World War II and the Korean and Vietnam wars. There are, of course, many others who were renowned for their risky reporting assignments, anti-authoritarian attitude, strong personalities, ability to 'keep up with the men', and possession of a working attitude that earned them the labels of 'insubordinate' or 'difficult'. While only some are widely known, history records the journalistic exploits of female reporters such as Kit Coleman (Spanish–American War); Florence Dixie (First Boer War); Inez Milholland (World War I); Margaret Bourke-White, Lorraine Stumm, Martha Gellhorn, and Marjorie McDonald (World War II); and Denby Fawcett, Laura Palmer, and Kate Webb (Vietnam War). What is evident, however, is that the gender ratios of war and conflict reporters have traditionally suggested that more men than women received opportunity and encouragement to cover these areas, largely due to the historical and cultural constraints that were (and sometimes still are) placed on women during the corresponding historical eras (Conboy 2004). In contrast to men's experience, women often had to fight for the chance to cover conflict, and in some cases were compelled to leave their employment in order to freelance. As James E. Caccavo outlines, then:

Denby Fawcett of the *Honolulu Advertiser* quit her job at the higher-paying *Honolulu Star-Bulletin* when that paper refused to send her to Vietnam. Fawcett had to pay her own way to Vietnam to freelance for the *Advertiser.* Of the nine contributors to *War Torn* (a collection of memoirs by female war reporters) five had to pay their own way over. The most novel was Jurate Kazickas' winning $500 on the TV game show *Password* to fund her one-way ticket to Vietnam in 1967. Laura Palmer followed a boyfriend doctor to Vietnam and got a job with ABC radio in 1972. (2002)

Female reporters have often had to battle the industry's hyper-masculinity to bring news from the front lines to audiences across the globe. In order to work their way through a sometimes hostile landscape of industry gender politics, some female reporters have historically had to adopt hyper-masculine traits in order to be seen as competent enough to cover war and conflict. As such, the 'hard-bitten' style of these female journalists matched and met the demands of the hyper-masculine style of the industry in which they operated (Hanitzsch 2007). There have now been decades of employment of women as police and court reporters, foreign correspondents, and hard news reporters. Therefore, assertions that most newsrooms consist of mainly male staffers are not necessarily correct. However, while it can be argued that the gender balance of newsrooms is now more equitable than ever before, and in some cases even dominated by women, journalist's 'gendered and professional identities' are still ongoing issues (Harden and Whiteside 2009), and largely male-dominated areas in journalism remain, such as in sports reporting and editorial management. To better understand the pressures placed on female journalists, it is necessary to gain a further understanding of the history of hyper-masculinity within the industry, using feminist perspectives of hyper-masculinity as part of the analysis of the myth of the hard-bitten journalist.

HYPER-MASCULINITY

The attributes accorded to a 'quality' reporter—tenacity, curiosity, cynicism, determination, aggression, purposefulness, honour (among others)—are those attributes that have been traditionally, and problematically, attributed to masculinity. Hyper-masculinity is characterised as involving 'stereotypically masculine or macho traits and the rejection of traits perceived as the antithesis of machismo' (Scharrer 2001, p. 160).

This perspective was identified more than 30 years ago in Donald L. Mosher and Mark Sirkin's seminal work (see Fisher et al. 2011) which highlighted three main characteristics of hyper-masculine behaviour in the development of the Hyper-masculinity Inventory for the field of psychology. These include callous sex attitudes, violence, and danger. Hyper-masculinity has also been identified as 'a coping mechanism used to ease feelings of vulnerability' (Corprew 2011, p. 1) with links to an individual's emerging identity, so that '[t]he construct of the macho personality is viewed as a script—a set of rules, magnified by affect, for predicting, interpreting, controlling and evaluating a family of related scenes—developed through socialisation and enculturation' (Mosher and Sirkin cited in Fisher et al. 2011, p. 472).

However, gender is not regarded as an identifying factor in the display of hyper-masculine traits within journalism, as both men and women can exhibit these traits (Deuze 2005). A journalist's acceptance and embodiment of exaggerated masculine traits in order to succeed in journalism may help form a collective memory through the 'organisational identity' which operates within journalism (Torkkola and Ruoho cited in Krijnen et al. 2011). Additionally, many journalists are compelled to pursue objectivity, an ideal that creates distance between the journalist and the story. This may be especially true for female journalists who, in displaying typically ascribed 'feminine' attributes such as empathy, sympathy, and sadness, place themselves at risk of being seen as 'unprofessional'. Hyper-masculinity, therefore, involves a rejection of sympathy, and sometimes empathy, in order for the individual to function as they desire (Scharrer 2001). Journalists' collective memory, which I argue is based on the myth of the hard-bitten journalist, is also reflected in the five 'ideal-typical' traits of a journalist: public service, objectivity, autonomy, immediacy, and ethics (Deuze 2005). These traits have been accepted and even celebrated in collective memory, both within and outside the profession, from the superheroes of popular culture (Clark Kent/Superman, Peter Parker/Spider-Man), to the champions of counter-culture movements that kicked against established authority (*Rolling Stone* magazine, 'gonzo' journalist Hunter S. Thompson), to fictional investigative journalists who operated like gumshoe detectives or private investigators.

According to the definitions above, both myth and hyper-masculinity can be used by journalists as coping mechanisms in situations of trauma and conflict. The myth of the hard-bitten journalist, which remains a universally powerful construct for journalists, both attracts journalists to reporting and can offer a comforting or affirming identity within the industry itself, thereby assisting in the creation of a collective memory. It is often the very thing that attracts people to the profession in the first place, and inspires journalists working within the profession. It is also underpinned by the 'keep the bastards honest' ideology of the Fourth Estate tradition within journalism.

Pre-9/11, this apparent hyper-masculine nature of the industry and its complex relationship with the history of journalistic practice was often an obstacle for female journalists. Post-9/11, journalists must also consider geopolitical change, increased surveillance, the nature of modern war/conflict and violence, increased militarisation and intelligence in policing, and changed methods of gathering and disseminating material. By examining the individual case studies of female journalists, we can see how their practice has been affected by the events of September 11, 2001.

Logan, Adie, and Colvin

Lara Logan is a seasoned reporter who has covered conflict in numerous regions, including the wars in Kosovo, Afghanistan, and Iraq. Joe Hagan (2014) used the term 'bombshell' to describe her because of both her physical appeal and her tendency to blast her way through a story. Logan said she always recognised that, as a woman, she had to work harder than her male colleagues in order to be taken seriously: 'The reason that people at work think I'm psychotic is because without even thinking about it I knew that as a young woman I had to work harder, and know more, than anybody else...You can strap three of these guys together and I can still leave them in my trail, you know?' (cited in AWRT 2009). Some have labelled her reporting style as 'risky' and 'aggressive' (Hagan 2014), but Logan uses the search for truth and justice to describe her career (cited in AWRT 2009). Indeed, Hagan suggests it may be her 'masculine' practice and her 'feminine' appearance that have been overriding factors in her career trajectory, and has made employers happy to have her reporting from the front line. Indeed, he points out that '[a]s Ed Bradley, the late *60 Minutes* correspondent and a strong advocate of Logan's, memorably if crudely observed, "She's got tits and balls"' (2014).

Arguably, Logan's defining post-9/11 moment was the widely publicised sexual assault that occurred in Tahrir Square during her coverage of the revolution in Egypt during the 'Arab Spring' in 2011. Logan reported she was assaulted and repeatedly digitally penetrated by a group of 200–300 men. This event taps directly into some key post-9/11 issues experienced by journalists, most notably the deliberate targeting of journalists in conflict, increase in the use of sexual assault as a weapon, and the increasing need for safety and risk training for journalists.

Kate Adie is a veteran journalist who has extensive experience in the coverage of war and conflict (Allison 2010) around the world. She supports the view that journalists have an obligation to their audience to responsibly cover events as they happen, even though there may be risk involved (Allison 2010). She has a reputation for being uncompromising, tenacious, confrontational, and exceptionally dedicated to her profession, but Adie also questions her role at times: 'I will admit that at times in my working life I have found myself caught in crossfire, or stunned by a grenade, or trying to ask directions from a corpse during a gun battle, and the first response of this reporter has been "Why am I doing this?" rather than "What's going on?"' (Adie 2008, p. iii). Adie has also raised concerns about an increasing focus on spectacle in war reporting, rather than a dedication to reporting the grim realities of war, implying that attention to visually striking events such as military bombardment may overlook important stories that can be more difficult to source and tell (Hutchinson 2006).

US journalist Marie Colvin was as famous for her tenacity as she became for her eye patch, which she wore after losing an eye in a rocket-propelled grenade explosion in Sri Lanka in 2001. Colvin covered conflicts all over the world—East Timor, Libya, Kosovo, Chechnya, Iran, Iraq—before heading to her final reporting task: the Syrian civil war in 2012. Marie Brenner's *Vanity Fair* piece on Colvin (Brenner 2012) notes conditions in Syria were extremely grim, with journalists named as specific targets for killing, yet Colvin smuggled herself into Syria in order to tell the stories of the civilians wracked by an indiscriminate conflict. Despite the months of extremely high-risk reporting, Colvin's approach was steely, but contrasted with the 'war-dog' persona many people think of when referring to journalists on the front line. In Brenner's terms, '[s]he pushed into combat zones that made her drivers sometimes vomit from fear. Yet she dreaded becoming "this smelly, exhausted pseudo-man," as she wrote in British *Vogue* in 2004 when explaining her "defiant preference" for satin and lace underwear in the trenches' (2012).

Colvin highlighted her femininity, becoming famous for wearing expensive lingerie under her flak jackets and reportedly, on the day she was killed in a besieged media centre, a double strand of pearls gifted to her by Palestinian Liberation Organisation (PLO) leader Yasser Arafat (Brenner 2012). Colvin had reached 'legend' status long before her untimely death. Like Adie, she was admired by her audience, respected by colleagues, and renowned for her grit and determination (Witherow 2012). In a *New York Times* interview in 2012, Colvin's mother highlighted her late daughter's dedication to her job, even in the face of danger:

> 'If you knew my daughter,' she said, 'it would have been such a waste of words. It just wasn't something that would even be on the plate at all. She was determined, she was passionate about what she did, it was her life. There was no saying 'Don't do this.' This is who she was, absolutely who she was and what she believed in: cover the story, not just have pictures of it, but bring it to life in the deepest way you could. (cited in Barron 2012)

It can be argued that Colvin's work practices were a result of her embodiment of the myth: she not only espoused the ideals of the Fourth Estate, but regularly undertook significant personal risk in order to fulfil her 'duty' as a journalist. Deuze's 'ideal-typical' traits of journalism can be identified in Colvin's practice, and in her continuous efforts to cover war and conflict.

JOURNALISM AFTER SEPTEMBER 11, 2001

The diverse sectors of the information industries have all been affected in some way by the events of September 11, 2001. From various restrictions imposed via legislation, to heightened sensitivities around access to data, the industries that deal in information are each faced with an ever-changing, ever-challenging landscape in which to do business (Zelizer and Allan 2011). In journalism, these changes are multi-dimensional and include the emergence of whistle-blower websites such as Wikileaks; the increase in the use of web routers such as Tor (originally The Onion Router) to avoid external surveillance; and the changing nature of audiences. Ultra-competitive, with fickle news consumers and stretched resources, newsrooms are struggling to meet the challenges of reporting in the twenty-first century. While the public may have traditionally had a love/hate relationship with journalists, it is now more sceptical of truth and cynical over a perceived media agenda, partly in response to some subjective post-9/11 reportage (Hutchinson 2006), arguably resulting in the reshaping of public memory by conspiracy theories, political ideologies and expediencies, and the speed and availability of social media. The reportage of the events of September 11 was a catalyst for change and created a turgid relationship between traditional and new media, and exacerbated the influence of social media. Indeed, '[i]t could be suggested that, while journalism has failed to live up to its initial investigative or objective roles, weblogs offered a polyglot of voices crying from the Babel Tower, demanding a media that actually mattered' (Champion cited in Carey 2002). While journalists may have historically divided the loyalties of the public, what Champion appears to suggest is that public memory has now shifted *en masse*. Journalists may no longer be seen as upholders of truth and battlers for the underdog; instead they may be increasingly looked upon as irrelevant and possibly even corrupt. In a post-9/11 world, the industry's hyper-masculinity has endured: regardless of geographic location, the 'typical' successful journalist, one who is consistently visible to the audience and is turning out what is deemed as 'quality' work, remains young, male, better educated than the general population, and from a dominant cultural group (Hanitzsch 2007). Gender does still have *significant* impact on the professional growth of female journalists, particularly in (but not limited to) newsrooms located in developing nations (Poindexter et al. 2008).

A common complaint among female journalists is that they still do not enjoy the same career trajectory as their male counterparts. Of the bylines published in Australian newspapers from July 1–15, 2005, only 34% were of female journalists, and female journalists were often given 'second-tier' (that is 'softer') stories to report on, such as human interest pieces or feature stories, while their male counterparts were more often given 'first-tier' stories, such as politics or business (Strong and Hannis 2007). In 2009, the International Federation for Journalists (IFJ) released a declaration outlining the state of gender equity in journalism, demanding particular attention be paid to the situation of female journalists in Africa, Asia, Latin America, Europe, and the Middle East. Logan says her career, both pre- and post-9/11 has observed this inequity:

> When I was working at *Reuters Television*, I literally ran that entire operation. And I'd always been second. And now I was running it, and they

decided to hire somebody else...he'd never done that job before, he was an editor, and he negotiated a salary that was three times my salary—and I trained him...I'm a terrible negotiator. I was always so grateful to get the job that I never negotiated anything ever and I was consistently underpaid. Consistently, my whole career. (cited in AWRT 2009)

Colvin's war reporting was partly fuelled by intense competition and a desire for truth which could be mistaken for 'a form of derring-do or addiction to the poison elixir of battle' (Brenner 2012). In contrast, Adie, who did not shy away from volatile events to report directly from those sites—even if that meant she risked (and sustained) physical injury—retired from the front line for the BBC in 2003 in order to freelance. Adie maintains that she never relished her work on the front line. She described the need to feed the 24-hour news cycle, the framing of agendas, and an addiction to the spectacle of war (or 'war porn'—the spectacle of explosions, missile launches, and the like) as major issues in post-9/11 reportage (Hutchinson 2006), which began in earlier conflicts but expanded in line with audience demands and developments in media technology. Feeding these demands requires immediate and constant attention and review across various media platforms, therefore satisfying the vagaries of traditional and news audiences can exacerbate another increasingly concerning area of post-9/11 reportage: the increase in personal risk in order to obtain a story.

Politics and war is risky business for journalists. The post-9/11 Wars on Terror have exacerbated the risk of physical harm because of factors that include the indiscriminate nature of modern warfare that implicates the increasing incidence of reports of sexual assault as a weapon in conflict, and the cultural differences between the states involved in war (Mason 2013). In 2014, a study found that, at that time, only 11 countries in the world were free from conflict (Withnall 2014). Figures from the Committee to Project Journalists (CPJ) highlight that, of journalists killed in the course of their reporting between 1992 and 2014, 45% were covering politics and 38% were covering war. By comparison, 22% were covering corruption, 17% were covering crime, and 19% were covering human rights issues (1180 Journalists Killed since 1992' 2016). Overwhelmingly, the majority of journalists killed were men (93%), many as a result of being directly targeted (66% of male journalists were murdered, with only 20% caught in crossfire during combat).

The increasing use of sexual violence is a growing threat to journalists, and while this has been exemplified in the experience of Lara Logan, it is important to recognise that in the same year as Logan's attack, numerous other female journalists were sexually attacked, although these attacks did not warrant the same global attention as Logan's, raising questions about the capacity of journalists to report sexual violence; the ethno-centricity of attack coverage; and the use of attractive reporters as 'war porn' to seize the attention of a mobile and distracted audience. A report for the CPJ highlights that sexual violence is often used against journalists as a form of reprisal, as abuse in detention, or is mob-related and public (Wolfe 2011). Concern over an increase in gender-based violence against female reporters reflects increased concerns regarding violence against women in general and global security since September 11 (Mason 2013). An International Women's Media Foundation and the International News Safety Institute survey showed 64% of female journalists had been assaulted or threatened in the course of their work, however most of these attacks were perpetrated by coworkers or, to a lesser degree, law enforcement in the areas in which they were reporting (Hess 2013). The majority of women killed, attacked, jailed, or sexually assaulted are from within the regions of conflict, rather than foreign journalists. In addition, women have historically not reported assaults to either law enforcement or editorial management due to a concern it would negatively affect their careers or preclude them from reporting in areas of conflict for 'fear they would be perceived as vulnerable and be denied future assignments' (Wolfe 2011). Some news organisations may also capitalise on the appeal of women journalists and may specifically seek out women journalists to report from conflict zones, and potentially increase their audiences:

> [M]ale editors, and particularly television editors, are exploiting women. More women than men graduate in media studies. They don't know how to find a fixer; they don't know about weaponry; they don't know where is safe, where is not safe — they just want to prove themselves. So they might end up in a really dangerous trouble spot without adequate preparation. And because you're hardly paid, it's often the young, inexperienced girls who are prepared to do it. And the editors are prepared to exploit them because it makes exciting news. It's vicarious thrill. You see a gorgeous woman on your screens in a flak jacket, and it's almost like entertainment. (Sebba cited in Chertoff 2013)

In the post-9/11 landscape, news-linked organisations such as Dart Centre for Journalism and Trauma, the International News Safety Institute (INSI), and Reporters Instructed in Saving Colleagues (RISC) help journalists minimise risk to their personal safety. These organisations provide training and support and can advise organisations and individuals about the specific requirements of female journalists, such as their need for smaller protective gear like flak jackets in areas of conflict. For those who maintain female journalists are deliberately targeted to make a political or religious statement, the increase in sexual assault may be seen as another propaganda tool used in the conflicts arising from the Wars on Terror (Kellner 2004). The use of media as a propaganda tool continued post-9/11 with kidnappings and executions of journalists, and while traditional news media has pulled back from graphic depictions of war and terror, web-based publishing, especially via social media, has provided audiences with the opportunities to witness rapes, decapitations, executions, and war crimes (Simon and Libby 2015) and provided ready access to press releases from organisations such as the military, security providers, and non-government organisations, resulting in a shift in how public memory is created.

CONCLUSION

In examining the experiences of Logan, Adie, and Colvin, it is evident that the impact of September 11 has potentially exacerbated pre-existing issues and created new ones for women. The myth of the hard-bitten journalist, and the hyper-masculinity historically associated with the industry, are ongoing issues for women in journalism and the complexity of this relationship remains: it is part of the collective memory of industry. The effects of September 11, while individually experienced by each journalist, still exhibit commonalities (such as increased threat to personal safety while on assignment). While their practice may differ, the journalists are linked by a shared memory that stems from their desire for truth and accountability—the tenets of journalism—that creates a complex, collective memory.

NOTE

1. The Islamic State (IS) was originally called the Islamic State of Iraq and Syria (ISIS) or the Islamic State of Iraq and the Levant (ISIL). Each of these acronyms refers to the same jihadist organisation which strives for the unification of Muslims across the globe and violently rejects all other interpretations of Islam but its own (Gulmohamad 2014).

WORKS CITED

1180 Journalists Killed since 1992. 2016. *Committee to Protect Journalists.* Available from: https://cpj.org/killed/.

Adie, Kate. 2008. *Into Danger.* London: Hodder & Stoughton.

Adie, 2005. *Nobody's Child.* London: Hodder & Stoughton.

Allison, Maggie. 2010. Roles in conflict: The woman war reporter. *Miranda*, vol. 1, no. 2. Available from: http://www.miranda-ejournal.fr/1/miranda/article.xsp?numero=2&id_article=article_07–586.

Alphonse, Lilah M. 2011. Do Female Journalists Belong in War Zones? *Lilah M. Alphonse* weblog, 17 Feb. Available from: http://www.lylahmalphonse.com/2011/02/do-female-journalists-belong-in-war.html.

American Women in Radio and TV (AWRT). 2009. Lara Logan: Female Journalists in War Zones, *Women's Media Forum*, 2 June. Available from: http://www.youtube.com/watch?v=JBUzACbVjqA.

Barron, James. 2012. Recalling Her Determined Daughter, a Journalist Killed in Syria, *New York Times*, 23 Feb. Available from: http://www.nytimes.com/2012/02/23/nyregion/marie-colvin-mother-recalls-determined-journalist-killed-in-syria.html?_r=1&.

Brenner, Marie. 2012. Marie Colvin's Private War. *Vanity Fair*, Aug. Available from: http://www.vanityfair.com/politics/2012/08/marie-colvin-private-war.

Caccavo, James E. 2002. Up close and Personal, *LA Times*, 22 Sept. Available from: http://articles.latimes.com/2002/sep/22/books/bk-caccavo22.

Carey, James W. 2002. American Journalism On, Before, and After September 11. *Journalism After September 11*, eds. Zelizer and Allan, 71–90.

Chertoff, Emily. 2013. It's More Dangerous than Ever to be a Female War Reporter, *Atlantic*, 21 Feb. Available from: http://www.theatlantic.com/sexes/archive/2013/02/its-more-dangerous-than-ever-to-be-a-female-war-reporter/273322/.

Conboy, Martin. 2004. *Journalism: A Critical History.* London: Sage.

Corprew, III, C.S. 2011. *Men at the Crossroads: Revisiting the Definition, Dimensionality, and Function of Hypermasculinity within the Collegiate Context*, Unpublished PhD diss., Tulane University.

Deuze, Mark. 2005. What is Journalism? Professional Identity and Ideology of Journalists Reconsidered. *Journalism Review* 6 (4): 442–464.

Djerf-Pierre, Monika. 2007. The Gender of Journalism. *Nordicom Review* 28: 81–104.

Ethics and Gender: Equality in the Newsroom, Brussels Declaration 2009. *International Federation of Journalists*, 1 Jun. Available from: http://www.ifj.org/nc/news-single-view/browse/4/backpid/128/category/news-8/article/ethics-and-gender-equality-in-the-newsroom-brussels-declaration/.

Fahmy, Shahira, Sooyoung Cho, Wayne Wanta, and Yonghoi Song. 2006. Visual Agenda-Setting after 9/11: Individuals' Emotions, Image Recall, and Concern with Terrorism. *Visual Communication Quarterly* 13 (1): 4–15.

Fisher, Terri D., Clive M. Davis, William L. Yarber, and Sandra L. Davis. 2011. *Handbook of Sexuality-Related Measures*, 3rd ed. London: Sage.

George, Alexander L., and Andrew Bennett. 2004. *Case Studies and Theory Development in the Social Sciences*. Cambridge, MA: MIT Press.

Gulmohamad, Zana Khasraw. 2014. The Rise and Fall of the Islamic State of Iraq and Al-Sham (Levant) ISIS. *Global Security Studies* 5 (2): 1–11.

Hanitzsch, Thomas. 2007. Deconstructing Journalism Culture: Towards a Universal Theory. *Communication Theory* 17 (4): 367–385.

Hagan, Joe 2014, Benghazi and the Bombshell, *New York Magazine*, 4 May. Available from: http://nymag.com/news/features/lara-logan-cbs-news-2014-5/.

Harden, Marie, and Erin Whiteside. 2009. Token Responses to Gendered Newsrooms: Factors in the Career-Related Decisions of Female Newspaper Sports Journalists. *Journalism* 10 (5): 627–646.

Hess, Amanda. 2013. Most Female Journalists have been Threatened, Assaulted, or Harassed at Work. Here's Why We Don't Talk About It, *Slate*, 3 Dec. Available from: http://www.slate.com/blogs/xx_factor/2013/12/03/sexual_harassment_in_journalism_a_new_study_shows_that_the_majority_of_female.html.

Hutchinson, William. 2006. Information Warfare and Deception. *Informing Science* 9: 213–223.

Kellner, Douglas. 2004. 9/11, Spectacles of Terror, and Media Manipulation: A Critique of Jihadist and Bush media Politics. *Critical Discourse Studies* 1 (1): 41–64.

Kitch, Carolyn. 2008. Placing Journalism Inside Memory—and Memory Studies. *Memory Studies* 1 (3): 311–320.

Krijnen, Tonny, Claudia Alvares, and Sofie van Bauwel (eds.). 2011. *Gendered Transformations: Theory and Practices on Gender and Media*. Chicago: University of Chicago Press.

Mason, Corinne L. 2013. Global Violence Against Women as a National Security "Emergency". *Feminist Formations* 25 (2): 55–80.

Mosher, Donald L., and Mark Sirkin. 1984. Measuring a Macho Personality Constellation. *Journal of Research in Personality* 18: 150–163.

Niglas, Katrin. 2004. The Combined Use of Qualitative and Quantitative Methods in Educational Research. *International Journal of Special Education* 18 (2): 62–72.

Poindexter, Paula, Sharon Meraz, and Amy Schmitz Weiss (eds.). 2008. *Women, Men and News: Divided and Disconnected in the New Media Landscape.* New York: Routledge.

Scharrer, Erica. 2001. Men, Muscles, and Machismo: The Relationship between Television Violence Exposure and Aggression and Hostility in the Presence of Hypermasculinity. *Media Psychology* 3 (2): 159–188.

Scheufele, Dietram A., and David Tewksbury. 2007. Framing, Agenda Setting, and Priming: The Evolution of Three Media Effects Models. *Journal of Communication* 57 (1): 9–20.

Simon, Joel, and Samantha Libby. 2015. Broadcasting Murder: Militants Use Media for Deadly Purpose, *Committee to Protect Journalists*, 27 Apr. Available from: https://www.cpj.org/2015/04/attacks-on-the-press-broadcasting-murder-militants-use-media-for-deadly-purpose.php.

Strong, Cathy, and Grant Hannis. 2007. The Visibility of Female Journalists at Australian and New Zealand Newspapers: The Good News and the Bad News. *Australian Journalism Review* 29 (1): 115–125.

Witherow, John. 2012. Marie Colvin, a Journalistic Force of Nature, *Australian*, 27 Feb. Available from: http://www.theaustralian.com.au/media/marie-colvin-a-journalistic-force-of-nature/story-e6frg996-1226282016460.

Withnall, Adam. 2014. World Peace? These are the Only 11 Countries in the World that are Actually Free from Conflict, *Independent*, 14 Aug. Available from: http://www.independent.co.uk/news/world/politics/world-peace-these-are-the-only-11-countries-in-the-world-that-are-actually-free-from-conflict-9669623.html.

Wolfe, Lauren. 2011. The Silencing Crime: Sexual Violence and Journalists, *Committee to Crotect Journalists*, 7 Jun. Available from: http://cpj.org/reports/2011/06/silencing-crime-sexual-violence-journalists.php.

Zelizer, Barbie, and Stuart Allan (eds.). 2011. *Journalism after September 11.* London: Routledge.

Zelizer, Barbie. 2008. Why Memory's Work on Journalism does not Reflect Journalism's Work on Memory. *Memory Studies* 1 (1): 79–87.

AUTHOR BIOGRAPHY

Rebecca Te'o took up an academic position at the University of Southern Queensland, where she is a Senior Lecturer in Journalism. Rebecca's grounding as a feature writer and sub-editor for (then) APN News and Media has provided a solid foundation for her continuing interest in industry-relevant research. She has investigated the myth of the hard-bitten journalist and the changing nature of journalism in the contemporary media landscape. Her current research is an extension of this interest, and focuses primarily on journalism and terrorism.

CHAPTER 13

Death and the Maiden: Memorialisation, Scandal, and the Gendered Mediation of Australian Soldiers

Jessica Carniel

The first decade of the twenty-first century has been marked by Australia's longest military involvement since Vietnam. Australia was among the first to pledge its assistance to the United States of America in the wake of 9/11, leading to its participation in both Afghanistan and Iraq, with the former resulting in over ten years' commitment. Such a high-profile, global engagement placed the Australian Defence Force (ADF) firmly within mainstream media focus, yet tense relations between the media and the ADF, driven by their competing interests of security and saleable copy, limited public understandings of this conflict, and of contemporary experiences of warfare and military life in general. Furthermore, cultural representations of twenty-first-century Australian soldiers in the form of film, television, and literature have been limited and backward-looking. Focused predominantly on the two World Wars, particularly in light of the centenary of World War I, these cultural texts focus on national memorialisation of historical events rather than

J. Carniel (✉)
University of Southern Queensland, Toowoomba, Australia
e-mail: jess.carniel@usq.edu.au

© The Author(s) 2017
J. Gildersleeve and R. Gehrmann (Eds.), *Memory and the Wars on Terror*, Palgrave Macmillan Memory Studies,
DOI 10.1007/978-3-319-56976-5_13

the exploration of contemporary experiences, which are almost entirely absent from Australian popular culture. Consequently, the Australian soldier—or the digger, as he is popularly known—has failed to become an active and realistic figure in the Australian popular imaginary. Rather, he—the gendering here is deliberate and important—has remained an abstracted and idealised figure still shaped by the historical image of the ANZACs carefully crafted by CEW Bean during and after the Great War from Ellis Ashmead-Bartlett's original infrastructure; contemporary Australian soldiers are still imagined as white and male like the original, and their voices and experiences continue to be vetted and edited for public consumption. The figure of the contemporary Australian soldier is obscured by the national memory of the digger, rather than the lived reality of current military personnel.

The careful control of the ADF's media and public relations machine and its combative relationship with the media have inadvertently led scandal and death to be the defining themes in popular understandings of contemporary Australian military personnel. These themes are highly gendered, working to simultaneously underscore women's apparent unsuitability for the military environment while reinforcing the white, male soldier as the ideal. On the rare occasion that female soldiers are present in mainstream media coverage, it is predominantly as cadets, as victims of sexual assault, or at the centre of debates about front line roles; this is to be compared to ADF-produced media, including internal newspapers and recruitment materials, such as advertisements, which is able to produce a more nuanced and holistic representation of female soldiers. Such mainstream media discussions rest upon traditional understandings of femininity and womanhood as vulnerable to the violence of men, both sexually and physically, and require women to defend their claims to sexual agency and military prowess, which are both constructed as unfeminine. Representations of male soldiers, on the other hand, are usually dominated by death and injury, with occasional images of tearful deployment and triumphant return. The dominance of death and injury places male soldiers at the centre of an Australian necronationalistic fetishisation that promotes a discourse of masculine sacrifice for nation, yet rests upon a very superficial understanding of soldiers' roles and experiences at war.

Focusing predominantly on media coverage, but drawing also on a small selection of other cultural texts, such as film and television, this chapter explores these gendered representations of Australian soldiers in the twenty-first century within the context of contemporary debates about Australia's military role, misogyny and sexism, and the very nature of Australian national identity. While perpetuating a problematic gendered culture within the defence forces themselves, these representations of military personnel, whether in media coverage of scandal and death or those cultural representations that focus predominantly on Australia's military past, also work to maintain traditional ideas of the typical Australian as white, rugged, and masculine. These have long been criticised for their failure to adequately and accurately represent contemporary Australians. This chapter does not seek to lay responsibility at the feet of either the media or the Australian Defence Force for these limited representations, nor does it argue that the ADF should compromise on matters of security. Rather, it contends that the fraught relationship between the two institutions adversely affects the national narratives and representations that are emerging about contemporary operations and military personnel that will have long-term social and cultural effects.

REMEMBERING ANZAC: NEGOTIATING THE MILITARY PAST AND PRESENT

Although Australian colonial troops had participated in nineteenth-century conflicts, such as the Boer War, World War I signalled the first deployment of troops from the newly federated nation of Australia.[1] Commanded by British generals, the Australian Imperial Force (AIF) was joined with New Zealand forces to form the Australian and New Zealand Army Corps, or ANZAC. The acronym has since evolved to Anzac, appropriated by soldiers at the time (Carter 2006, p. 109) and is now used to refer to a particular iconography of Australian military tradition, 'signifying a citizen soldier with the distinctive qualities of the settler societies from which he sprang, resourceful and willing' (Macintyre 2009, pp. 158–159). Various factors, including the inaugural military exercise of the new nation, the high enlistment and casualty rates, the volunteer basis of the AIF, and the coincidence of young soldiers fighting for a young nation (Carter 2006, p. 110), galvanised both the real and symbolic significance of Anzac in Australian national history and public memory.

Anzac is at the centre of Australia's military mythology and, by extension, its national mythology. Its place here does not pass uncontested.

Historians such as Marilyn Lake argue that a focus on a military tradition and iconography in national narrative and public memory does not adequately reflect Australia's past, let alone its present. Lake occupies a feminist and pacifist position that lends itself easily to critique of this myth, yet even those emerging from this military tradition, such as former soldiers James Brown and Ben Wadham, are critical of its usefulness for both the Australian Defence Forces and Australia's civilian population. It is important to emphasise, however, that Brown and, to a lesser extent, Wadham are less critical of the perceived militarism of the myth than Lake. To some extent, both suggest that Anzac 'celebrations' distract from rather than provide any deeper understanding of Australia's military traditions, contemporary culture, and experiences. In short, Anzac encourages a preoccupation with the memorialisation of the military past that contributes to the obfuscation of contemporary, lived military experiences. As a result, the Anzac mythology becomes a core component of national culture and memory, but contemporary soldiers are, for many communities, distant from military barracks and outposts, not integrated into the daily life of Australian society and its contemporary culture.

Lake is a long-standing critic of the Anzac tradition as a central national mythology and of what she terms to be the militarisation of Australian history. Although the focus of her criticisms has shifted over time, the nexus of citizenship, gender, and nation remains at the core of Lake's concerns. With a consistent focus upon the gendered dimensions of national history, Lake argues that Anzac has long served as Australia's creation story (Lake 1992, p. 305; Lake 2009). In her highly controversial lecture for the History Teachers Association of Victoria 'Mythologies' lecture series at the University of Melbourne in 2009, Lake targeted the Anzac tradition's 'imperial, masculinist and militarist baggage'. Rather than a history centred upon wars sought on foreign soil for ostensibly foreign powers, Lake advocated a national history located within Australia and focused upon its civic achievements.

Like Lake, Brown presents an argument that centres upon contemporary Australia's relationship with its past, but he is more concerned with the effect that Australia's backward-looking habits have upon its understanding of its contemporary military rather than a criticism of militarism's centrality. Writing as Australia approached the centenary of its Anzac tradition, Brown urges,

I want to be sure that all this effort, all this attention, all this emotional investment has a purpose. The sheer effort we are expending on the Anzac centenary is utterly irreconcilable with the parlous state of our defence forces, our ignorance of the war in Afghanistan and the marginal status of the serving military in our society. We need to look hard at the reality of Anzac, the bad as well as the good. (2014, p. 14)

Brown's criticisms are levelled in part at what he terms the 'Anzac industry', rather than at the core tradition itself. He also critiques political and cultural systems that paradoxically shield Australian civilian society and, perhaps even more problematically, politics and politicians from military realities while placing them unproblematised at the centre of the national mythology. Brown presents criticisms of what he considers to be ill-considered practices as part of his *defence* of the importance of Anzac and the ADF, rather than an attack of these institutions. Similar concerns about the dangers of mythologising the military past can also be found in Colonel EG Keogh's essay on the importance of studying military history, included in the *Chief of Army's Reading List* (Grey ed. 2012). While Keogh advises studying Gallipoli in order to understand the logistics of mounting an amphibious operation, throughout his chapter he emphasises the importance of being a critical reader and advises against 'thoughtlessly accept[ing great military myths] at their face value' (2012, p. 10). Keogh cautions, '[s]ometimes these myths grow after the event. Sometimes they are deliberately created at the time and ever afterwards are accepted as truth, too often even by soldiers' (2012, p. 11). In his view, mythologies may be good for morale and public imagination, but less so for professional soldiers who must understand strategy and make difficult decisions.

Brown and Lake's criticisms about the Anzac myth share a preoccupation with questions of inclusion. Lake argues that a militaristic focus within a national history overlooks various social and political achievements that are arguably more pertinent to contemporary Australia, while Brown argues that Australia's historical, commemorative focus works to exclude current military issues, experiences, and servicemen and women from contemporary society and public debate. This is a concern echoed in the debate about the relationship between the military and media and its broader effects: public understanding of conflicts and experiences is pivotal to maintaining public interest and sympathy. Neglecting this dimension can have deleterious effects on returned servicemen's reception within society, as there is no pre-established framework for understanding their contribution to Australia's involvement. Lake raises important issues about the inclusivity of national narratives, and seeks to better incorporate pacifist and other civic achievements into Australian mythology, but it is important to be aware of the attendant risk of excluding military narratives completely. While contemporary troops are imbued with the spirit of the Anzac and are affectionately referred to as diggers, public knowledge and appreciation of military action is very much anchored in the past.

Such criticisms highlight the tensions between past and present that occur in the process of memorialisation. Journalist Sally Neighbour is critical of the 'sentimental reverence' and 'jingoistic puffery' that a focus on Anzac encourages in most discussions about Australians' actions in Afghanistan. She argues that the platitudinous invocation of the legend distracted from a much-needed 'hard-headed, self-interested assessment' of the involvement and its national worth (2011, p. 10). Historian Mark McKenna is more scathing in his assessment of how the Anzac mythology impacts public understanding and objective public debate of contemporary events, arguing that 'the cult of the warrior stands in the way of critical appraisal of Australian engagement in overseas wars' (2010, p. 165).

One of the major criticisms of this is that this mythology has not adjusted to the significant social changes Australia—and by extension the ADF—have undergone in the past 100 years. One such significant criticism is the masculinism of the image of the digger and the Anzac legend itself. While women have served in the Australian armed forces since the Boer War, the popular image of the Australian serviceperson is predominantly male. Many criticise the ADF for continuing to be a male-dominated environment and masculinist culture, despite its equity policies and initiatives. Another significant criticism to be made—one that emerges from Brown's analysis of the myth—is that a focus on the 'glorious dead' distracts from the service of the living, and can even detract from adequate policy-making in terms of service provision to veterans. These criticisms are explored in later sections, subsequent to a discussion of the problematic relationship between the military and the media.

FRENEMIES AT ARMS: THE MILITARY AND THE MEDIA

The long relationship between the Australian media and the ADF is complex. In earlier wars, such as the two World Wars, war correspondents were given honorary military ranks of captain and posted with particular regiments in a militarised version of what we would now describe as media embedding. They were issued with uniforms and military rations, used military transport, were subject to military law and observed the usual discipline of the army (Anderson and Trembath 2011, p. 7). As journalists, they were subject to heavy censorship; although field reporters found this everywhere, it was reported to be worst in Australian forces. Embedding also works on a principle of self-censorship that is built through reliance upon protection by the troops and the resulting camaraderie (or mateship, in Australian terms) of close quarters. In later wars, the military no longer distributed war accreditation to journalists, consequently 'civilianising' war correspondence and changing the relationship with the media, arguably making it even more combative.

Distance grew between the military and media during the Gulf War in the 1990s, but tensions reached their zenith during the Afghanistan conflict. Some journalists see the change of attitude to the media as occurring during conservative Prime Minister John Howard's government (1996–2007), which was increasingly attached to military solutions. The difference between East Timor in 1999 and Afghanistan in Burton (2001) is rather acute, but can be accounted for by incidents of leaked defence intelligence documents leading to the embarrassment of people in senior political and bureaucratic positions. Kevin Foster is particularly critical of how this tense relationship between the military and media has worsened throughout the operations in Afghanistan, with the ultimate casualty being the Australian public. He argues that the 'Australian public's access to objective information about and understanding of the longest military commitment in the nation's history has been correspondingly impoverished' (Foster 2013, p. xiv).

More positive shifts in the fraught relationship between the Australian military and the media occurred in the final four years of Australian involvement in Afghanistan. The introduction of a media-embedding program in 2009 has been credited with easing this tense relationship and improving public understanding of the war in Afghanistan. Lt. Colonel Jason Logue observes that '[t]he program has done much to humanise what is perceived as an increasingly clinical and sometimes detached way of waging war' (2013, p. vi). He emphasises that a negative relationship with the media poses a greater risk than granting access, and that the primary goal for both parties in the embedding program 'must be about sustaining public understanding, not just facilitating media demands' (p. vii).

It is not simply the tension between the media and the military that shapes public misunderstanding, but the complicity of the government in avoiding substantial debate on Australia's conflict involvement for many years. An anonymous soldier writing for the Lowy Institute in 2010 lays equal blame at the feet of the government, the media, and the ADF. 'That Australians neither understand the war nor why its soldiers' sacrifice is needed in Afghanistan is shameful', he wrote; 'If we are to risk life and go to war, the policy must be properly articulated' (Soldier Z 2010). Later that year, the Australian parliament held a much-needed debate about Australia's involvement in Afghanistan which had been leveraged by Independent MP Andrew Wilkie as part of his shared king-making role in the 2010 hung parliament. Although Wilkie had supported the initial incursion into Afghanistan, ten years later he was highly critical of Australia's continued involvement, stating that 'Afghanistan is no longer relevant to Australia's security in the way it was in 2001' (cited in Commonwealth of Australia 2010).

A common theme in discussions about the relationship between the military and the media focuses on a concern about national security; specifically, what strategic information could potentially be leaked from media reportage of military operations. Yet what several commentators suggest, including Brown and Logue, is that it is possible to generate a qualitative and empathetic exploration of soldiers' experiences of service in both peace and conflict that does not involve a compromise in issues of military security. Furthermore, such coverage could generate more positive and holistic popular understandings of what military service entails, fostering respect for a living institution rather than awe for a sacred and distant national legend. It is important to have a debate about national narratives like Anzac and to consider the very real impact that they can have upon public knowledge and understanding of military policy and operation with, of course, due respect for attendant security issues.

DEATH: SACRIFICE, NECRONATIONALISM, AND MASCULINITY

The media may be quick to criticise the impenetrable veneer of Australia's military iconography, but it is also complicit in both its creation and its perpetuation. It is important to remember that the Anzac tradition finds its origins in the reportage of WWI correspondents Ellis Ashmead-Bartlett and CEW Bean, from Britain and Australia respectively. Bean was also Australia's official war historian and the inaugural curator of the Australian War Memorial; it can thus be said that journalists, if not the media as an institution, played a pivotal role in the construction of the mythology as it now plays in its maintenance. As Fay Anderson and Richard Trembath observe, 'The chasm between the media and the military is curious, because the troops are largely quarantined from criticism, and the media continues to embrace the sanitised narrative of the Anzac hero' (2011, p. 339). While the Australian media reflected critically upon the disproportionate attention to the deaths of soldiers in Afghanistan, these outlets also willingly participate in what has become an almost ritualistic invocation of Anzac and diggers that relies upon these very deaths.

This focus on the glorious dead is a form of what Michael Cathcart calls necronationalism—a nationalism that is based on death—which he critiques as a problematic focus for a living nation (2009, p. 154). In his cultural history of the pursuit of water in colonial exploration, Cathcart connects this concept of necronationalism to Marcus Clarke's celebration of Australia's 'weird melancholy'; that is, the silent, solitary, and 'fear-inspiring' gloomy landscape, which in literature often required the sacrifice of youth. Gallipoli eventually usurped the earlier necronationalistic impulse of lost explorers consumed by the harsh Australian landscape; the tragic tale of Gallipoli is well suited for a 'nationalism that longs for stories of defeat, death and the sacrifice of the young' (Cathcart 2009, p. 163).

Australia's necronationalistic approach to military memorialisation does allow space for the recently fallen, but in a de-contextualised and almost ahistorical manner. Contemporary casualties are subsumed into the Anzac tradition, which is arguably defined more by the lost than by the returned. International editor for the *Age*, Tom Hyland, argued in 2011 that official public mourning for those lost in Afghanistan is disproportionate to the military commitment in place, especially in comparison to the gross loss of life in previous wars. He pondered, 'Perhaps we are trying to make up for the perceived public indifference to our losses in Vietnam, where the dead were brought home in silence and buried in obscurity' (2011). In *Anzac's Long Shadow* (2014), Brown also analyses the deleterious effects of national coverage focused on death in his chapter on the ADF's relationship with the media. He draws upon a Canadian response to troop fatalities, in which the Canadian defence minister posited that military deaths in times of conflict should not be viewed as extraordinary as it promotes an unhealthy bloodless myth of war, and the Afghanistan mission in particular.

It is important to emphasise that Hyland and other commentators do not actually intend any disrespect to serving members of the ADF, those who have lost their lives, and their mourning families and friends. What Hyland and many other Australian journalists argue is that they cannot access this information themselves in order to provide any sort of information or commentary on activities in Afghanistan. What results is an inability to have any sort of meaningful and informed debate about Australia's involvement. Consequently, they focus upon what they can—the death and injury of troops—but this, in turn, raises public alarm about exactly what 'our boys' are doing over there and why they are dying. As Anderson and Trembath observe, '[t]he media play an essential role in any democracy as a channel for information, a vehicle for dissent and a watchdog over authority' (2011, p. 4). This is what various commentators, ranging from journalists to politicians to the general public, are concerned is not currently able to happen in Australia.

While Anzac's necronationalistic dimensions recall the tragedies of war, its focus on the past works as what Ben Wadham conceptualises as camouflage for contemporary military issues. Camouflage, he suggests, is the means through which less savoury elements of military culture are obscured from public attention, or prevented from remaining in view long enough to endure intense scrutiny. He observes that 'the Skype Affair and the history of such incidents arrive to us, civil society, via the media portrayal of a military sex scandal but are quickly forgotten among the news of the next Australian soldier death in Oruzgan Province, Afghanistan, the tales of heroism as the next VC winner is announced or put on hold while the nation celebrates ANZAC Day' (2013, p. 220). Valiant, sacrificial masculinity and national memorialisation mask scandal. Also suggested here is the complicity of the media; unable to penetrate the ADF's public relations walls, the media will fall back to reporting what they are able to, rather than scrutinising what they cannot.

Several individual soldiers have breached the ADF's media policy and spoken of their experiences from under a veil of anonymity, such as the anonymous soldier writing for the Lowy Institute discussed above. In 2009, the ABC's youth-oriented current affairs program *Hungry Beast* produced a special edition on Afghanistan. This episode included a dramatisation of a real interview conducted with a soldier. To obscure the soldier's identity, actors of varying ages and builds were used to play 'Tom' in a dramatised monologue of the interview content; notably, the character remained white and male, which is indicative of the general demographic deployed in Afghanistan at the time. Titled 'Dust, Mud and Shit: A Soldier's Life' in reference to the 'three things that are a constant in a soldier's life', Tom details the monotony and frustrations of life on base in Afghanistan.

During the interview, Tom responds to a question about the death of Trooper David Pearce, the second Australian casualty by enemy fire,[2] with poignant honesty:

> It didn't shock anyone. We were all expecting our luck to end. People used to talk about it within the military—it was this phenomenon of, you know, 'Fuck, the uniform must have a force field around it or something like that'. So many close calls, no one killed. A second thing was, well, that's broken the spell and we can expect more now. It brings it home. It's not a game anymore. I've felt no fear for myself in the face of the deaths. I even felt comfortable with the idea of being killed in Afghanistan. There's two ways of looking at it. It's either a bullet with your name on it, or it's one marked, 'To whom it may concern'. Dying quickly, doing a job I loved and being remembered for it held an appeal that living a long, safe, dull existence only to die unloved and forgotten of old age would never have.
> (cited in Drysdale 2009)

Tom's account humanises the official announcements of Australian casualties, adding a realistic—almost nihilistic—dimension to the characteristics of bravery touted by the media and the ADF. Just as the death of Pearce brought home the reality of war to Tom and his fellow soldiers, his account of proximity to death in Afghanistan works to bring home this experience to the viewers.

Arguably, the soldier's story was no different to stories of soldiers from America, Britain, and other nationalities that Australians readily had access to, but the fact of the Australian perspective—even the Australian accent—works to give viewers a greater sense of connection to the individual soldier and his experiences, underscoring how he represents Australia in that context. Such a representation is significant given the dominance of American film and television in portraying experiences of contemporary conflict. Excluding the section about the Australian Army and its history, the *Chief of Army's Reading List* (Grey ed. 2012), compiled by Lieutenant General David Morrison and several colleagues, includes ten Australian books, two of which are World War II memoirs, again reflecting the more historical focus to be found in Australian representations and memorialisation of the military tradition. It must be acknowledged, however, that not only is the list selective rather than exhaustive, but also that several military memoirs have been published since the release of the reading list, such as Mark Donaldson's *The Crossroad* (2013) and Garth Callendar's *After the Blast* (2015), and these may appear on future revisions of the list.[3] Morrison has also included a selection of popular films, as these 'can provide vivid insights into issues of wartime leadership, military cultures and the realities of combat' (2012, p. 112), yet Australian military culture is significantly underrepresented in his selection. Notably, *Beneath Hill 60* (2010) is the only Australian feature film included in the list alongside the documentary series *Australians at War* (2001). The exclusion of classic Australian war films, such as *Gallipoli* (1981), *Forty Thousand Horsemen* (1941), *The Rats of Tobruk* (1944), and *The Odd Angry Shot* (1979) is interesting as the defining characteristic of such films, as well as the inclusions in the reading list, is their historical nature. Morrison does not include any contemporary Australian representations in his list because, quite simply, such films are not available. When depicting war and the military, Australian cinema and television is more focused on the historical rather than the contemporary. The exception to this is the television show *Sea Patrol* (2007–2011), which received mixed reviews about the veracity of its representation of the Royal Australian Navy, but the impact of this is eclipsed by the various miniseries produced to commemorate the centenary of the Anzac landing.[4] The relative absence of contemporary representation is a more recent development; *The Rats of Tobruk* appeared while World War II was still being waged, and *The Odd Angry Shot* was released only four years after the end of the Vietnam War. In short, Australia has not produced the equivalent of, for example, *The Hurt Locker* (2008) or *Generation Kill* (2008), films and series that depict fictional (or fictionalised, in the case of *Generation Kill*, which is based on a book by media embed Evan Wright) experiences of contemporary combat.

In the absence of contemporary explorations, the media is the primary means through which the public can access knowledge and understanding of contemporary combat and military culture, returning us to the dilemma produced by the often combative relationship between the military and media. As discussed above, limitations in reportage lead to narrow depictions of contemporary operations and personnel. Furthermore, by focussing on past interventions, such representations are both malefocused and, perhaps inadvertently, still centred more on the lost than even the returned, let alone those still serving.

THE MAIDEN: WOMEN ON THE FRONT LINE OF SCANDAL

In December 2013, ADFA 'Kate', the female cadet at the centre of the 2011 so-called 'Skype sex scandal', was named Woman of the Year by *Daily Life*, Fairfax's woman-centric supplement with an evident broadly feminist editorial agenda. The title was determined by both readers and a panel of judges who nominated Kate as 'the Australian woman who had advocated for and instigated the most positive change this year' (Dumas 2013). This admiration for Kate emerges from two sources: her resistance against sexual discrimination and harassment in the broadest sense, and the fact that this resistance occurred within the Defence Force as an institution representative of firmly entrenched male dominance in Australia. Similarly, then Prime Minister Julia Gillard (2010–2013) was awarded the inaugural title in 2012 for her landmark misogyny speech that hit out at sexism in Australian politics.[5] Gillard's nomination was the culmination of an eventful year for public debate about sexism, feminism, and Australian women. The launch of *Daily Life* by Fairfax in February 2012 gave space to discussions about gender and Australian society within the mainstream press. This was followed by various successes in paid parental leave and workplace gender equality legislation, and significant backlash throughout the year to highly gendered criticisms of Gillard as both an individual and as a leader. Further social and cultural successes were found in the form of the inaugural Stella Prize for women writers, preceding the journal *Overland*'s declaration that 2012 was the year of the woman writer, and the overwhelming public response to issues of women's safety on the streets after the rape and murder of Jill Meagher.[6] Although many of the events of 2012 were highly problematic, their positive outcome was the stimulation of significant public debate about issues of gender in various facets of Australian culture. Although the Skype sex scandal preceded this, it can and indeed should be understood as part of this revitalised debate about perceptions of women in Australian culture that has marked the early years of this decade, and which coincides with Australia's first female prime minister and first female governor-general.

The Gillard Labor government era is marked by debate about Australia's military and its activity. As discussed above, parliamentary debate about Afghanistan was nominated by independent MP Andrew Wilkie as a condition of his support for Labor in the wake of the hung parliament of 2010. In April 2011, then defence minister Stephen Smith announced the fast-tracking of changes to women's front line combat opportunities, which was confirmed in September that year, after the support of senior defence personnel had been secured. The opening of front line combat roles to women was already on the government's agenda, but the coincidence of this decision with the announcement of reviews into the ADF's treatment of women in the wake of the Skype sex scandal raised questions about the political and institutional motivations for this change (Cox 2011; Dodd 2011; Jamieson 2011).

The Skype sex scandal was undoubtedly a catalyst for change in the ADF, and it is also exemplary of the adversarial relationship between military and media. To summarise this incident, Kate was secretly filmed having sex with a fellow cadet, Daniel McDonald; while Kate consented to the sexual relationship with McDonald, she did not consent to a recording of the encounter being broadcast to other cadets in another room. Kate discovered what had occurred from military investigators who told her it was likely the other cadets would receive a charge of 'prejudicial conduct'; this prompted her to take her story to the media rather than rely on the academy's due process. Both McDonald and the other cadet involved, Dylan Deblaquiere, were sentenced to good behaviour bonds and have subsequently left the military, while the five cadets who viewed the incident were also eventually dismissed from ADFA. Disciplinary and legal measures were eventually taken, but it was clear from her actions that Kate was initially not confident in how the allegations would be handled within the institution, and so she sought support from the public. As with fully trained military personnel, there are restrictions on cadets' interactions with the media, thus Kate's decision to approach the media with her story can be seen as a deliberate break with ADFA and the ADF that was likely to inflame sensibilities. As a result of her disclosure, Kate allegedly experienced bullying from both fellow cadets and senior officers; while this behaviour cannot be excused, the hostility can be seen as a negative manifestation of the expectation (or, indeed, the requirement) that issues are dealt with in-house rather than aired publicly. However, Kate's individual response is indicative of broader concerns regarding the ADF's ability to deal effectively with issues of sexual harassment and discrimination. Public opinion about the ADF's approach to sexual harassment and abuse was already weakened by investigations into the *HMAS Success* throughout 2009–2011.[7] As Kate herself observed upon receiving *Daily Life*'s Woman of the Year award, '[i]n the past three years, every time the military is in the news, it's because of another indiscretion. Until the culture within the defence has changed, I don't think that the defence is going to have the support of the public' (Dumas 2012).

Cultural change is at the centre of the various reports into the ADF prompted by this scandal. From 2011 to 2013, the Australian Human Rights Commission (AHRC) conducted a three-stage review into the treatment of women in the ADF. The first stage focused on the treatment of women in the Australian Defence Force Academy as a direct response to allegation of sexual harassment and discrimination, such as that encountered by Kate. The second stage examined the ADF itself, and the third stage was an audit of the implementation of the recommendations made in the first two reviews. The AHRC review made 31 recommendations for ADFA and 21 for the ADF, and the review conducted in the third stage found that both had made significant progress on implementing positive change. The review found that most staff found the ADF to be a supportive and inclusive employer, but that there were still areas where poor leadership impeded institutional progress, there was still a disproportionate representation of men in senior officer positions, and recruitment of women remained low.

The ADF released their own response to the review and to concerns about military culture beyond gender, *Pathways to Change: Evolving Defence Culture* (Department of Defence 2012), which in turn involved specific reviews into sexual abuse, personal conduct, incident and complaint management, and career pathways for women, as well as specific responses to the AHRC review. The AHRC argued that promoting diversity in leadership and better addressing issues of sexual ethics and misconducts would significantly strengthen the military institution.

Similarly, the ADF's *Pathways to Change* policy emphasised that the principle of cultural change was consistent with the ADF's commitment to professionalism and excellence. *Pathways to Change* explicitly places cultural change within the context of the ADF as a proud, core national tradition. In the sections addressing this, its language is gender neutral and draws upon key concepts of nationalism without devolving into jingoism. It states that service within the ADF 'represents the best of the Australian character', and that defence force personnel are 'icons in Australian society' (2012, p. 8). Interestingly, *Pathways to Change* avoids reference to mateship and instead draws upon the idea of 'community' to articulate the important bonds that are formed through military training and service. Like Anzac, the concept of mateship has been criticised for its implicit masculinism and for its connections to war (Page 2002, p. 195). Although the ethos aims to promote a sense of inclusion, its cultural and historical terms of reference have problematised this process. For example, the Australian government's cultural portal acknowledges the concept's bush origins and attempts to include women and other races in its scope, but ultimately emphasises its role for men at war—and more specifically, men at war in the past. In elaborating upon 'community', the *Pathways to Change* document carefully constructs this concept in terms of formal and informal professional networks, as well as family. The effect of this is both a de-militarisation and gender-neutralisation of the mateship ethos, yet one still bounded by the ADF as an institution.

Despite this reshaping of mateship into the more inclusive, although perhaps less motivating, concept of community, it is still important to interrogate mateship and its role in Australian military culture. According to Wadham (2011a), there is a paradox inherent in militarism when it comes to mateship: '[it] motivates bravery, courage and sacrifice, the stuff our national legends are built upon. But the flip side is an unrestrained potential for violation, exclusion and hostility that includes sexual predation, excessive alcoholism, racism and intimidation'. Thus, in the male-dominated domain of the military, mateship becomes the purpose of male bonding exercises that can draw upon the characteristics of that negative flip side, even as it is aiming for the more positive goal of cohesion and *espirit de corps*. At the time of the Skype sex scandal, Wadham observed that in a 'highly masculinised institution...[the ADFA incident] highlights the way men bond together at the expense of women, and others, in order to buttress their privilege' (2011b). Parallels can also be drawn between the use of Kate for male bonding in the Skype scandal and the use of other women in sexual assault cases allegedly perpetrated by footballers, such as the Cronulla Sharks incident of 2002 made notorious by a *Four Corners* investigation seven years later (Cover 2013).[8] Without women, male bonding exercises are focused on other men, but with women there is a risk that they will be seen as a conduit for this bonding, involved in the process but ultimately excluded from the outcome. The problem with this conclusion, however, is that the blame rests upon women's presence rather than men's behaviour.

A similar conundrum emerges from debates about women on the front line, which also draw strategically upon the concept of mateship from its traditional masculine dimensions. Put simply, women on the front line are a dangerous distraction, based upon criteria that range from questionable competence to sexual vulnerability. Furthermore, as discussed by Richard Gehrmann and Heather Smith in relation to the first death of a female soldier from New Zealand, there is greater public acceptance of male deaths in combat than female deaths (2013). Australia did not suffer female casualties in either Iraq or Afghanistan but, as Former Chief of Army Peter Leahy emphasises, '[a] dead or wounded soldier should not be judged on the basis of their sex but on their service and sacrifice on behalf of the nation' (cited in Summers 2011, p. 26). Focusing on the shift in US policy in January 2013, Megan M. MacKenzie criticises contemporary debate about women in combat for being trapped in an analytical rut, caught between the questions of 'can they?' and 'should they?', which rest upon arguments about physical differences and capabilities and normative claims about gender respectively (2013, p. 239). She argues that this narrow focus limits discussion about gender, equality, and militarisation. Furthermore, the emphasis on the imagined effects of female combat inclusion—that it will improve all gendered dimensions of the military experience—places pressure upon a single policy reversal and fails to acknowledge the fact that women are indeed already at the front line in many militaries, yet other gender issues persist (p. 240).

In an analysis of mateship from consequentialist and duty ethics perspectives, Jim Page laments that women's inclusion within the ideology is predicated upon being 'actively involved in the male practices of war and warfare' (2002, p. 195). Counter to this, Eleanor Hancock highlights that war is not a result of male aggression, but rather a clash between states and opposing value systems; to simplify warfare to male aggression denies women's role and complicity in this (1993,

p. 93). There is, therefore, already space for women within a militarised conception of mateship, provided war itself is not imagined as an exclusively male domain. The issue remains, however, as to how women's role within warfare is imagined. In Australia's Anzac past, women's roles were confined primarily to the home front, which is imagined as a fairly feminised space, or to nursing. Even as women moved into military roles, the iconic digger remained male. Lake argues that the Great War, and specifically its legacy of the Anzac myth, established the citizen soldier as the exemplar of Australian citizenship. Women's citizenship was expressed via their maternal role, breeding the national population while men bred the nation itself through their sacrifice. Unable to physically bear new life, men gave birth to the nation. Lake further argues that soldiers' deaths were constructed as a means of bringing forth new life in these nationalistic terms (see also Grimshaw et al. 1994, p. 218). While such arguments are clearly embedded in a specific cultural context, the legacies of this gendered construction of citizenship remain, arguably influencing the position women can take up in this idea of soldier citizen in contemporary Australia. With reference to both leadership and combat, Hancock argues, '[a]ccess to all aspects of the military is important in both practical politics and in concepts of citizenship' (1993, p. 97). The Gillard Labor government's announcement that front line roles would be open to women therefore constitutes one of the most significant challenges to the traditional image of the Australian soldier as male and by extension interrogates the gendered dimensions of militarised exemplary citizenship.

This shift has been reflected in the ADF's recruitment campaigns since 2011. Gender and racial diversity is a marked feature of its 2014 'This Is Us' campaign (Defence Jobs Australia 2014). Women are shown in a variety of roles, including several scenes of physical labour and training. The shorter 30-second version of the advertisement is even more telling of this shift in marketing and representation. It opens and closes with shots of individual female soldiers gazing directly into the camera, thus consolidating the push for women to be the 'face' of the contemporary ADF. Furthermore, the song used on the advertisement soundtrack features a female rock vocalist, Mia Dyson. In addition to the 'This Is Us' campaign, in 2015 the ADF launched an additional campaign, 'Do What You Love', specifically targeting women (Defence Jobs Australia 2015a, b, c, d, e, f). The campaign focuses on themes of leadership, travel, health, education, family, and the pursuit of a meaningful vocation in response to a survey of what Australian women most want out of their lives. The high level and positive representation of women in the ADF found in their recruitment campaign is reflected also within its internal media, such as *Army News*, which similarly aims to emphasise the career, lifestyle, and community opportunities and achievements of its female personnel; such internal media representations are markedly different to those available within the mainstream media. Similar to the 'This Is Us' campaign, 'Do What You Love' features a female vocalist on the soundtrack, although Phebe Starr's composition is perhaps more whimsical than motivational, tapping into contemporary trends. The visual and aural features of both 'This Is Us' and 'Do What You Love' are in marked contrast to the ADF's 2008–2009 'Rise' campaign (Defence Jobs Australia 2008). The full version of this advertisement included historical footage of men at war, as well as from the then-current Afghanistan campaign, set to a fairly rock-based song with a male vocalist. Women are not entirely excluded from this advertisement, but are certainly less prominent than in the 2014 campaign, as are non-white soldiers. These differences can be explained by the fact that Australia no longer has a large deployment in Afghanistan, therefore is no longer recruiting for a sustained conflict, and as a response to the 2011 AHRC and internal reviews in the aftermath of the Skype sex scandal.

A sceptical view of such advertising material is that the ADF is working hard to repair damage to its reputation wrought by scandals and reviews. Certainly, this must be a factor, but it must also be acknowledged that the ADF itself may not necessarily find such elements of its current culture conducive to a healthy institutional and workplace environment. Such a perspective emerges from Chief of Army, Lieutenant General David Morrison's address released in June 2013 in response to investigations into the so-called 'Jedi Council' email ring, in which male personnel exchanged stories and images of sexual encounters with women, some of whom were also ADF staff. In this powerful video address, Morrison derides the behaviour of those in the email network as being 'in direct contravention to every value that the Australian Army stands for' and pledges to rid the army of any who cannot live up to the institution's values.[9] Most notably, Morrison closes with an invocation of the army's historical legacy, but frames this in terms that promote a dynamic understanding of the army as both a national institution and a particular workplace that can and should exemplify particular national values:

If we are a great national institution, if we care about the legacy left to us by those who have served before us, if we care about the legacy we leave to those who, in turn will protect and secure Australia, then it is up to us to make a difference. If you're not up to it, find something else to do with your life. There is no place for you amongst this band of brothers and sisters. (Australian Army HQ 2013)

Morrison's speech is a continuation of sentiments expressed in another speech presented at the United Nations International Women's Day conference earlier that year in which he reflected upon the importance of dismantling cultures of bullying and degradation in order to foster a more cohesive defence force, rather than allowing bullying and degradation to be the means by which such cohesion is forged. Morrison has proven to be a driving force in implementing cultural change within the ADF, which is in turn manifested in the tone and style of its recruitment campaigns. While such advertisements can and should still be viewed with a critical eye, as urged by Keogh in his exhortation for the critical study of military history, they should also be seen as evidence of efforts to implement positive change.

Ultimately, the Skype sex scandal was a catalyst for positive change within the ADF, which has been reflected in its emphasis upon diversity, equality, and opportunity in its various recruitment campaigns, but this is not necessarily reflected in mainstream media representations of women in the Australian armed forces. Where death and sacrifice still dominate representations of male soldiers, female soldiers are often defined by sex and scandal; just as the focus on death can work to erode public faith in military operations, the focus on sex and scandal can be detrimental to discussions about women's changing roles in the defence force.

Conclusion

Although the scale of deployment is smaller than World War I, post-9/11 operations have been far more protracted: Australians have spent the first decade, and much of the second decade, of the twenty-first century as a country engaged in overseas conflict. Yet understanding, interest, and sympathy with this engagement is eclipsed by its preoccupation with its first rather than its most recent war. An examination of representations of Australian military personnel and changes to operations since 2001 reveals disconnection between public memory, public image, and institutional identity. Fostered by a focus on Anzac as Australian core national military imagery, public memory is driven by an increasingly distant history. There are significant tensions in the memorialisation of Australia's military tradition and its need to recognise and represent its contemporary military culture. While Anzac should not necessarily be dismissed as a national tradition, it may be time to displace it from the centre of how the public know and understand Australia's military actions, integrating it into a broader military tradition that actively creates space for those currently serving. This could be facilitated by a movement away from a necronationalistic memorialisation on death and sacrifice toward a more dynamic recognition of service as a broader concept.

Such a change needs to be supported by more nuanced reportage and representation of the ADF in the Australian media in order to develop a public image for Australian military personnel that does not trap them into a dichotomy of virtue and vice, but rather another public institution that negotiates the same pitfalls of modern Australian society as other industries and workplaces. As both the AHRC and ADF reviews demonstrated, the ADF as an institution does have strong infrastructure to facilitate positive change and progress. That the communication of such progress seems to be limited to recruitment campaigns and internal media is problematic, lending itself to criticisms of propagandising rather than self-representation and reportage. Increasing the number and diversity of cultural representations of the ADF, its personnel, and its operations may assist with dismantling nostalgic and propagandistic imagery.

NOTES

1. The various colonies of the Australian continent federated in as the nation of Australia in 1901. While governed by its own constitution and parliament, Federation did not indicate 'independence' from Britain. Australia remained part of the British Commonwealth and its citizenry were defined as British subjects; the institution of Australian citizenship as a separate entity occurred in 1949. At the time of World War I, Australia was constitutionally bound to provide support to Britain in times of war (Macintyre 2009, p. 157).
2. The first Australian casualty was Sergeant Andrew Russell in 2002.
3. Donaldson is an SAS soldier and in 2009 became the first recipient of the Victoria Cross since 1969.

4. These series include *Gallipoli* (2015); *Deadline Gallipoli* (2015), which focusses on the experiences of journalists such as Charles Bean, Ellis Ashmead Bartlett, and Philip Schuler; and *Anzac Girls* (2015), a series focussed on the Australian Army Nursing Service.

5. On 9 October 2012, Gillard delivered a speech addressing endemic issues of sexism within Australian politics. Specifically, the speech focused on the alleged sexism of the (then) Opposition Leader Tony Abbott. Controversial in many ways, the speech led to a revitalisation of debate about gender issues in Australian public life and a redefinition of misogyny in the Macquarie English Dictionary.

6. Jill Meagher was a Melbourne woman of Irish origin who was raped and murdered on her way home from drinks with work colleagues in September 2012. Initially treated as a disappearance, her body was found six days later almost 50 kilometres from the original site of her disappearance. Adrian Ernest Bayley, a parolee unknown to the victim and who acted opportunistically, pleaded guilty to Meagher's rape and murder, and was sentenced to life imprisonment. The Meagher case was notable for its use of social media to spread awareness of her disappearance, which in turn raised issues about the courts' ability to source an unbiased jury. It also galvanised anti-violence against women campaigns and revitalised the Reclaim the Night tradition in Melbourne.

7. A judicial inquiry into the operations of the *HMAS Success* commenced in 2009 and its report released in 2011. The inquiry was in response to allegations of sexual harassment, assault, bullying, and intimidation by and against crewmembers. The inquiry found that female crewmembers were particularly vulnerable to such behaviour, but also that the overall culture of the ship favoured excessive use of alcohol, drug abuse, and fraternisation. An additional scandal emerged in 2011, after the inquiry was closed, in which a female sailor was indecently assaulted by a colleague.

8. In 2002, while on pre-season trip in New Zealand, several players engaged in sexual intercourse with a local woman while other team members watched. The woman made a complaint to the police several days later, but no charges were laid. The scandal re-emerged in 2009 as part of a *Four Corners* expose into sexual misconduct in the National Rugby League (NRL). The exposé, as well as responses to it by the NRL, players involved in the incident, and other members of the rugby community prompted public debate about attitudes to sex, sexuality, and male bonding in football culture in Australia.

9. Lieutenant General David Morrison was subsequently named the 2016 Australian of the Year.

Works Cited

Anderson, Fay, and Richard Trembath. 2011. *Witnesses to War: The History of Australian Conflict Reporting*. Melbourne: Melbourne University Publishing.

Australian Army HQ. 2013. *Chief of Army Lieutenant General David Morrison Message about Unacceptable Behaviour*. YouTube. Available from: https://www.youtube.com/watch?v=QaqpoeVgr8U.

Australian Human Rights Commission. 2011. *Report on the Review into the Treatment of Women at the Australian Defence Force Academy, Phase One of the Review into the Treatment of Women in the Australian Defence Force*.

Australian Human Rights Commission. 2012. *Report on the Review into the Treatment of Women at the Australian Defence Force, Phase Two of the Review into the Treatment of Women in the Australian Defence Force*.

Australian Human Rights Commission. 2013. *Audit Report: Review into the Treatment of Women at the Australian Defence Force Academy*.

Australian Human Rights Commission. 2014. *Audit Report: Review into the Treatment of Women at the Australian Defence Force Academy*.

Bigelow, Kathryn (Director). 2008. *The Hurt Locker*. Summit Entertainment.

Brown, James. 2014. *Anzac's Long Shadow: The Cost of Our National Obsession*. Collingwood: Black Inc.

Burton, Geoff et al. (Directors). 2001. *Australians at War*. ABC TV.

Callender, Garth. 2015. *After the Blast: An Australian Officer in Iraq and Afghanistan*. Collingwood: Schwartz Publishing.

Carter, David. 2006. *Dispossession, Dreams and Diversity: Issues in Australian Studies*. Frenchs Forest: Pearson Education.

Cathcart, Michael. 2009. *The Water Dreamers: The Remarkable History of Our Dry Continent*. Melbourne: Text.

Chauvel, Charles (Director). 1941. *Forty Thousand Horsemen*. Universal Pictures.

———. 1944. *The Rats of Tobruk*. RKO.

Commonwealth of Australia. 20 Oct. 2010. Parliamentary Debates, House of Representatives, HR7790-3. Available from: http://parlinfo.aph.gov.au/parlInfo/download/chamber/hansardr/2010-10-20/toc_pdf/7790-3.pdf;fileType=application%2Fpdf#search=%22chamber/hansardr/2010-10-20/0000%22.

Cover, Rob. 2013. Suspended Ethics and the Team: Theorising Team Sportsplayers' Group Sexual Assault in the Context of Identity. *Sexualities* 16 (3–4): 300–318.

Cox, Eva. 2011. Women in the Frontline...Fighting Dinosaurs in the ADF. *Conversation*, 12 Apr. Available from: http://theconversation.com/women-in-the-frontline-fighting-dinosaurs-in-the-adf-766.

Defence Jobs Australia. 2008. *Rise TVC*, YouTube. Available from: https://www.youtube.com/watch?v=FqyhoXACnpw.

———. 2014. *The Australian Army: This Is Us*, YouTube. Available from: https://www.youtube.com/watch?v=rXnpZ4A0Vfs.

———. (2015a). *Do What You Love—TVC—Fly*, YouTube. Available from: https://www.youtube.com/watch?v=p2P7EaEAI0s.

———. (2015b). *Do What You Love—TVC—Keep Learning*, YouTube. Available from: https://www.youtube.com/watch?v=LxZmyudueSE.

———. (2015c). *Do What You Love—TVC—Lead*, YouTube. Available from: https://www.youtube.com/watch?v=H2_aj5TIsDc.

———. (2015d). *Do What You Love—TVC—Make an Impact*, YouTube. Available from: https://www.youtube.com/watch?v=jpul5koAMB0.

———. (2015e). *Do What You Love—TVC—Push Myself*, YouTube. Available from: https://www.youtube.com/watch?v=ZrCOOhktl4I.

———. (2015f). *Do What You Love—TVC—See the World*, YouTube. Available from: https://www.youtube.com/watch?v=vXXqdYDJ9mU.

Department of Defence. 2012. *Pathway to Change: Evolving Defence Culture*. Commonwealth of Australia, Canberra.

Dodd, Mark. 2011. Combat Roles Offered to Women. *Australian*. 12 Apr.

Donaldson, Mark. 2013. *The Crossroad*. Sydney: Pan Macmillan.

Drysdale, Kirsten. 2009. Dust, Mud and Shit: A Soldier's Life. *Hungry Beast*, ABC TV, 19 Nov.

Dumas, Daisy. 2013. Woman of the Year Is ADFA Skype Sex Scandal Cadet. *Daily Life*, 16 Dec.

Foster, Kevin. 2013. *Don't Mention the War: The Australian Defence Force, the Media and the Afghan Conflict*. Clayton: Monash University Publishing.

Gehrmann, Richard, and Heather Smith. 2013. Bronzed, Buffed and Tattooed: The New Brand of Soldier Shaped and Shipped by Popular Culture. In *Proceedings of the 4th Annual Conference of the Popular Culture Association of Australia and New Zealand (PopCAANZ 2013)*. Popular Culture Association of Australia and New Zealand, 129–137, Brisbane.

Grey, Jeffrey (ed.). 2012. *Chief of Army's Reading List*. Canberra: Land Warfare Studies Centre.

Grimshaw, Patricia, et al. 1994. *Creating a Nation*. Ringwood: McPhee Gribble.

Hancock, Eleanor. 1993. Women, Combat and the Military. *Journal of Australian Studies* 17 (37): 88–98.

Hyland, Tom. 2011. Media Squabbles Miss the Real Questions about War. *Sunday Age*, 5 June.

Jamieson, Amber. 2011. Women on the Front Line. *Crikey*, 12 Apr. Available from: http://www.crikey.com.au/2011/04/12/women-on-the-front-line/.

Jeffrey, Tom (Director). 1979. *The Odd Angry Shot*. Village Roadshow.

Keogh, E.G. 2012. The Study of Military History. In Grey, *Chief of Army's Reading List*. 5–20.

Lake, Marilyn. 1992. Mission Impossible: How Men Gave Birth to the Australian Nation: Nationalism, Gender and Other Seminal Acts. *Gender and History* 4 (3): 305–322.

———. 2009. Beyond the Legend of Anzac. *ABC Radio National*, 26 Apr. Available from: http://www.abc.net.au/radionational/programs/hindsight/beyond-the-legend-of-anzac/3145132.

Logue, Jason. 2013. *Herding Cats: The Evolution of the ADF's Media Embedding Program in Operational Areas*. Canberra: Land Warfare Studies Centre.

Macintyre, Stuart. 2009. A Concise History of Australia. Cambridge: Cambridge University Press.

MacKenzie, Megan H. 2013. Women in Combat: Beyond "Can They?" or "Should They?". *Critical Studies on Security* 1 (2): 239–242.

McElroy, Hal, and Di McElroy creat. 2007–2011. *Sea Patrol*. Nine Network.

McKenna, Mark. 2010. Anzac Day: How Did It Become Australia's National Day? In *What's Wrong with Anzac?*, ed. Marilyn Lake, and Henry Reynolds, 110–134. Sydney: New South Publishing.

Neighbour, Sally. 2011. The Anzac Spirit. *Monthly*, Apr. pp. 8–10.

Page, James Smith. 2002. Is Mateship a Virtue? *Australian Journal of Social Issues* 37 (2): 193–200.

Sims, Jeremey Hartley (Director). 2010. *Beneath Hill 60*. Paramount Pictures.

Soldier Z. 2010. Token: Australian Debate about Afghanistan. *Interpreter*, 1 July. Available from: http://www.lowyinterpreter.org/post/2010/07/01/token-australian-debate-about-afghanistan.aspx.

Summers, Anne. 2011–2012. The Lady Killers: Women in the Military. *Monthly*, Dec–Jan. pp. 24–27.

Wadham, Ben. 2011a. The Dark Side of Mateship in Australian Military Ranks. *Crikey*, 6 Apr. Available from: http://www.crikey.com.au/2011/04/06/the-dark-side-of-mateship-in-australian-military-ranks/?wpmp_switcher=mobile&comments=50.

———. 2011b. Will Defence Ever Stop Defending the Indefensible? *Punch*, 6 Apr. Available from: http://www.thepunch.com.au/articles/will-defence-ever-stop-defending-the-indefensible/desc/.

Wadham, Ben. 2013. Brotherhood: Homosociality, Totality and Military Subjectivity. *Australian Feminist Studies* 28 (76): 212–235.

Weir, Peter (Director). 1981. *Gallipoli*. Village Roadshow.

White, Susanna, and Simon Cellan Jones (Directors). 2008. *Generation Kill*. HBO.

AUTHOR BIOGRAPHY

Jessica Carniel is a Lecturer in Humanities within the School of Arts and Communication at the University of Southern Queensland. Her broad research interests encompass race and ethnicity, cultural studies, popular culture, and gender studies, with a particular interest in Australian social and cultural issues.

CHAPTER 14

Reflecting on the Wars on Terror

Frank Bongiorno

Is it reasonable to talk of a post-9/11 world? Should we call the era since September 2001 the 'War (or Wars) on Terror' in the same way we might call 1914–1945 the era of 'The World Wars', or the 1950s and 1960s 'The Cold War'? Tony Judt called his monumental history of Europe since 1945 *Postwar* (2005); historians seem attached to the idea of dividing up time according to its relationship to war. To the extent that we accept that we live in the era of the 'War on Terror', we follow this habit, even as we might acknowledge the metaphoric aspect of the use of war in this phrase—terror is a practice, not an enemy—and its apparent indebtedness to phrases such as the 'War on Poverty' and the 'War on Drugs'.

Certainly, 2001 is widely understood as a landmark year in world history, one to sit alongside 1789, 1848, 1914, 1917, 1945, 1968, and 1989 as epoch-making. 1979 has recently emerged as yet another 'year that changed the world', and it was indeed a time of dramatic change in China, Britain, Poland, Afghanistan, and Iran, the significance of which seems only greater for what has happened since (Caryl 2013). No doubt a case can be made for the significance of any of these years as world-changing or epoch-making. Sometimes, they represent seeming

F. Bongiorno (✉)
Australian National University, Canberra, Australia
e-mail: frank.bongiorno@anu.edu.au

J. Gildersleeve and R. Gehrmann (eds.), *Memory and the Wars on Terror*, Palgrave Macmillan Memory Studies,
DOI 10.1007/978-3-319-56976-5_14

possibilities that remain unrealised, promises unfulfilled. 1848 and 1968 are good examples: A.J.P. Taylor famously declared that in 1848, 'German history reached its turning-point and failed to turn' (1945, p. 68). In other cases, much that happens afterwards seems to have flowed from a particular year, sometimes even from a few moments in a year: 1789 and 1914 stand out in this respect. Some signal the end of an era, rapid changes that transform whole economies, polities, and societies: 1914 surely has this kind of status, the end of a century of relative peace in Europe after Waterloo compared to the periods before and afterwards. 1989—and its emblematic moment, the fall of the Berlin Wall—has assumed a powerful status as the end of an era, bringing to a close either the period beginning with *The Communist Manifesto* (1848) or with the Bolshevik Revolution (1917). But 1914 is perhaps, for the twentieth century at least, 'the year that changed the world' *par excellence*. Apart from producing mass slaughter on an unprecedented scale over the next four years, it also 'made' other events and years that 'changed the world': 1917, 1939, 1945, and 1989.

These dates are essentially landmarks in political history, although they would often have powerful consequences for culture, the economy, and society. Cultural historians might look at the world somewhat differently, a point dramatised by Virginia Woolf's comment, paraphrased by Jessica Gildersleeve and Richard Gehrmann in the introduction to this collection: 'And now I will hazard a second assertion, which is more disputable perhaps, to the effect that on or about December 1910 human character changed' (1924). Sometimes, culture and politics come together in unexpected ways to produce a defining 'year', such as the coincidence of the Salman Rushdie affair in 1989 with the end of the Cold War, a hint, at least in retrospect, of the kinds of religious and cultural conflicts that do so much to define the early twenty-first-century world; the post-9/11 world, if you like.

'World-changing years' also reflect the Western biases of contemporary historiography. A Chinese perspective might look rather different, with 1911, 1937, and 1949 figuring as years of war and revolution rather than 1789, 1848, 1917, and 1939. Even for the United States, 1917 and 1941 are more meaningful as landmarks than 1914 and 1939.

Does 'world-changing' 2001 also contain such cultural or national biases? Being an attack on the American mainland and on civilians going about their daily business, it was seen to represent a new kind of warfare and a new era of brutality. The Japanese bombing of Pearl Harbor, as a surprise attack by a ruthless enemy that produced about 2500 deaths, was inevitable yet problematic as a point of comparison, being rejected in the *New York Times* almost immediately by the eminent historian David M. Kennedy: 'a blow to a military outpost at Pearl Harbor, far removed from the American heartland, is scarcely comparable to strikes against the nation's largest city and its capital' (2001). September 11 also seemed novel, if understood as 'warfare', in being the work not of a state as such but of a terrorist organisation, although the neo-conservatives of the Bush Administration quickly chose to identify state actors—Afghanistan and, most controversially and opportunistically, Iraq—as carrying a burden of responsibility for the attack and, with various allies, the US launched invasions of both countries.

In terms of the number of casualties it produced in New York, Washington DC, and Pennsylvania, the 9/11 attacks were comparable with the world's worst industrial accident at the Union Carbide plant in Bhopal, India in 1986, where some 3800 people died immediately and many more prematurely. Bhopal, like 9/11, produced deeply shocking images for the international media, but it was not seen in the West to have changed the world or 'human character'. Bhopal was not widely seen to define an era; not in the West, at any rate. It is unnecessary here to untangle the complex histories of race, empire, and capitalism that would help account for these 'differences', to use a more polite term than 'hypocrisies'. But one of the points exposed by such a comparison is the politically and culturally implicated nature of historical periodisation in general, and of the habit of identifying particular years and historical landmarks as world-changing times. When we—or our political masters—say that 'the world will never be the same again' after a tragedy of this kind, we and they are making a statement about history, culture, and politics; about how the world is ordered, and how it should be ordered.

Before the Iraq War, Tony Blair received a briefing from Michael Williams, a Middle East expert. He explained to the prime minister the nature of the religious and ethnic divisions in Iraq, and the dangers that this would pose to the country's stability once Saddam Hussein had been removed from the picture. 'That's all history, Mike', replied the upbeat prime minister, 'This is about the future' (Rawnsley 2010, p. 185). An emphasis on the novelty of a set of circumstances can, as in this instance, be used by political leaders to give themselves a freer hand in dealing with a crisis than knowledge and prudence ought to have dictated. Rather, such conflicts might be better understood as having 'a long global history', as Gildersleeve and Gehrmann suggest, in which the past might be a better guide to the present than the dominant rhetoric of crisis implies.

Silence, in these matters, is also meaningful. When opinion-formers refrain from such commentary about some event or other in a media-soaked world, when they decline to announce a tragedy as 'historic', they are likely to be expressing values that reflect a global order characterised by great inequalities of wealth and power. When the language of trauma that has come to dominate western cultural understandings of war is applied to one group of sufferers but not another—say, civilians in constant fear of drone strikes—we are ultimately witnessing a political choice. It is nothing as simple as valuing the human lives of one group of people more than another, or of imagining the poor and the oppressed have a greater capacity to bear suffering and to resist traumatic remembering than the wealthy West; although such biases surely still exist. It is rather the role that cultural, diplomatic, military and economic power play in framing international crises in one way rather than another. For leaving aside those who are actual eyewitnesses to a Pearl Harbor, a Bhopal or a 9/11, we mainly encounter such events through the media or, rather, through the dynamic relationship of media and state.

There is, of course, nothing new about that. The role played by the media in representing war has been a major theme in modern historical writing including, as recognised by Jessica Carniel in this collection, in the creation of Australia's Anzac Legend by Great War correspondents such as Ellis Ashmead-Bartlett and Charles Bean. Several chapters in this collection take as one of their central themes media-military relations. The failure of the Australian media to move beyond a nostalgic and unrealistic portrayal of the Australian soldier in Afghanistan and Iraq has attracted critics such as James Brown (2014), a former army officer, as well as some of the contributors here. This preoccupation with the representation of war and terrorism—so prominent in this collection—should not be seen as merely a continuation of an older scholarly preoccupation. Rather, it is recognition of a more intense and dynamic relationship between the media and war that includes the potential, if not always the reality, of almost instantaneous circulation of news and images as crises unfold. These technological advances, in turn, intensify some of the political and ethical 'problems' associated with the representation of war in culture, a matter taken up in this collection, for instance, by Christa van Raalte in her discussion of *Zero Dark Thirty*.

The reception of such images in any particular context, however, remains conditioned by local cultures and histories. A revealing example of this process is explored by Gehrmann, in his examination of the frustrations felt by Australian defence personnel at the lack of opportunities for participation, alongside their allies, in direct combat. No doubt the Anzac ideal continues to shape soldiers' sense of personal and community expectation of their war experience. The Anzac Legend has, in its modern reinvented form, placed considerably more emphasis on sacrifice, suffering, and death than on killing, and it is more comfortable celebrating mateship and compassion than the traditional warrior virtues. There is surely a cultural squeamishness about one of the most important roles performed by soldiers in warfare: killing the enemy. Does this help explain why Australian defence officials fail to draw attention to the numbers of the enemy killed by Australian soldiers in Afghanistan, a reluctance reported by Kevin Foster in his essay? Are Australians better able to accept the occasional death in combat than the idea that large numbers of the enemy are being killed in their name, in a campaign shrouded in great secrecy? Certainly, the idea of the Australian 'as more victim than victor' echoes a familiar national cultural sensibility, about war and much else besides.

These considerations underline some of the complexity of the post-9/11 cultural terrain. For the Australian public, the dominant images of the modern soldier—in Afghanistan and Iraq—are to be found not only (and perhaps not primarily) in Australian culture but in American culture's preferred version of military masculinity. By way of contrast with the US situation, the lack of media discussion of Australian participation, which is partly a result of the lack of openness of the Australian Defence Force in dealing with the media, as Foster shows, means that there is little understanding in Australia of the wars or the reasons for Australia's participation in them. The public's wars are, to a great extent, those that have been fought by the United States but, in the Australian case, without the sense of connection to real communities that the scale and nature of the US involvement have ensured. The combined effect of the cult of Anzac and US military culture is to fill a vacuum left by Australian media reporting about the real wars being fought in the Middle East. The longer-term impact on collective memory of this disengagement, as Amanda Laugesen speculates, must remain uncertain, but it is not difficult to imagine some kind of echo of the kinds of anger and trauma of returned Vietnam veterans concerning a lack of sympathy and understanding, even allowing for the very considerable differences between the fighting and politics of the wars concerned.

The focus of this collection on war in culture is itself a marker of the way that 9/11 and the War on Terror have contributed to a wider sense of the meaning of contemporary history and culture. It is impossible to imagine a collection on this theme being produced by a group of Australian scholars 30 years ago, when it seemed that war had become, and was likely to remain, a marginal aspect of the Australian experience. By that time (the mid-1980s), the Anzac revival was gathering momentum, but it was not seen as having any powerful implications for attitudes to international conflict in the present. It was a matter of history, identity, and culture; a site for nostalgia, popular culture, and historical enquiry; and (as some politicians, such as Prime Minister Bob Hawke, gradually came to realise) a safe topic for political speech-making and cultural diplomacy. Those innocent days, if that is what they were, are long over: collective memory of Australia's military history inevitably has powerful implications for military commitments in the present, with particular interpretations of past commitments being deployed by supporters and opponents of present wars rather like guided missiles (Bongiorno and Mansfield 2008).

The apparent ease with which the scholars here move across national boundaries to some extent replicates the way that war and terrorism, and their cultural representations, function in today's globalised world. As two of the later essays in this collection demonstrate, diasporic communities in Australia of Latin Americans, and of Jews, have responded to 9/11 in terms of historical trauma, collective memory, local experience, and shifting transnational identities and allegiances. The global language of trauma—increasingly prominent since the 1980s—offers a powerful vocabulary for understanding the ruptures associated with war and terror. Meanwhile, these transformations are taking place in an increasingly complex gender terrain, one in which the male soldier remains dominant, yet less so than a generation ago. Carniel, in the final essay in the collection, raises the possibility of 'a movement [in Australia] away from a necronationalistic memorialisation on death and sacrifice toward a more dynamic recognition of service as a broader concept'. The strength of this collection of essays lies as much in its foreshadowing of such possibilities as in its effort to make sense of the cultural topography of a post-9/11 order.

Works Cited

Bongiorno, Frank, and Grant Mansfield. 2008. Whose war was it anyway? Some Australian historians and the great war, *History Compass* 6 (1): 62–90.

Brown, James. 2014. *Anzac's Long Shadow: The Cost of Our National Obsession.* Collingwood: Redback.

Caryl, Christian. 2013. *Strange Rebels: 1979 and the Birth of the 21st Century.* New York: Basic.

Judt, Tony. 2005. *Postwar: A History of Europe Since 1945.* London: William Heinemann.

Kennedy, David M. 2001. *Fighting an Elusive Enemy. New York Times.* Sept. 16. Available from: http://www.nytimes.com/2001/09/16/opinion/fighting-an-elusive-enemy.html.

Rawnsley, Andrew. 2010. *The End of the Party.* London: Viking.

Taylor, A.J.P. 1945. *The Course of German History: A Survey of the Development of Germany Since 1815.* London: Hamish Hamilton.

Woolf, Virginia. 1924. *Mr Bennett and Mrs Brown,* Leonard and Virginia Woolf at the Hogarth Press: London. Available from: https://ebooks.adelaide.edu.au/w/woolf/virginia/mr-bennett-and-mrs-brown/.

Author Biography

Frank Bongiorno is Professor of History at The Australian National University, and has also lectured at King's College London, the University of New England, New South Wales, and Griffith University, Brisbane. His most recent books are *The Sex Lives of Australians: A History* (2012) and *The Eighties: The Decade that Transformed Australia* (2015). He has published widely on Australian history, including war and society.

INDEX

© The Editor(s) (if applicable) and The Author(s) 2017   271
J. Gildersleeve and R. Gehrmann (eds.), *Memory and the Wars
on Terror*, Palgrave Macmillan Memory Studies,
DOI 10.1007/978-3-319-56976-5

Printed by Printforce, the Netherlands